# GÓRECKI

*Oxford Studies of Composers*

# Górecki

ADRIAN THOMAS

CLARENDON PRESS · OXFORD

1997

Oxford University Press, Great Clarendon Street, Oxford OX2 6DP

Oxford New York
Athens Auckland Bangkok Bogota Bombay
Buenos Aires Calcutta Cape Town Dar es Salaam
Delhi Florence Hong Kong Istanbul Karachi
Kuala Lumpur Madras Madrid Melbourne
Mexico City Nairobi Paris Singapore
Taipei Tokyo Toronto
and associated companies in
Berlin Ibadan

Oxford is a trade mark of Oxford University Press

Published in the United States
by Oxford University Press Inc., New York

British Library Cataloguing in Publication Data
Data available

Library of Congress Cataloging in Publication Data
Thomas, Adrian, 1947–
Górecki / Adrian Thomas.
p.  cm.—(Oxford studies of composers)
List of composer's works:
Includes bibliographical references (p.  ) and index.
1. Górecki, Henryk Mikolaj, 1933–  —Criticism and interpretation. I. Title. II. Series.
ML410.G6448T5  1997  780'.92–dc20  96-26034
ISBN 0-19-816393-2 (cloth)
ISBN 0-19-816394-0 (pbk.)

1 3 5 7 9 10 8 6 4 2

Typeset by Best-set Typesetter Ltd., Hong Kong
Printed in Great Britain
on acid-free paper by
Biddles Ltd., Guildford & King's Lynn

*for my parents*

# PREFACE

HENRYK MIKOŁAJ GÓRECKI has become known throughout the musical world in the past few years as the composer of *Symphony of
Sorrowful Songs* (1976). Its phenomenal success, however, should not
be allowed to mask a forty-year career stemming from the post-
Stalinist era of the mid-1950s and embracing over seventy acknowledged compositions. Polish writers have generally approached
Górecki from philosophical and aesthetic viewpoints. But because
much of his output remains relatively unknown, this study is designed
rather as a sourcebook for readers who wish to find out more about
Górecki's music, along with relevant background material. I hope
that, as a non-Pole, I have adequately reflected the essence of Polish
folk and sacred music as it pertains to Górecki, although such is the
range of his allusory references that others will undoubtedly discern
further resonances in his compositions.

The starting-point for my fascination with Górecki came in 1970
when I was introduced to a recently issued Polish LP of his music by
a fellow postgraduate, Jim Samson, to whom my sincere thanks must
go for his encouragement as I have pursued my own study of Polish
music over the intervening years. In Poland, I have been assisted
selflessly by a number of colleagues, notably Kazimierz Nowacki
(former librarian of the Polish Composers' Union), Michał Kubicki
(of Polish Radio 5, English Language Section), and Jolanta Bilińska
(former secretary of the Warsaw Autumn), who have provided a
wealth of information and recordings, delved for source material, and
helped with translations from the Polish. Welcome assistance has
also come from Elżbieta Szczepańska (who was my guide and inter-
preter on my visit to Górecki in 1984) and Zbigniew Dzięgiel in
Warsaw, Rafat Augustyn in Wrocław, Louise Lerche-Lerchenborg in
Denmark, and Leszek Paul and Tomasz Walkiewicz in London. The
staff at Boosey & Hawkes, particularly Susan Bamert and David
Allenby, and James Rushton and his colleagues at Chester Music,
have been unfailingly helpful, as has David Drew, who, during his
time at Boosey & Hawkes, was instrumental in bringing Górecki's
name to the attention of promoters and performers. The music exam-

ples are reprinted by kind permission of Boosey & Hawkes, Music Publishers, Ltd. I must also thank the National Library in Warsaw and the Polish Library in London for giving me access to materials, and The Queen's University of Belfast for generously supporting my leave of absence in 1993–4 and many previous research visits to Poland. Much of this study would have been impossible without the help given by Górecki himself, who played his unpublished scores for me and filled me in on many biographical details. With his wife and family, he has welcomed me in Chochołów and Katowice as one of the family, and I hope that this study will be accepted as a token of my thanks and in deep appreciation of one of the most distinctive musical voices of our time.

A.T.T.

*Cardiff*
*1996*

# CONTENTS

# MUSIC EXAMPLES

# PRELUDIUM

OTYLIA GÓRECKA died on 6 December 1935; it was her son's second birthday. From this day, what had promised to be an unassuming but musically encouraging childhood for her son all too rapidly became one of hardship and misfortune. And, without overstressing the significance of this private tragedy, it is evident that the resilience and acuteness with which he absorbed this and later afflictions have played an integral part in shaping his distinctive personal and musical character.

Otylia was born in 1909 to Emilia and Florian Słota in Zabrze, Upper Silesia, part of a chain of cities (including Gliwice, Bytom, Chorzów, and Katowice) which still constitutes one of Europe's largest steel and coal-mining belts (Fig. 1).[1] Florian Słota died a few years later following a mining accident, and Emilia married Emanuel Buchalik, a restaurateur and hotelier. Both Otylia and her brother Alfred were encouraged to aim for the higher things in life: Alfred wrote poems, composed, and played the violin and accordion, while Otylia played the piano and, at one time, harboured the intention of entering a religious order. How she met her future husband is not clear, but in October 1932 she married Roman Górecki (1904–91), a railway employee and amateur musician. Roman's family came from near Rydułtowy, a town some twelve kilometres outside Rybnik, the main city to the south-west of Zabrze and Katowice. Rydułtowy was a coal-mining and agricultural centre, and Roman and Otylia settled on the Górecki family farm on the outskirts of the nearby village of Czernica. It was here that their only child, Henryk Mikołaj Józef, was born on 6 December 1933.[2]

---

[1] Upper Silesia became fully part of Poland after World War II, but it had a chequered history earlier in the century. It had been governed by the Prussians since Poland was partitioned in 1795 and remained so until after World War I. Discontented with its exclusion in 1918 from the newly independent Poland, the populace of this heavily industrialized region instigated three insurrections against the German authorities (1919–21). After the third, successful, uprising, parts of Silesia (including Katowice but excluding other cities such as Bytom and Zabrze) were incorporated into the new Polish republic. Also incorporated was the more rural area to the south-west where Górecki was born and raised.

[2] Polish pronunciation is consistent with its spelling. Of the names so far mentioned, the following will give an indication of pronunciation patterns and the normal emphasis on the

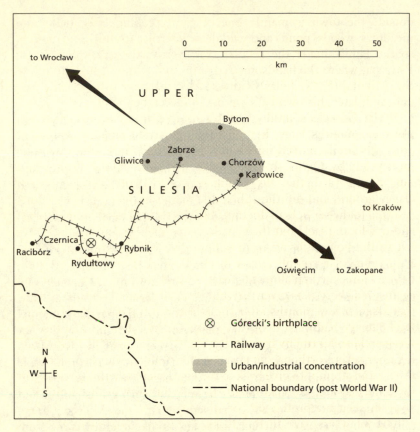

FIG. 1. Map of Upper Silesia

The Górecki family lived modestly. Their cottage was too small for Otylia's grand piano, so she brought an upright with her instead. The house and barn (now rebuilt) are overlooked by an embankment along which branch-line trains from the ancient Piast town of Racibórz still run to Rybnik via Rydułtowy, where Roman Górecki worked all his life in the goods office at the railway station. Louring over the station is the 'Leon III' pit-head, one of many in the area, but the landscape

penultimate syllable: Mikołaj (Mee-*koh*-why), Górecki (Goo-*rets*-kee), Buchalik (Boo-*hah*-leek), Katowice (Kah-toh-*vee*-tseh), Czernica (Chair-*nee*-tsah).

outside the town is mainly one of gently rolling hills, fields and meadows, woods, ponds and wild deer. Czernica itself had no church, so the family made the regular trek westwards across country to Pstrążna, where the handsome red-brick and whitewashed church of Św. Mikołaj (St Nicholas) witnessed the marriage of Górecki's parents and, later, his own baptism on 26 December 1933.

Otylia Górecka's sudden death ruptured this pastoral existence. Fourteen months later, her husband remarried and in September 1937 the family moved into a new house, built in Rydułtowy with money left by Otylia. It was during this time, while playing in a neighbour's yard, that the young Henryk Mikołaj slipped on the clayey ground and did the splits, dislocating his left hip. The family resorted to the services of doctors in hospitals in Katowice and Istebna and to a local quack, but their inadequate remedies and misdiagnoses led to the boy suffering from suppurative inflammation of the hip with tubercular complications in the bone. It took over two years before Górecki (then almost 6 years old and with his leg bunched up against his chest) was given anything like adequate treatment; but by that stage, a few months after the outbreak of World War II, near-fatal damage had been done. He spent the next twenty months in a German hospital run by nuns in Bytom. Górecki owes his life to a fine if rather severe orthopaedic surgeon, Dr Seifert, who operated four times in an attempt to give back to the youngster something approaching a normal life. Górecki returned to Rydułtowy in the summer of 1941 and began a protracted convalescence.[3]

The war years were further blackened when his step-grandfather, Emanuel Buchalik, perished in the Dachau concentration camp, a loss which served to emphasize the sad fact that, since his mother's death, Górecki had been deprived of almost any contact with her family. And yet it was during the early 1940s that Górecki demonstrated that he had inherited his mother's musical interests. What he really wanted was to be able to play the piano she had left to him. But despite his father's earlier musical activity—he had led dance bands at local weddings before his first marriage—Górecki received little or no encouragement either from him or from his stepmother. He was strictly forbidden even to touch the piano, although he did sneak in to

---

[3] Ill health has dogged him since his childhood and has several times led to major surgery, including his first kidney operation in 1958 and another operation on his hip in 1982. His safe deliverance from this particular 'dangerous journey' is commemorated in the foreword to *O Domina nostra* (1985).

play it when he chanced to be alone in the house.[4] But in 1943 he was allowed to begin violin lessons with a local teacher, Paweł Hajduga. This amateur musician was also an instrument-maker (from mouth-organs to violins) as well as being a sculptor, painter, and poet: a 'chłopski filozof' (peasant philosopher), as Górecki recalls him. Rydułtowy's musical life centred on Hajduga: enthusiastic but untrained, he was Górecki's only contact with the outside world of music and culture. In addition to attending group violin lessons (and, later, piano lessons) with Hajduga, Górecki started to compose. These first attempts were mostly little songs and miniatures, although by the start of the 1950s he had progressed to composing a larger-scale *Sonata in the Style of Corelli* for string quintet.

Górecki's normal schooling had continued meantime at the Rydułtowy gymnasium, from which he gained his secondary school certificate in the summer of 1951. Instead of joining his contemporaries at university (there had been an idea that he might study economics), Górecki set about realizing his burning ambition to study music. He applied to several Intermediate Schools of Music, including those in Rybnik, Bytom, and Katowice, but to his immense frustration he found that he was regarded as too untutored and too old (normal entry to intermediate schools was at the age of 15). But after all the emotional, physical, and musical disadvantages he had overcome, Górecki was not going to be deterred. He enrolled for a year at a music learning centre in Rybnik (open to all ages), where he studied the piano, and at the same time he took on a full-time job as a primary school teacher.

For two years (1951–3), Górecki taught 10- and 11-year-olds in a school in Radoszowa, a suburb of Rydułtowy, covering a wide range of subjects, including Polish history, maths, biology, natural history, and art. Here he also gained experience conducting choirs, teaching the violin and the piano, and writing the music and verse for school drama productions mounted in local villages. In 1952, he succeeded in winning a place on the teacher-training course at the Intermediate School of Music in Rybnik, enabling him not only to have professional lessons on the piano, clarinet, and violin but also to catch up on subjects such as harmony and counterpoint, instrumentation, and folklore. He was nothing if not determined, particularly as life at home remained difficult and not very supportive. On a typical weekday, after a full day's teaching, he would take the train to Rybnik for several

---

[4] In the end, Górecki did inherit this piano, which he has installed in his studio in Katowice.

hours' tuition, coming home in the evening to do more studying and composing. And when he started going to orchestral concerts in Katowice, two hours away by train, he would use the journey to study Beethoven symphonies or analyse some Bach. He often missed the last connecting train home and would then spend the night composing or sleeping on the table in the waiting-room at Rybnik before returning home at 5.30 a.m., just in time to leave again for his job at the primary school.

Something had to give, so Górecki left his teaching post in 1953 and concentrated solely on music in Rybnik. He tapped every source he could to slake his thirst for music. He listened avidly to Polish Radio broadcasts and continued his periodic trips to Katowice for symphonic concerts. Early on he had developed a love for the printed score, and his first acquisition—a straight swap for his valued table-tennis bat—was the score of Beethoven's Ninth Symphony. This was followed by the purchase of the mazurkas by Karol Szymanowski (1882–1937), and his shopping list in the early 1950s continued this twin track of classics and Polish music with works such as Beethoven's Violin Concerto, Chopin's mazurkas and Adolf Chybiński's collection of Polish folksongs *Od Tatr do Bałtyku* (From the Tatras to the Baltic). Any musical enrichment in those impoverished times was welcome: he went repeatedly to see Aleksander Ford's 1952 film *Młodość Chopina* (Chopin's Youth) because, despite its propagandizing depiction of Chopin as an active participant in the revolutionary fervour of the 1830s (the film ends with action at the Paris barricades), it was an opportunity to relish the power of his compatriot's musical vision.[5] In fact, as a student in a distant Polish province, Górecki was barely touched by the Stalinist dictates of socialist realism, which at its height in the early 1950s affected most creative artists living and working in the major cities. He was able to develop his compositional skills away from such inhibiting dogma, although his compulsory classes in Leninist theory and the singing of exhortatory 'mass' songs were always a reminder of the pressures affecting everyday life.

By studying intensively at Rybnik, Górecki was able to cover his teacher-training course in only three years. Compositionally, he was still essentially self-taught, although his piano teacher would play through his pieces with him—still mainly songs and piano miniatures. Occasionally he attempted something big: perhaps the most tantaliz-

---

[5] For a detailed account of the making of *Młodość Chopina*, including the use of Chopin's music in the score by Kazimierz Serocki, see Jerzy Giżycki's *Film o młodym Chopinie* (Warsaw, 1953).

ing, and unfinished, project was a ballet, *Świtezianka* (The Water-Nymph), adapted by Górecki in 1952–3 from Adam Mickiewicz's well-known ballad of 1821. The impulse to write was irresistible, and his ambition as a composer was clear. When he applied to study composition at the Higher School of Music in Katowice (by then renamed Stalinogród)[6] in 1955, Górecki had a folder bulging with compositions which were sufficiently strong to impress his future teacher, Bolesław Szabelski (1896–1979). Although Górecki later destroyed most of the pieces he composed before he started with Szabelski, the ten or so which he simply withdrew from his last year in Rybnik give a good indication of his ability and expressive potential. Most of them are understandably for small forces: four works for piano solo, two lyrical songs to words by Maria Konopnicka, a fairly chromatic *Preludium* for violin and piano, a *Terzetto quasi una fantasia* for oboe, violin, and piano, and a String Quartet.[7]

At one end of the spectrum are some of the *Five Mazurkas* and *Obrazki poetyckie* (Poetic Pictures), where modality and open-fifth oscillations (Mazurka in C major) are spiced by folk-inspired sharpened fourths ('Wieczor'—Evening—from *Poetic Pictures*). A darker side to Górecki's emerging musical persona is felt in the Ten Preludes, where melancholy and chromaticism (shades of Rachmaninov and Skriabin) are sometimes animated by stormy tempos, as in the crowning tenth prelude, an *angst*-ridden study in double octaves. Dissonance resurfaces in the *Romans* (Romance), whose central 'molto agitato'—a dramatic recitative—is surrounded by a Szymanowskian 'lento cantabile' in C minor. The most ambitious of these now-discarded compositions is the last, the Piano Concerto. The outer movements are rhythmically flamboyant, and the central Interludium is particularly fine. It starts with a piano soliloquy, whose dark-hued dissonances are followed by an orchestral monody interrupted by violent piano interjections. The Piano Concerto's combination of rhythmic energy, melancholic introspection, and dynamic aggression was a powerful taste of things to come.

---

[6] Katowice regained its name after Krushchev denounced Stalin in his now famous 'secret' speech in Moscow in the spring of 1956.

[7] In May 1995, Górecki brought out the two songs by Konopnicka from his 'bottom drawer' for performance, alongside a newly composed song to a text by the same author, at the Kościuszko Foundation in New York with his long-standing friend, Andrzej Bachleda. For details see List of Works.

# I

# SONGS OF JOY AND RHYTHM

BOLESŁAW SZABELSKI was a man of few words, but his role as Górecki's composition mentor and as a figure *in loco parentis* was crucial. His taciturnity was complemented by Górecki's enthusiasm, and they shared a profound admiration for the music of Szymanowski, who had been Szabelski's teacher in Warsaw in the late 1920s. They seem to have talked rarely about compositional technique or even Szabelski's own music.[1] Instead, Szabelski encouraged his pupil's growing confidence and independence by giving him considerable space in which to develop his own ideas and projects. Several of the first pieces Górecki wrote in 1955–6 were straightforward examples of the type of neo-classicism written in the post-war decade by older Polish composers such as Grażyna Bacewicz (1909–69), Kazimierz Serocki (1922–81), and Tadeusz Baird (1928–81). Characteristic of the style are the twists and turns introduced into fairly four-square rhythmic and metric patterns, uncomplicated formal structures, the frequent use in the fast movements of a broad melody set against a pulsating background, and a harmonic language that seeks consistency less in the diatonic triad than in perfect intervals, tritones, and chromatic ostinatos.

Many of these early student works highlight the two instruments with which Górecki was most at home, the violin and the piano. Simplest among them are the brief *Sonatina in One Movement*, Op. 8, and the three-movement *Quartettino*, Op. 5, written for the unusual combination of two flutes, oboe, and violin. The influences of folk-music and Bartók are evident, not least in the delicate dissonances of the unpublished piano pieces, *Kołysanka* (Lullaby), Op. 9, and the nine miniatures in *Z ptasiego gniazda* (From the Bird's Nest), Op. 9a.[2]

---

[1] A 1973 Polish Television documentary on Szabelski includes a vivid sequence in which Górecki waxes energetically on Szabelski's music while his teacher sits more or less silently beside him.

[2] *From the Bird's Nest* may be viewed as an incidental throw-back to the small-scale pieces of 1954–5 (the unadorned 'Folksong', for example, is a mere ten bars long).

Sometimes, the allusions to folk-music can be very direct (as in the Lutosławskian treatment of a Lydian tune towards the end of the Toccata, Op. 2, for two pianos). In the Variations, Op. 4, for violin and piano, however, Górecki tests his ability to create a more extended structure out of a folk theme.

More by accident than design, the short motif of the introduction and the related theme of the Variations bear a striking resemblance to the soprano's opening theme in Szymanowski's *Stabat mater* (1926). It is an early example of Górecki's natural affinity with the music of Szymanowski, particularly that of his last, 'Polish', period (from the mid-1920s onwards). The theme, chromaticized beyond its initial sharpened fourth, is put through its paces in nine short variations and a finale, each with a clear individual purpose and character. Nos. 2, 5, and 7 are the only fast variations, the fifth characterized by scherzando superimpositions of duple and triple metres while the seventh is an energetic, foot-stomping mazurka. Finest of all, perhaps, are the slower variations. The fourth (andante cantabile) is indicative of how imaginatively Górecki was shaping his material (Ex. I.1). It clearly recalls Szymanowski in its melodic development of the folk motif, in its gritty harmonic language, and in its texture where, as it soars into the high registers of both instruments, it is counterweighted in the bass of the piano by tolling six-part chords. The two adagio variations (Nos. 3 and 9) are sombrely funereal, following in the wake of the most touching of Górecki's early pieces, *Trzy pieśni* (Three Songs), Op. 3.

*Three Songs* is dedicated to the memory of Górecki's mother. If the third song, 'Ptak' (The Bird), by Julian Tuwim (1894–1953), seems skittish in the context, it does provide a certain relief from the sadness and anger expressed in the first two songs. The poems of 'Do matki' (To Mother) and 'Jakiż to dzwon grobowy' (What was this funereal bell) are both by Juliusz Słowacki (1809–49), whom Górecki views as the most significant Polish poet of the nineteenth century. 'What was this funereal bell' pictures a procession in which a man bears his mother's coffin. Górecki emphasizes the almost confrontational outrage of the bereaved son, the piano's thundering ostinato in the outer sections vividly capturing the image of a man 'tormented by black despair'.

The text of 'To Mother' is worth quoting in full because it symbolizes for the first time in Górecki's published work the continuing impact of his mother's death:

2

Ex. I.1. Variations, variation 4, bb. 1–8

Within the darkness I see the image of my mother,
As if walking towards the source of the rainbow—
Her turned face looks over her shoulder,
And her gaze reveals that she is looking at her son.[3]

Górecki's response here is veiled, even laconic, and the musical language distanced from neo-classical elegance. He marks the song 'Lento, recitativo', and the low-lying melodic line is noticeably subdued. A pair of alternating chords (an early example of a quintessential Góreckian device), graced here by sighing appoggiaturas, reiterates a rooted C minor tonality. The less precise tonalities introduced at the start of the two middle lines of the verse illustrate Górecki's early attachment to dense chording in the bass register. Only once does the gloom lift, at the end of the third line, when the chord of C major unexpectedly appears as the resolution of a clouded perfect cadence. For a moment, the silence hangs in the air. The singer softly reiterates an unaccompanied G♮, realizing the mood of empathy implicit in the last line. But Górecki ultimately takes a bleaker view, and the piano reasserts the opening chords under the final phrase. The mother's backward glance is little solace for her absence.

There are four works from this period of Górecki's studies in which he essays larger-scale formal structures than the works already cited: *Four Preludes*, Op. 1, Piano Sonata, Op. 6, *Pieśni o radości i rytmie* (Songs of Joy and Rhythm), Op. 7, and Sonata for Two Violins, Op. 10. *Four Preludes* for piano may be regarded as a statement of intent by a youthful composer acknowledging that serious matters are now at stake. Not that this is a large-scale composition (it lasts only eight minutes), but the four preludes together constitute a mini-sonata in all but name. A monothematic sonata principle lies behind the first prelude (the most substantial of the four), a swirling toccata spiced with metrical surprises. There are echoes of Szymanowski and Bacewicz, but the strong contrasts between its cantabile andante sections and the impassioned *sfff* chordal climaxes are very much Górecki's own. The second prelude—another Lento-recitativo (see the first of the Three Songs, Op. 3)—is a masterful lament in which a diatonic, four-note folk motif is repeated and explored. The motif is offset by jabbing bass sevenths which in turn influence the climactic statement of the melodic line. The leanness of the textures and the composer's understanding of the piano as melody instrument mark this prelude out as

---

[3] Trans. by Andrew Okrzeja and Krystyna Rogacka (reproduced with kind permission of Chester Music).

4

something special. The final two preludes are intended to run together: a mischievous little scherzo followed *attacca* by a whirlwind study in semiquavers whose ancestry might be traced as far back as the finale of Chopin's Third Piano Sonata.

Górecki's own Piano Sonata was composed during the vacation at the end of his first year of study. It is a three-movement structure in which the short, twenty-four-bar second movement (Grave pesante e corale) is so dwarfed by the tempestuous allegros on either side that it functions really as a momentary respite from the prevailing hyperactivity rather than as a substantive statement in its own right. Its delicate pensiveness is, however, partly balanced by reflective episodes in the outer movements. The pounding quavers of the opening Allegro molto, con fuoco (its lineage goes back to Bartók's *Allegro barbaro* and Stravinsky's *The Rite of Spring*) are offset by a central section, molto lento, with its distinct echoes of motivic intervals in the second of the *Four Preludes*. The last movement's folk-dance (a mazurka with three main themes) pauses towards the end—much as Bartók was fond of doing—to enjoy a quiet rumination on four statements of a simple F sharp major phrase, whose final G♯ is pointed up by different second-inversion major triads (E flat, C, B flat, G, and C once more). Even if the Piano Sonata emerges less as a traditional structure and more as a pair of muscular allegros with an interlude as 'the still point', what is certain is that Górecki had released a dynamic energy which was capable of supporting large-scale works.

Górecki's first attempt at a composition for more than four instruments, juvenilia excepted, was also his most unusual, *Songs of Joy and Rhythm* for two pianos and chamber orchestra, the original version of which was written at the same time as the Piano Sonata in the summer of 1956. In this version, it is scored for single woodwind, trumpet, timpani and percussion, celeste, two pianos (one solo, one concertante) and, unusually, eight violins playing in pairs. The structural proportions are also unconventional. It opens with a Preludium and Toccata lasting under one minute and continues with a similarly slow–fast 'Recitativo–etiuda', which lasts for less than two. The 'Przygrywka lyriczna' (Lyric Prelude) which follows brings some stability to the design, although the weight of the overall structure lies squarely on the shoulders of the finale, dubbed 'Mały koncert fortepianowy' (Little Piano Concerto) by Górecki, perhaps to distinguish it from the concerto he had composed the previous year. And, while there are many highly original features (and Górecki sometimes toys with the idea of reviving it), the overall impression is of a collec-

5

tion of four separate pieces insufficiently balanced and developed in terms of material and proportions.

And yet *Songs of Joy and Rhythm* continued to exercise a hold on the composer: lists of his principal works often begin with this one. It was premièred in Katowice in February 1958, but was subsequently withdrawn for major reworking, carried out in the winter of 1959–60.[4] Part of Górecki's loyalty to the idea of the piece may stem from its extramusical associations. Its title is taken from Julian Tuwim's youthful (and singularly titled) poem 'Song of Joy and Rhythm', in which he describes a moment of ecstatic understanding as he contemplates universal truth under the stars—'Truth which is living, visible, unique | Eternal'. It is reasonable to infer that Górecki's composition, and his attachment to it, are the result of his identification with such a revelatory experience. Not that we hear anything approaching Szymanowski's seductive Third Symphony, 'Song of the Night' (1916): for Górecki, the impulse is more down-to-earth and extrovert.

It is perhaps surprising that the 1960 version of *Songs of Joy and Rhythm* is as impervious as it is to the radical changes that Górecki's music had undergone since 1956. The finale's first theme, for example, has a rhythmic *élan* that Poulenc would have recognized, and the ensuing combination of bravado and introspection, while rooted in the world of gruff neo-classicism that Górecki had developed during 1956, is only occasionally coloured by the intervening years. Much of the work's thematic material—apart from a totally new second movement—is carried over into the new version, although the textures are generally more elaborate, with the second piano playing more of an equal role with its partner.[5] A gritty vitality is evident from the up-beat to the first movement, where the momentum is achieved from increasingly intense statements of irregularly alternating chords on both piano 2 and strings. With emphatic punctuation from piano 1, wind, and percussion, one might be forgiven for recalling Edgard Varèse, but, like the quiet Ivesian coda to this brief movement, such an interpretation would only point up coincidences, given that the music of Varèse and Ives was virtually unknown and unperformed in Poland until the 1960s.[6]

---

[4] It then lay unplayed until 1990—Górecki has never taken any interest in pushing his own works for performance.

[5] The orchestration has some changes from the 1956 version, notably a complement of twenty-four strings (no double basses) and the addition of a trombone. But Górecki cuts the oboe, an instrument for which he has said he has no particular fondness.

[6] It took a couple of decades for certain aspects of the canon of 20th-cent. music from the West to surface fully. Polish premières of Varèse's music, for example, include *Density 21.5*

The new second movement, like the replaced 'Recitativo–etiuda', is short (just over two minutes) and split into two parts, con moto and secco. It displays an increased motivic sophistication. All the thematic material derives from the opening discursive violin pizzicato (Ex. I.2*a*). On each of its three subsequent statements, a new contrapuntal voice is added in the pizzicato strings and the theme itself is extended by new motivic insertions, such as may be observed in the central section of the Toccata, Op. 2. Despite its accumulative nature, the con moto has an air of impermanence which is seized on by the two pianos in the secco section. Phrases drawn from the con moto theme are then counterpointed, partly in canonic imitation, in an exhilarating race for the line (Ex. I.2*b*).

Like those in the earlier version, the first two movements from 1960 are so short and breathless as to require some complementary stability. The third movement—closely modelled on the Lyric Prelude of 1956—provides it. In a real sense, this captures the contemplative essence of Tuwim's poem:

> Here I am resting joyfully in myself,
> Wrapped in deep silence on all sides,
> And my heart beats in the rhythm of everything
> Which surrounds me.

But this is no self-indulgent reverie. The arch structure reflects Tuwim's image of a 'huge starry dome', and at its apogee is an extended solo for piano 1, culminating in a tart harmonization of a chant-like motif and in multiple repetitions, involving the full orchestra, of the piano's final stark chord. On either side of this centre-piece are reiterated chords of E major/minor, and these are flanked by another chant-like melody (shared by piccolo and clarinet) whose origins lie in the material of the second movement.

One of the most striking aspects of the 1960 version of *Songs of Joy and Rhythm* is its underlying thematic unity. At the heart of the

---

(1959), *Octandre* (1960), *Hyperprism* and *Offrandes* (1961), and on to *Nocturnal* (1983), while those of Charles Ives include *Tone Roads No. 3* (1964), *The Fourth of July* (1965), *Three Places in New England* (1976), and *Central Park in the Dark* (1978). On the other hand, Górecki had spotted in the most important Polish book on orchestration—Feliks Wrobel's *Partytura na tle współczesnej techniki orkiestracyjnej* (The Score against the Background of Contemporary Techniques of Orchestration, Kraków, 1954)—some very short examples from a few 'modern' scores: Schoenberg's Third String Quartet, Berg's Violin Concerto, and Varèse's *Ionisation*. These inclusions, rather surprising for the time, reinforce the observation that Polish composers had known for a while that certain Western composers were exploring new techniques: what they craved were actual scores and performances (tape recordings and machines were still only a dream).

Ex. I.2. *Songs of Joy and Rhythm*, second movement: (*a*) bb. 1–11; (*b*) ⑦

various cross-references lies a tiny intervallic sequence which was to prove a central 'motto' in Górecki's music from the mid-1960s onwards. It is the essence of modal simplicity and is a thematic component in all four movements, but it is heard in its most direct form in the coda of the finale (Ex. I.3*a*; see also Ex. V.5). Given the ubiquity of the motif's outline, it would seem unrealistic to assign it to any particular source. But Górecki has commented that it comes from Poland's

Ex. I.3. (*a*) *Songs of Joy and Rhythm*, fourth movement, ⑱; (*b*) 'Bogurodzica', opening phrase; (*c*) *Songs of Joy and Rhythm*, fourth movement, ③

oldest notated music, 'Bogurodzica' (Ex. I.3*b*).[7] Although the connection here is notional rather than actual, the influence of the incipit of 'Bogurodzica' on the finale's earlier second theme is clear (Ex. I.3*c*). But the real significance lies not so much in identifying the origins of this manipulated material but rather in Górecki's acknowledgment of his youthful rapport with old Polish music and, in part, its associ-

---

[7] 'Bogurodzica' is an early medieval hymn to the Virgin Mary and Jesus Christ and was sung by Polish troops going into battle. Several contemporary Polish composers have quoted directly from it.

Ex. I.4. Sonata for Two Violins, first movement, bb. 133–44

ated modality, long before they became major elements in his compositional thought.

The most consistently impressive achievement of this period is the Sonata for Two Violins. It is a remarkably assured work in a medium which hitherto had invited miniatures, notably Bartók's Forty-Four Duos (1931), and also Prokofiev's Sonata (1932), to which Górecki's own work bears a close kinship. It was the major composition of Górecki's second year in Katowice, alongside small-scale pieces for one and two instruments and the first of several ventures during his student years into writing incidental music for the theatre.[8] The sonata's opening bars grab the listener by the throat: neo-classical niceties are brutalized, conventional melody and accompaniment textures are dislocated by a composer burning to move on. And yet, at the centre of the movement lies one of Górecki's lyrical quasi-improvisations. Even this becomes impassioned, particularly in its concluding double-octave unison, and the lead-back into the recapitulation is wild (Ex. I.4). Technically, this is the most closely argued and contrapuntal movement, and the thematic exploration incorporates both inversion and retrograding of material.

From early in his career, Górecki relished the potency of sharp contrasts, be they of texture or the full range of dynamics. The change from first to second movement in the sonata is from the guttural to the ethereal. The cool high lyricism of the unison muted violins gradually disintegrates into gentle imitative phrases but, unlike the sustained quietude of the Piano Sonata's central movement, the calm here is imperilled by intimations of the finale. This emerges as a slow grotesque Con anima a la danse, marked by *sul ponticello* snippets on muted first violin (shades of Stravinsky's *The Soldier's Tale*). The second violin moves from perfunctory articulation of a C major/minor ostinato to frantic hustle as the first violin attempts a more lyrically tonal line. Having reached an impasse, the process is repeated, essentially up a tone. This time, there seems to be a greater air of confidence, but the disruptive invasion of a fragment from the first movement leads to a brief thematic contest and a rapid denouement. This is certainly an odd movement, although the element of the grotesque was to resurface much later in Górecki's career. The sonata as a whole is a dramatic and virtuoso conclusion to his first compositional phase. If there are signs of creative impatience, they may be taken as symptomatic of Górecki's continual desire to move forward.

---

[8] Between 1957 and 1960, Górecki wrote incidental music for several productions at the Teatr Śląski (Silesian Theatre) in Katowice. Among them were two American plays in translation: Robert Ardrey's *Thunder Rock* and Arthur Miller's *A View from the Bridge*. The director in both instances was Jerzy Jarocki, who went on to become one of Poland's foremost theatre directors, principally associated with the Stary Teatr (Old Theatre) in Kraków.

# II

# COLLISIONS

AFTER Stalin's death in 1953, cultural life in Poland began to break free of the bonds of socialist realism. No single event heralded the so-called 'thaw'; it was rather a series of hair-line and a few major fractures in the system that increasingly encouraged individual initiatives and opened up communication with the West.[1] The most important musical event was the four-month nationwide Second Festival of Polish Music, whose final stretch occupied most of May 1955. Its significance was less the fact that it was held than that it failed to galvanize both professional musicians and the public. This spurred its organizers, the Presidium of the Polish Composers' Union, to advance its plans, mooted the previous year, for an international festival of contemporary music to be held in the autumn of 1956. Thus was born the Warszawska Jesień (Warsaw Autumn), a catalytic event in Polish musical life.[2]

Along with his future wife, Jadwiga Rurańska, Górecki travelled up from Katowice for the first Warsaw Autumn (10–21 October 1956). The programme was fairly innocuous in comparison with those of the following festivals (from 1958 onwards). There were few brand-new Polish compositions but several Polish premières of mainstream twentieth-century pieces, including Bartók's Fifth String Quartet, Berg's *Lyric Suite*, and Schoenberg's Piano Concerto. Foreign performers

---

[1] Among the many contributory events in Poland may be counted the first legal jazz concert since 1949 (in Kraków, 13 Mar. 1954), the arrival in Warsaw at the end of July 1955 of 30,000 young people from all over the world for the World Festival of Youth and Students for Peace and Friendship, the publication of Adam Ważyk's searing poem about everyday life in Poland 'Poem for Adults' (in *Nowa kultura*, 21 Aug. 1955), and the opening of Tadeusz Kantor's Cricot II theatre in Kraków on 24 May 1956. On the political front in 1956, First Secretary Bierut died in Moscow in March, during the Soviet Congress when Krushchev denounced Stalin, Włodzimierz Sokorski was removed as Minister of Culture (17 Apr.), and the Polish Communist government was severely shaken at the end of June by riots and dozens of fatalities as workers in Poznań protested against living conditions.

[2] For a comprehensive account of the early Warsaw Autumn festivals, see Cynthia E. Bylander, 'The Warsaw Autumn International Festival of Contemporary Music, 1956–1961: Its Goals, Structures, Programs, and People', Ph.D. thesis (Columbus, Ohio, 1989).

12

came from elsewhere in the Eastern bloc and, more significantly, from the West: the Vienna Symphony Orchestra under Michael Gielen, the Quatuor Parrenin and the ORTF from Paris under Jean Martinon. It was not least an opportunity, rare in those days, for composers and performers from both sides of the Iron Curtain to discuss new directions in an atmosphere of excitement and optimism.[3] In the coming years it acted as the major focus for Polish composers as they pieced together the jigsaw of new idioms and techniques filtering through from Western Europe and America. It was a slow and haphazard process: scores and recordings from abroad continued to be virtually unobtainable and the general level of national and international communications remained extremely poor. Like his compatriots, Górecki was compelled to chart his own path towards the new horizons.

Back in Silesia, life for Górecki continued to be difficult. He had little or no money and no radio, and manuscript paper was often in short supply. He kept himself informed by buying the periodicals *Ruch muzyczny* (Musical Movement) and *Muzyka*, and he put money aside to buy one score each week, even if that meant going without food. After a period of alternately commuting from home and staying briefly in lodgings (including with his maternal grandmother, Emilia, with whom he had meantime renewed contact), he eventually moved into a tiny, sparsely furnished room in Katowice, which he was to occupy until his marriage in 1959.[4]

There had been a notable toughening in his music between the works immediately preceding the Warsaw Autumn (the Piano Sonata and the first version of *Songs of Joy and Rhythm*) and the Sonata for Two Violins, written in the spring of 1957. But a more significant change came later that year when he composed the Concerto for Five Instruments and String Quartet, Op. 11. The concerto still retains elements from the early pieces—particularly the repeated chordal fortissimos in the second and fourth movements—but its overall tone clearly points in a new direction. Given that Katowice was even more off the beaten track for contemporary music than Warsaw, it is remarkable how Górecki had assimilated or developed of his own accord

---

[3] On the last day of the festival, a new complexion was put on the ruling PZPR (Polish United Workers' Party) with the election of Władysław Gomułka as First Secretary. He promised a 'Polish [as distinct from a Soviet] road to socialism'. It may have seemed a symbolic coincidence to some—a new dawn for both culture and society. But whereas the Warsaw Autumn more than fulfilled its potential, the reality of everyday existence in Poland remained grim.

[4] Given Górecki's deep antipathy to the Communist authorities, it is ironic that two floors beneath his room in Marie Curie-Skłodowska Street lived Edward Gierek, who succeeded Gomułka as First Secretary of the PZPR in 1970.

Ex. II.1. Concerto for Five Instruments and String Quartet, second movement, bb. 1–7

Ex. II.2.  Concerto for Five Instruments and String Quartet, first movement, bb. 1–13

technical and textural ideas which approached those of twelve-note composers in the West. Many of the stylistic innovations relate to Webern, as can readily be seen at the start of the second movement (Ex. II.1). Gone are the traces of neo-classicism already being shouldered out in the Sonata for Two Violins, and in come fragmented, contrapuntal textures, octave displacements, and an atonal if not a thoroughgoing twelve-note concept of pitch organization.[5] Górecki's concerto lacks the crystalline motivic integration of Webern's own Concerto for Nine Instruments (Polish première, Warsaw Autumn, 1960) and prefers a looser, quasi-improvised sequence of intervals. In the first movement, for example, the opening flute solo unfurls in a manner akin to that in Varèse's *Density 21.5* (although less patiently) (Ex. II.2), while the coda of the movement outlines a chain of rising perfect fourths that has no counterpart elsewhere in the work. Ostinatos appear in all four movements; the first of these is a passage for pizzicato viola on the notes D–E♭–C♯, a chromatic rumination which is returned to frequently in Górecki's music of the mid-1960s onwards.

[5] There had been occasional fully chromatic passages in earlier pieces, e.g. in the introduction to the finale of the Sonata for Two Violins.

Two further aspects stand out in the concerto. Firstly, the instrumental ensemble is very much of its time in its incorporation of pitched percussion and in its generally high tessitura. Górecki designs the succession of instrumental combinations carefully: the first movement is essentially a duet for the flute and viola (subsequently the first violin), while the finale brings all nine instruments regularly into play (Górecki has consistently paid great attention to deploying his forces for maximum expressive effect, often at the end of a work). Secondly, the four movements anticipate later instances of a structural model which may be summarized as 'slow–fast–slow–fast' (or 'reflective–active', etc., already a characteristic pattern). And while Górecki seems to be on his way to discursive, non-goal-oriented formal schemes, the second movement still revels in forward drive. It is an enormously expressive and vivid piece of writing, each of its three sections (dolce–animo–feroce) distinct in instrumentation and texture, the whole movement brimming with confidence not in strict compositional procedures but in what comes across as an instinctive creative force.

Already Górecki was recognized at the Higher School of Music as a student of rare quality, and he received the unusual honour of a public concert on 27 February 1958 in the Philharmonic Hall in Katowice. On the programme were six premières: the Toccata, Variations, *Quartettino*, *Songs of Joy and Rhythm*, the Sonata for Two Violins, and, with two performances (before and after the interval), the Concerto, Op. 11. The audience included the Warsaw-based composers Witold Lutosławski (1913–94) and Andrzej Dobrowolski (1921–90); they were full of praise for the sonata, but the concerto was beyond comprehension for most of the audience. Górecki was a leap ahead of his colleagues. Although a few other composers were treading warily towards dodecaphony, most were not yet abreast of Webernian or more recent Western techniques.[6] A comparison with contemporary premières of other Polish scores reveals that Baird was dressing his twelve notes in a neo-classical idiom (String Quartet, 1957), Lutosławski's *Funeral Music* ('à la mémoire de Béla Bartók') was premièred in Katowice (26 March 1958), and only Włodzimierz Kotoński (b. 1925) was moving quickly in a radical direction; Baird's Quartet and Kotoński's *Six Miniatures* for clarinet and piano (1957)

---

[6] The first Polish article on twelve-note technique (by Bogusław Schäffer) had just been published, in *Ruch muzyczny* (1958), no. 1, 9–19. Schäffer's substantial book *Nowa muzyka: Problemy współczesnej techniki kompozytorskiej* (New Music: Problems in Contemporary Compositional Technique) was published later that same year in Kraków.

were premièred in Warsaw the day after Górecki's concert. Krzysztof Penderecki (b. 1933) had not yet surfaced as part of the Polish avant-garde.

The second Warsaw Autumn in 1958 introduced new Polish pieces by Bacewicz, Serocki, and Baird, whose *Four Essays* revealed him as a new master of twelve-note lyricism in the tradition of Alban Berg. The festival highlighted the music of the Second Viennese composers; it also welcomed Karlheinz Stockhausen (b. 1928) and Luigi Nono (1924–90) as guests.[7] Stockhausen introduced a concert of electronic music (by Eimert, Berio, Pousseur, Maderna, himself, and Ligeti) combined with solo piano works by himself, Nilsson, Wolff, and Cage. Later that same evening (3 October), Górecki's *Epitafium*, Op. 12, was premièred alongside music by Kotoński, Serocki, and Webern (*Das Augenlicht* and *Five Pieces*, Op. 10).[8] It was a heady day in the festival, and Górecki did not disappoint; even alongside Webern, *Epitafium* seemed terse.[9]

For the third time since commencing his studies in Katowice, Górecki turned to the poetry of Julian Tuwim. But the contrast with the earlier poems could not be greater; where 'Song of Joy and Rhythm' was positive, Tuwim's final poetic aphorism seems bitterly ironic:

> . . . for the sake of economy put out the light eternal,
> if it were ever to shine for me.

Tuwim wrote it on a serviette in a coffee shop in the Tatra mountain resort of Zakopane, just an hour before collapsing and dying in his hotel. Górecki found the fragment in a Polish periodical a few years later and remembered it for its fateful atmosphere. But there is a further twist to the story: Tuwim appears to have been parodying Goethe's own last words, 'Macht doch den zweiten Fensterladen auch auf, damit mehr Licht hereinkomme' (Open the second shutter, so that more light can come in). In his evocative setting, Górecki stresses

---

[7] Unfortunately, a performance of Nono's *Composizione per orchestra* (1951) had had to be cancelled. Instead, a concert of tape recordings of this work and two other pieces—*Il canto sospeso* (1956) and *Coro di Didone* (1958)—was held in the Zachęta Gallery (I am grateful to Jolanta Bilińska for this information). Górecki was among the audience.

[8] Górecki recalls that *Das Augenlicht* was the first score by Webern that he actually held in his hand.

[9] *Epitafium* was written in the space of a week, with his left hand (his right was in plaster). Górecki was quite used to composing in unconducive circumstances: the Variations were partly written on the train from Kraków to Katowice, the Quartettino in the Cyganeria café in Katowice, and the Sonata for Two Violins on a wooden board that his father made to go over the wash-basin in his bed-sitter.

17

the words 'światło wiekuiste' (the light eternal) at the start and finish, reserving Tuwim's second phrase for the climax. Attention is naturally focused on the choir, and the sharp-edged complement of instruments—side-drums, cymbals, piccolo, C trumpet, and viola—continues the emphasis on high registers noted in the concerto.

For all its brevity, *Epitafium* is constructed of four named sections—Preludium (mainly for percussion), a slow bipartite 'Chorał' (Chorale), a brief climactic 'Antyfona' (Antiphon), and a Postludium. The Preludium–Chorale–Antiphon sequence (a pared-down successor of the tripartite second movement of the concerto) creates momentum towards the textual culmination when the choir, now in eight parts, utters Tuwim's final line in rhythmic unison. But Górecki's musical language elsewhere in the work is more splintered than in the concerto, a shift emphasized by his treatment of dynamics, *Klangfarbenmelodie*, and rhythmic flow. After a sustained opening in the Chorale, the text's syllables become increasingly dislocated as they are passed from one voice to another, often using *Sprechstimme*. The instrumental resources are used sparingly, the percussion providing a dispassionate framework (again, parallels with Varèse), and the three 'melody' instruments contribute an equally unpredictable commentary.[10]

## Symphony No. 1

Górecki acknowledged at the time of its première that *Epitafium* was composed using 'a free serial technique'.[11] In fact only the first hexachord of the series outlined at the start of the Chorale makes any further impression, and that is marginal to the other compositional parameters that command attention. His tussles between following the twelve-note path and obeying other instincts are evident in the next two works, the *Pięć utworów* (Five Pieces), Op. 13, for two pianos and Symphony No. 1 '1959', Op. 14, both completed in 1959, although the symphony was the first to be finished and performed.[12] The First Symphony is a major landmark in Górecki's own *œuvre* and was a radical jolt to Polish music of the time. The first movement has

[10] The score of *Epitafium* is the first of several to give specific layouts for the performers (see also Symphony No. 1, *Monologhi*, *Scontri*, the *Genesis* cycle, and *Choros I*). In this instance, the 'melody' instruments in the foreground are deliberately separated from each other by the percussion.

[11] In the 1958 Warsaw Autumn programme book.

[12] The première, at the 1959 Warsaw Autumn, was incomplete: the second movement was omitted because of its performing difficulties.

claimed much attention, but the remaining three are just as interesting in terms of both style and technique. Górecki gives the four movements 'old' titles, borrowing two of them from the individually headed sections in *Epitafium*: 'Inwokacja' (Invocation), 'Antyfona' (Antiphon), 'Chorał' (Chorale), and 'Lauda'. Although the primary forces are unpitched percussion and strings, the scoring includes the 'antique' sounds of the harpsichord as part of a substantial pitched percussion and keyboard section, which comes into its own in the second movement.

The Antiphon (omitted from the première) illustrates the panache with which Górecki brings together different strands in his technical armoury. While the coda typifies a spare, pointillistic approach—generally soft pinpricks of sound across instrumental families—the opening section enriches this both with a mixture of sustained string chords and unisons and with the antiphonal contrast of the string tutti set against a concertante quartet drawn from front and back desks. The central section ( 5 – 12 ), with its own coda ( 12 – 15 ), is in marked contrast. From a duo for snare drum and violas, Górecki builds up a helter-skelter of eleven lines, sometimes surging individually and sometimes acting in rhythmic co-ordination, leaping from one dynamic extreme to the other, giving the impression of intersecting diagonal planes (Ex. II.3). This highly colourful texture, dominated by the pitched percussion, harp, and piano, comes to what seems like a premature halt, out of which emerge robust repeated string chords, *quasi recitativo*, and a harpsichord solo.

The Chorale and 'Lauda' continue Górecki's exploration of his deliberately chosen orchestral palette. The Chorale is a restrained development of the *Klangfarbenmelodie* in the Antiphon, including a short duo for *sul ponticello* violas and piano. The two lines have consistent and opposing dynamics (*pp* and *ffff* respectively), a polarity that recurs in subsequent works. They are also restricted in their pitch content, which in the case of the viola line brings forward one of a number of unorthodox, if subliminal external references in the symphony. In this case, the oscillation between D and C♮ (itself an echo of the unison notes in the Antiphon) is an oblique reference to the opening notes of 'Bogurodzica', which had already appeared in *Songs of Joy and Rhythm*.[13] A second, but different citation comes at the very end of 'Lauda', where the *pppp* perfect fifth A–E on the violins is an

---

[13] The opening seven notes of 'Bogurodzica' appear on one of the few pages which remain of the sketches for the symphony.

Ex. II.3. Symphony No. 1, second movement, [11]

allusion to the folk-music of the Polish mountains.[14] But the finale is dominated by the unpitched percussion, with a central 'cadenza' for the eight players capped by the entry of the timpani, *massima forza*.

The three last movements, with their mixture of solo and tutti, are a distinctive combination of influences and textures. The strongly stated, quasi-recitative string chords and the unpitched percussion which occur in all of them also act, in effect, as echoes and reinforcers of the character of the first movement, Invocation. This was the ground-breaker, because it was the first time in Polish music that there had been such a stark concentration on massed blocks of sound: four harmonically saturated string 'recitatives', alternated and subsequently interleaved with unpitched percussion. The strings' pitch organization is straightforwardly based on a twelve-note matrix, whose upper horizontal axis is Po (prime) and left-side vertical axis is Io (inversion). The four string passages move in turn through a horizontal presentation, in each of the twelve parts, of P, I, R (retrograde), and RI (retrograde inversion) forms of the series. The vertical layering of the lines is determined by the corner of the matrix from which Górecki begins each passage. At each appearance the string chords become dynamically and rhythmically more dramatic, with the exception of the third passage (scored for violas and cellos), which is clothed in softer dynamics and works through the twelve chords with the tutti providing a backdrop to an antiphonal concertino of a desk each of violas and cellos, anticipating the second movement (Ex. II.4). Elsewhere in the symphony, there is evidence that Górecki is using his matrix as a source of numerical sequences: the durational values of the viola's D–C oscillation in the Chorale derive from the reordering of Po's pitches 1–12 in RI4 (12.2.10.4.1.5.3.7.9.6.11.8), while the numbers of bars grouped between $\boxed{11}$ and $\boxed{22}$ in 'Lauda'—the percussion section of the finale—are drawn from R7's pitch order (9.8.11.7.3.6.1.4.12.5.10.2). The Invocation may be compared to a gigantic recitative without words, with minimal communication between percussion and strings, brutal and uncompromising.[15] The en-

---

[14] Conversation with the author, Aug. 1984. In 1958, Górecki and his fiancée had paid the first of many visits to the Tatras on the border with what was then the Peoples' Republic of Czechoslovakia.

[15] This movement in fact replaces an earlier one. Górecki recalls hearing a performance of a Tchaikovsky symphony during which a particular tutti triggered the idea for the Invocation, which he then wrote overnight. He cannot recall the precise passage, but it was from one of the last three numbered symphonies. It may have come from the finale of the Fourth Symphony, where the reiterative fate motif returns from the first movement and where one of the themes relates to the initial intervals of Górecki's row. Tchaikovsky's motif may be being echoed in the rhythm of the final twelve-note chord of Invocation, after the unison C♯ ($\boxed{7}$).

Ex. II.4. Symphony No. 1, first movement, 4

suing movements pick up on its characteristics as part of a wider expressive vocabulary, but its impact dominates the overall symphonic design.

It is perhaps surprising that Górecki's two other works from 1959, *Five Pieces* and *Trzy diagramy* (Three Diagrams), Op. 15, for solo flute, are for such small forces and eschew the monumental aspects of the First Symphony.[16] It is evident that *Five Pieces* absorbed more of the stylistic characteristics of the serial pieces emanating from Germany, France, and Italy in the early 1950s, although without showing much interest in the attendant theories. Górecki's move towards pointillist textures is reinforced by wide-ranging dynamic, rhythmic, and registral shifts, although there is no evidence that these are organized on strictly serial lines. A more rigorous approach to pitch organization is apparent, albeit one that is individually tailored to Górecki's needs from piece to piece. In the first, which acts as an exposition to the remaining four, the series is outlined in the opening bars (even here there is slight disarray: notes 5 and 6 are interchanged). The second is an early example of Górecki's love of mirror structures, an ingenious little set of pitch palindromes shared between the two pianos. The dramatic fourth piece is notable for its recurring, fixed-range forearm clusters, and, as in the symphony's Chorale, for its 'unorthodox' concentration in the coda on just two dynamic levels—*mp* (piano 1) and *ffff* (piano 2).

The fifth of the *Five Pieces* is the most elaborately worked out and is indicative of the possibilities Górecki now perceived in twelve-note partitioning. It is in two parts, the second for piano 1 alone. Part A, framed by Po and Ro flourishes, is a mirror of *ffff* chromatic clusters and chords. These are arrayed systematically between the two pianos to provide all twelve notes in each bar. Here, as in the fourth piece, Górecki reinforces his dynamic, chordal, and rhythmic brutism, a characteristic from his earliest pieces, but one which strikes a distinctive note in the generally pointillistic context. Part B is constructed of six short sections, each with its own tempo. Each in turn is divided into three subsections, delineated by separate twelve-note complexes rotated in three-, four-, and five-note partitions (Ex. II.5*a*). It seems evident, from the systematic sequence of partitions for each section of Part B (Section I—3–4–5/4–3–5/5–4–3; Section II—5–4–3/4–3–5/ 3–4–5; etc.), that Górecki originally planned a concurrently strict

---

[16] *Five Pieces* incorporates material from *Uderzenia* (Clashes), another work for two pianos, which Górecki wrote and withdrew in 1959.

Ex. II.5. Five Pieces: (a) No. 5, part B, section II; (b) RI4 and subseries

pattern for the twelve-note series. He created a subseries by permutating RI4, giving himself a certain latitude for troping the pitches in each of the three, four, and five-note partitions (Ex. II.5b). In Ex. II.5a, the three subsections are, respectively, permutations of RI4, RI8, and an unidentified re-partition. This last subsection confirms the progressive breakdown of the scheme by transposition or, more typically, by taking the permutation process further. By the time the piece reaches its final twelve-note complex, Górecki has reverted to a dense chromatic idiom, with an eleven-note chord (emphasizing perfect intervals), followed by a solitary C♯ as full stop. What emerges—and this is symptomatic of Górecki's attitude to pre-compositional planning—is that he is not interested in schematic perfection as such, but is quite prepared to explore and appropriate those elements in which he finds interesting material.

The other small-scale chamber work of 1959, *Three Diagrams*, is the first of only two works for solo melody instrument; the other, *Diagram IV* (1961), is also for flute. Given his fascination at the time with pointillistic textures and high rates of dynamic, registral, and rhythmic change, the flute proved an ideal instrument, and Górecki wrote

25

Ex. II.6. *Three Diagrams*, parent series and subseries

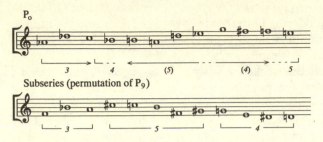

Subseries (permutation of $P_9$)

a work which features not only its lyrical possibilities but more particularly its capriciousness. Framed by a similarly designed 'Principio' and 'Fine' (acting as inverted commas), the three diagrams may be played in any one of the six possible orders. This back-reference to the 'six times three' structure in Part B of the last of the *Five Pieces* is paralleled in the methods of pitch generation. The work's parent series is never stated, but its subseries, devised through partitioning and reordering, is given out at the start of Diagram 2 (Ex. II.6). Górecki also returns to the 3–4–5 pattern which underpins a number of his designs of this period. Here, each diagram has twelve segments divided in rotations of 3–4–5 across three tempos—tardo–moderato–rapido. Diagram 3 demonstrates that the pattern 5–4–3 is deployed in groups of notes from one to twelve:

| | | | | | | | |
|---|---|---|---|---|---|---|---|
| rapido [5 groups] | 10 | 7 | 12 | | 3 | | 6 |
| moderato [4 groups] | | | | 8 | 5 | 1 | 4 |
| tardo [3 groups] | | 2 | | | 11 | 9 | |

This number sequence (and those for the other diagrams, although that for Diagram 1 is corrupted) is drawn from the numerical derivation (I10 in the above instance) from the parent series.

A number of observations may be made from this brief resumé of the basic serial manipulations in *Three Diagrams*. Górecki does not make direct connections between middleground substructures (manipulation of numerical series) and foreground pitches. This remote stratification is not untypical in serial techniques, but for audible results of the basic principles (not necessarily a relevant criterion) the different elements need to be distinctively presented. Górecki does not aid the listener in this respect. The three diagrams are only marginally characterized (No. 2 is arguably more reflective than the

26

others), so the large-scale structure too has minimal impact. Although the three tempos are nominally highly differentiated, their rhythmic material is not, rendering both the shifts between them and the under-lying 3–4–5 groupings largely notional. And the general lack of motivic consistency—despite a degree of spasmodic intervallic corres-pondences—gives the work a loose, improvisatory air. The pattern of dynamics (the ten-step range for *pppp* to *ffff* is the same as in *Five Pieces*) is equally mysterious. To criticize a small work may seem to be bullying a miniature for not being exquisitely formed. But that is not the nature of the puzzle: the perennial enigma is the relationship between end and means. *Three Diagrams* is a small instance of a problem which was to occupy Górecki for several years; in its un-published companion piece, *Diagram IV*, Górecki altered his compositional priorities and achieved a much more telling balance between the various parameters and their organization (see Chapter III).

Before *Diagram IV*, Górecki composed two major pieces as he concluded his studies in Katowice: *Monologhi*, Op. 16 (1960), and *Zderzenia*, Op. 17, otherwise known as *Scontri* (Collisions, 1960). *Monologhi* is Górecki's most committed statement of the serialist ethos espoused by Boulez and others. He combines a solo soprano with an ensemble of metal percussion (cymbals, gongs, and tam-tams) and high-tessitura instruments (two harps, bells, vibraphone, and marimba), refining further the example in *Epitafium*. The text is unusual. It is 'Monolog II', one of nine poems which Górecki wrote between 1958 and 1961.[17] Their tone and syntactical style recall, amongst others, the futurist verse of the Polish poet Stanisław Młodożeniec (1895–1959). And the syllabic reconfigurations of Górecki's already elusive poem become natural partners of the serial processes at work elsewhere in *Monologhi*. The original lines are al-most untranslatable and in English miss out on some of the sibilant sounds clearly relished by Górecki. The first of *Monologhi*'s three movements uses just the opening words: 'szeregowanie | bogów' (lit. arranging gods; the Polish word 'szereg' also has twelve-note conno-tations as a row or series). The second movement exploits the next four, elliptical lines: 'będący głębokością | krzywej | słowa |

---

[17] The poem 'Monolog II' was written during the preparatory phase (19 Mar.–14 Apr. 1960) in the composition of *Monologhi*. Two non-vocal works also shared titles with Górecki's poems: the withdrawn *Clashes*, for two pianos, with a poem written in Dec. 1958, and a later, abandoned work conceived as part of an extended *Genesis* cycle, Op. 19, with another poem from 1958, 'Kantata w formie postludium' (Cantata in the Form of a Postlude).

wymiarowości' (which is depth | the distorted dimensional quality of the word). The final movement's text is slightly more straightforward and, in its coda, recalls the opening lines:

| oni wszyscy grzebali | they all delved |
| w pustej materii | into the empty matter |
| krwi | of blood |
| martwota krzyku | the lifelessness of a scream |
| –czący | [scream]-ing |
| i | and |
| szukający | the searcher |
| szuka funkcji głosu | searches for the function of the voice |
| BOGOŁOWANIA | AT BEING GOD |
| SZEREGOWANIE | ARRANGING |

Górecki divides his forces into three groups: A (harp 1, soprano and tenor cymbals, three gongs), B (soprano, bells, vibraphone, marimba, mezzo and baritone cymbals), and C (harp 2, alto and bass cymbals, three tam-tams). The three groups are frequently intertwined, with the soprano's ferocious line ranging from straight vocal production through occasional *Sprechstimme* and on to unpitched utterances when combined with the metal percussion. The instrumental textures vary from the meditative (often created by small-scale palindromes) to the convulsive, reeking of a neurotic *angst* totally appropriate to the disjunct vocal delivery. *Monologhi*'s twelve-note matrix furnishes not just pitches but dynamic and durational patterns (the bar-lengths are controlled in this way). The most concentrated example occurs in the unpitched percussion accompanying the soprano's first entry in the third movement: the dynamic and durational values of each of the five groups (gongs, tam-tams, and three pairs of cymbals) are separately drawn from different numerical sequences in the matrix of the parent series. The pitch content of the work is heavily disguised, not least by the partitioning procedure already used in previous works; here, the subseries is derived from P7 (Ex. II.7). *Monologhi* represents something of a stylistic digression from Górecki's long-term goals, although his taste for intricate technical procedures continued in some works in the early 1960s. With *Scontri*, the work he completed immediately after graduation with first-class honours from the Higher School of Music in Katowice, he seems to have looked again at aspects of his technique, clarifying his procedures while at the same time astonishing the audience at the 1960 Warsaw Autumn with the explosive vitality in his handling of the orchestra and symphonic structure.

Ex. II.7. *Monologhi*, parent series and subseries

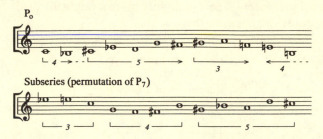

Scontri

*Scontri* is well named. It is the antithesis of Nono's *Incontri* (Meetings, 1955), and Górecki was well aware of the connection when searching for a foreign equivalent to the Polish title *Zderzenia*. There is nothing quite like it. It is a stupendous symbol of Górecki's extraordinary progress since his arrival in Katowice five years earlier. And yet, for all the stylistic and technical changes along the way, his musical stamp had always been clear from Op. 1 onwards. What *Scontri* represents is the most colourful and vibrant expression of the new Polish wave which he had headed since the première of the Concerto in 1958. The première caused an uproar, critical brickbats and bouquets, not least because of the irregular disposition of the large orchestra on stage (Fig. 2). The strings form an arc around the stage (not in a conventional sequence), the woodwind, trombones, and three of the eight percussion players are contained inside, the remaining brass scattered outside the strings, with harps, pianos, the remaining percussion, and conductor forming a loose circle on the periphery. The first trombone and third percussion are at the centre of this aural galaxy. It is possible that the score's difficulties have militated against frequent performances, in contrast to the many given of later Polish experimental works such as Lutosławski's *Jeux vénitiens* (Venetian Games, 1961) and Penderecki's *8′37″*, better known under its subsequent title *Ofiarom Hiroszimy tren* (Threnody to the Victims of Hiroshima, 1961). But *Scontri* remains a crucial work and is worth examining in some detail.

Its dedicatee, the conductor and composer Jan Krenz (b. 1926), was artistic director of the Polish Radio Symphony Orchestra in Katowice 1953–67 and had conducted the partial première of Górecki's First Symphony at the 1959 Warsaw Autumn. In the spring of 1960 he

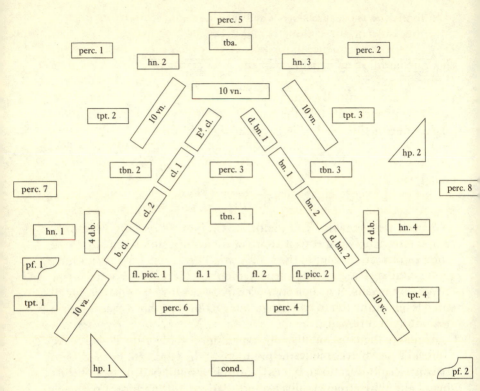

FIG. 2. *Scontri*, orchestral layout

commissioned a new work from Górecki for the orchestra's appearance at the next Warsaw Autumn and, after completing *Monologhi* at
the end of April that year, Górecki set about his new orchestral score.
He composed *Scontri* in the amazingly short time of five weeks (he
then copied out the parts himself), and perhaps this white-hot speed
contributed to the work's stunning fusion of futurist energy and
nervous repose. The technical means are directly related to the expressive ends, giving the composition a transparency absent in some
of its immediate predecessors.

Górecki divides the orchestra into its four constituent families:
woodwind (without oboes), brass, percussion with harps and pianos,
and strings. He tends to write for these families regardless of their
spatial dislocation on the platform, likening the aural principle to that
of the shared melody at the start of the finale to Tchaikovsky's Sixth

Symphony (on those occasions when the two violin sections are placed on either side of the conductor). Initially he planned to build the structure from a sequence of the twenty-four possible permutations of the four families, an expansion of the 3–4–5 principle used in earlier compositions. He intended to composed each of the permutations (which were eventually extended to twenty-eight) onto one *arkusz* (sheet of paper), but only the first seven sheets bear any significant correlation to this plan. The printed score still closely follows the overall design, with each double-page spread devoted to one sheet (and each marked by a new rehearsal number), although with occasional overlapping onto the following page. In practice, the structure is a series of twenty-eight mosaics, lasting anything from eighteen to seventy seconds. These coalesce into six larger sections: I (sheets 1–8), II (8–11), III (11–14), IV (15–17), V (18–24), and VI (25–28). The tempo moves between three markings (crotchet = MM 40, 72, 132), a development of the scheme in *Three Diagrams*, although here Górecki adapts a practice, already in use elsewhere, of indicating tempos by means of a continuous thick line that moves between the three levels at the top of each page. In every other respect, the score is laid out conventionally.

Arguably the most significant development is the rationalization of Górecki's serial techniques. He continues to apply these to pitch, dynamics, and durations, but seems for the most part to have abandoned the derivation of subseries through partitioning. Instead, he composes four separate series, a main one and three others assigned to different instrumental families. The first series is the main source in *Scontri* and happens to share its first four intervals with the last four of that in *Three Diagrams* (Ex. II.8). Like most of its predecessors, it is dominated by semitones (five), but whereas earlier series tend to have a sub-emphasis on one or two intervals (i.e. perfect intervals in that of the First Symphony), the main series of *Scontri* has a more even spread. Górecki shows no interest in cross-related intervallic substructures in any of his series. The other three series in *Scontri* are sparingly used and show a new concern for intervallic consistency allied to instrumental groups: the woodwind series is characterized by seconds, the brass series by thirds, and the string series by fourths (Ex. II.9).

Section I (sheets 1–8) leaves the listener in no doubt as to its volcanic temperament. The initial string texture is a gradual sustained accumulation, sparked off by accented semiquavers, of an unearthly sound-world created by playing the strings *pppp* below the bridge (Ex.

Ex. II.8. *Scontri*, main series and number matrix

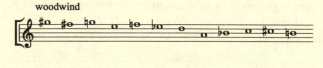

| P → | | | | | | | | | | | |
|---|---|---|---|---|---|---|---|---|---|---|---|
| I 1 | 2 | 3 | 4 | 5 | 6 | 7 | 8 | 9 | 10 | 11 | 12 |
| ↓ 9 | 1 | 11 | 8 | 10 | 4 | 3 | 6 | 2 | 12 | 7 | 5 |
| 10 | 5 | 1 | 11 | 8 | 3 | 2 | 7 | 12 | 6 | 9 | 4 |
| 8 | 4 | 5 | 1 | 11 | 2 | 12 | 9 | 6 | 7 | 10 | 3 |
| 11 | 3 | 4 | 5 | 1 | 12 | 6 | 10 | 7 | 9 | 8 | 2 |
| 6 | 8 | 10 | 9 | 7 | 1 | 5 | 2 | 4 | 3 | 12 | 11 |
| 12 | 10 | 9 | 7 | 6 | 11 | 1 | 3 | 5 | 4 | 2 | 8 |
| 4 | 6 | 12 | 2 | 3 | 9 | 10 | 1 | 8 | 11 | 5 | 7 |
| 2 | 9 | 7 | 6 | 12 | 8 | 11 | 4 | 1 | 5 | 3 | 10 |
| 3 | 7 | 6 | 12 | 2 | 10 | 8 | 5 | 11 | 1 | 4 | 9 |
| 5 | 12 | 2 | 3 | 4 | 7 | 9 | 11 | 10 | 8 | 1 | 6 |
| 7 | 11 | 8 | 10 | 9 | 5 | 4 | 12 | 3 | 2 | 6 | 1 |

Ex. II.9. *Scontri*, woodwind, brass, and string series

woodwind

brass

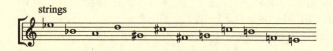

strings

II.10). This passage's metrical-rhythmical design is the precursor of
many such 'elasticated' patterns, which are often palindromic: the
accented notes are placed on the following semiquavers in different
half-bars (1&8; −|2; 7|3&6; 4&5|etc.) before reversing the process.
Some forty-five seconds later, this erupts in the other families in a

Ex. II.10. *Scontri*, opening of sheet 1

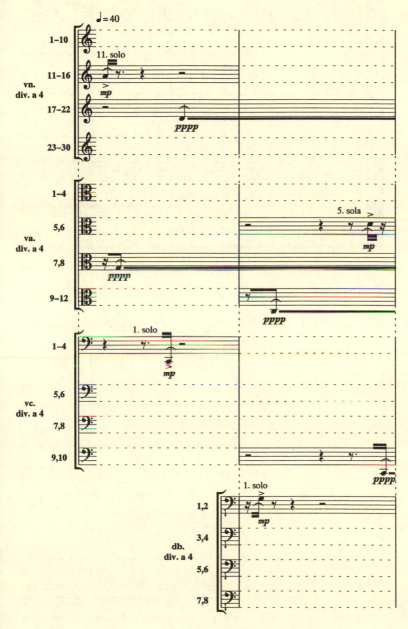

34

volatile mix of clusters and solo lines which emphasizes the registral extremes, notably high piccolo and low contrabassoon. This rate of timbral, rhythmic, and dynamic change will prove typical of this section, which has all the marks of a fertile exposition. Sheet 2 is galvanized into a pulsating hocket between the twelve woodwind instruments and a four-octave string cluster. The woodwind texture is a rhythmically animated version of the pitch matrix idea that Górecki used in the First Symphony's Invocation, but in this instance he partitions the matrix of the main series (a rare occurrence in *Scontri*) into the pattern 4–3–5 (notes 6–8, 9–12, 1–5). He then reverses the pattern to create another of the work's many palindromes. Sheet 3 disturbs the blocked use of instrumental families as the texture fragments among wind and strings. The music for individual woodwind and brass (a more extended palindrome) is the first instance in *Scontri* of the combination of three series: pitch (RI6), durations (R6), and dynamics (P4). The percussion family's contribution so far has been brief (piano and vibraphone in the early stages). Sheet 3 is punctuated on the last semiquaver by the bass drum, heralding the second phase of this section (sheets 4–8), where the unpitched percussion takes on a more prominent role. In sheets 4 and 6 the percussion elaborate their own durational-dynamic matrix while the brass and woodwind collide and the string clusters slide over one another like geological plates.[18] Sandwiched between sheets 4 and 6, sheet 5 is a more quixotic mix, comprising *ffff* chords and clusters on the two pianos, a web of rapid string glissandos pitched against the horns, and a recollection of the strings' sound-wall from sheet 1. The interlocking of ideas is a fundamental element in the design of Section I, as sheet 6 develops material from 4, and both 6 and 7 refine and bring to the fore the hocketing between orchestral families that lies at the root of Górecki's concept. Sheet 7, in fact, looks so clean-cut as to suggest collusion rather than collision. But the unpredictability of the rhythmic design gives it the necessary edge, with the wind's neat rhythmic-metric mirror pattern seismically rifted by several large string clusters and a now rhythmically united percussion section with its own simple durational-metrical palindrome (Ex. II.11).

After this display of muscular *Klangfarben*, the temperature cools, signalled by a sudden compression of the string cluster onto a solitary A♭ and some unusual textures from the pianos and harps (hitting the piano case with wooden beaters, playing harp glissandos with the

---

[18] The realization of the percussion matrix in sheets 4 and 6 is one of a number of instances in *Scontri* where Górecki departs occasionally from his adopted series.

Ex. II.11. *Scontri*, first half of sheet 7

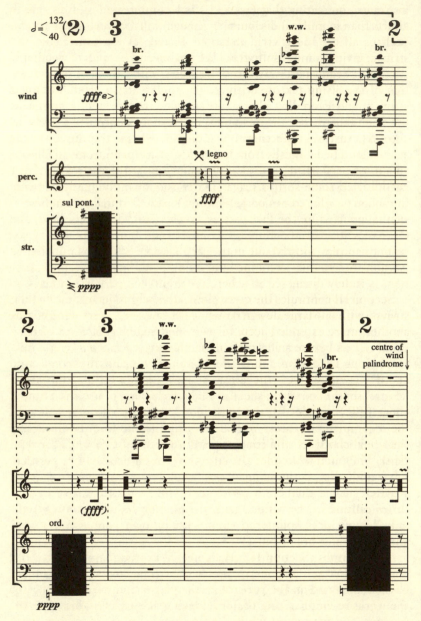

fingernails). There are relatively few unusual performance directions in *Scontri*, indicating that Górecki was less interested in avant-garde effects than in musical discourse by conventional means. The result is perhaps all the more vivid. Sections II and III are centred on the strings, giving some respite from the quakes and fissures of Section I. Section II begins part-way through sheet 8, with a distinct recapitulation of the string texture with which *Scontri* began, each sustained string note triggered by a harp note sounded by a metal plectrum near the soundboard. As the resultant twelve-note chord ebbs away in sheet 9 (a textural reduction to just one solo violin straining upwards against loud pedal noises from the pianos), the music seems to take on an almost personal nature, as if the unison Ab at the end of Section I has initiated some sort of private narrative. After the cosmic energy the solitary violin comes perhaps to symbolize a more human dimension, supported by the fact that writing for strings is second only to Górecki's love of the human voice. Sheet 10 instructs the string sections to play mostly soft notes, tremolo and sustained, as high as possible, before their combined unpitched *pp* chord (another recollection) is rudely dismissed in sheet 11.

Section III continues the quasi-developmental concentration on the strings, with one large design covering sheets 11–14. Very simply, it is another, more extended accumulation of string chords, devised consecutively as twelve solo notes (dynamic range: *pppp–mf*), six dyads (*ppp*), four triads (*pp*), three four-note chords (*p*), three five-note chords (*quasi p*), etc. (the durational values again derive from an 'elastic' rhythmic-metric sequence). At the arrival of the twelve-note chord (*ffff*) in sheet 14, the brass interrupts with its own version of the accumulation process while the strings hammer out twelve times their final chord (cf. the conclusion of the First Symphony's Invocation). The pitch source for the strings in this entire section, giving it its own identity, is the string series (see Ex. II.9).

After such a deliberate construction, Górecki feels the need to throw caution to the winds again, and Section IV (sheets 15–17) not only reintroduces splintered sounds on pitched percussion, woodwind, and later brass, but also steps up the tension by returning to variable tempos (Section II had a constant crotchet = MM 40, III a constant MM 72). The reappearance of high piccolo and low contrabassoon picks up on the registral extremes touched on at the start of the work, re-emphasizing the developmental quality of these central sections, and for a short while the woodwind and brass pitches come from their own series. A palindromic duet for the two pianos crosses from sheets 16 to 17 and is one of the few remnants in *Scontri* of the filigree writing in *Five Pieces* and *Monologhi*. But the woodwind and brass cannot contain their collective explosions much longer, and a short climax leads to the next stage of this elemental 'guide to the orchestra'.

Górecki's fascination with the percussion was to lead him to write a manual on percussion instruments, 'Uwagi o perkusjach' (Comments on Percussion, 1960–2, unpublished), and he had already accorded unpitched percussion instruments significant roles in *Epitafium*, Symphony No. 1, and *Monologhi*. In Section V (sheets 18–24), the unpitched percussion controls the timbral space, with their pitched cousins adding colour (sometimes recalling *Monologhi*), particularly to the exploration of wood and metal percussion in sheets 19–21. In sheet 22, the strings sneak in with a magnified version of its glissando web from sheet 5, although the percussion (now reverted to skins—bongos, timbales, tom-toms, and bass drums) is determined to assert its authority. In a sequence parallel to the percussion writing in sheets 4 and 6, sheets 22 and 24 each explore eight rhythmic series, while the intervening sheet 23 contains an exuberant passage of overlapping rhythmic mirrors.

The final section (sheets 25–8) acts as a conflation of recapitulation and coda. While the central four sections have largely concentrated on distinct timbres (strings, wind, percussion), section VI returns to the kinetic and vividly sculpted contrasts of the first section. Sheet 25 acts as a preparation for the main tutti, and for only the second time gives the brass and woodwind their own series. The tutti itself (sheets 26–7) is the least rhythmically defined passage in *Scontri*, each wind instrument having its own repeat-note accelerando or ritardando (although pitch and dynamics are carefully controlled). Representatives of wood, metal, and skin percussion take their part in this general cadenza, while pianos and below-the-bridge strings add to the general impression of aleatory chaos. The coda proper (sheets 27–8) gathers the orchestra together in a final wild hocket across the timbral strata before the brass unite on a *ffff* E♮ (only the second such unison, paralleling the string A♭ at the end of section I), leaving the strings to scamper tremulously into the ether with an almost defiant crescendo on the final note. For all its apparent artlessness and free-ranging invention, *Scontri* is a meticulously crafted score, with many layers of organization and cross-reference. On an expressive level, however, Górecki had unleashed a fire which scorched both his listeners and himself.

# III

# GENESIS

GÓRECKI'S personal circumstances had changed markedly since 1955, not least after his marriage to Jadwiga Rurańska in Katowice in the summer of 1959. On their honeymoon in July they visited Zakopane for the second time, and on this and subsequent walking holidays they continued to explore the foothill country to the north of the Tatra range—the regions of Podhale, Kotlina Nowotarska, and Gorce (Fig. 3). In 1959 they discovered the villages of Witów and Chochołów, where they were to spend many summer months from 1966 until the late 1980s.[1] Their home in Katowice was now a small flat north of the city centre in a block occupied by a number of musicians, although Górecki frequently returned to Rydułtowy (and occasionally to a summer-house in Szabelski's garden) to gain some peace and quiet for composition.

He was in no hurry to earn his living again as a teacher once he had graduated (he joined the staff of the Higher School of Music in Katowice a few years later). More importantly, he wanted to move beyond *Scontri* and investigate new possibilities. During the following year he completed three small chamber works, one of which was *Diagram IV* for flute. It is interesting for a number of reasons. Firstly, it extends the limited structural choice presented to the performer in its predecessor, *Three Diagrams*. *Diagram IV* consists of thirteen 'structure-fragments'. The player is given the freedom to choose the order of the twelve smaller structure-fragments (between $11''$ and $2'$ in duration), making sure that the longest (lasting $2'-4'$) is played centrally, that is, seventh. Secondly, it develops new notational devices governing duration, types of repetition, order of events, and rhythmic and performance indications.[2] Thirdly, Górecki devised a unique pitch structure to define and hold in check the new freedom he was

---

[1] These place-names are pronounced *Vee*-toof and Hoh-*hoh*-woof.

[2] An explanation of the beginning of the eleventh structure-fragment of *Diagram IV* is given in the author's article 'The Music of Henryk Mikołaj Górecki: The First Decade', *Contact*, 27 (1983), 10–20.

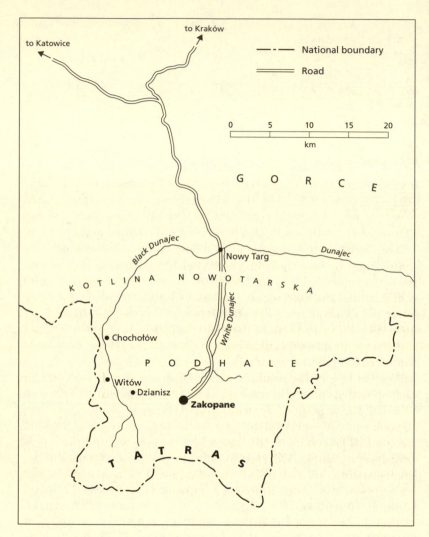

FIG. 3. Map of Podhale

giving to the performer to shape some of the interior details. In many ways, it bears a kinship to Lutosławski's sensibility to harmonic fields and their rhythmic and motivic animation, which he was developing at the same time in *Jeux vénitiens*. But the construction of a single fixed harmonic framework was a departure for Górecki and would not appear again in this guise.

Ex. III.1. *Diagram IV*: (*a*) outline pitch design; (*b*) pitch ranges of G♮ and F♯ structure-fragments

(*a*)

(*b*)

G♮ structure - fragment          F♯ structure - fragment

The central structure-fragment consists of a meticulously de-signed, step-by-step unfolding of a twelve-note series. Each note of the series, preceded by a *ffff* flourish of some of its neighbour-notes, is highlighted at a fixed register and dynamic (the lower the pitch, the lower the dynamic, etc.). These pitches then act as individual satellites, each located in one of the twelve shorter structure-fragments, and each with its own orbital pitch sphere. The spheres' radii range from zero (on G♯) to a minor ninth (around E♭)—Górecki excludes the tritone because of the resultant octave diameter (Ex. III.1*a*). Within each sphere of influence, most if not all of the chromatic pitches are sounded: the structure-fragment radiating from F♯, for example, uses all twelve pitches, whereas the G♮ structure-fragment not only fails to reach to its lowest note (B♮) but specifies only nine of the twelve available pitches (Ex. III.1*b*). Six of the structure-fragments have a single dynamic, six a variable dynamic range. It is an effective design, not only for a mobile, although it did not fully answer Górecki's question, 'Where next?'

Travel outside the Eastern bloc, although easier than before 1956, was still a dream for most Poles. Górecki's *Monologhi* had won the Composers' Union's youth competition in 1960, and the prize was a three-month trip abroad. This was to be Górecki's first foreign visit, and his intention was to study in Italy with Nono, whom he had met at the Warsaw Autumn.[3] The Polish authorities for some reason did

[3] Górecki would also have had the opportunity to renew contact with the composer Franco Evangelisti (1926–80), who had visited Poland in the late 1950s and early 1960s and whom Górecki acknowledged in 1962 as an important influence on aspects of his technical thinking (interview with Leon Markiewicz, *Ruch muzyczny* (1962), no. 17, 8).

not approve his plan, so Górecki headed on his own to Paris for the last three months of 1961. After Communist Poland, the shock of France can be imagined. Górecki's stipend was small, but he eagerly explored Paris by foot, visited galleries and museums, saw films, and went to a few concerts. He listened to Olivier Messiaen playing the organ at La Trinité on Sundays but, although he had a letter of introduction, he was too shy to make contact.[4] He did, however, introduce himself to Pierre Boulez at a concert of Schoenberg's music. He also met the *emigré* Polish composer Michał Spisak (1914–65) and had memorable conversations with Stravinsky's friend Pierre Souvchinsky.[5] Apart from a couple of poems, Górecki wrote nothing during his stay in Paris, but he thought long and hard about his future direction. Once back in Poland, he began work in earnest on a composition whose title symbolized a tough new compositional ethos.

## Elementi

*Elementi*, Op. 19 No. 1, for three string instruments was the first of a series of pieces in a cycle called *Genesis*. Ultimately, there were to be three pieces in Op. 19, the second being *Canti strumentali* (Instrumental Songs) for fifteen players (1962) and the third, *Monodramma* (Monodrama), for soprano, metal percussion, and six double basses (1963).[6] All three advance the notational experiments in *Diagram IV* and are witnesses to Górecki's radical exploration of the nature of sound, a conscious distancing from the pointillistic idiom of previous works. He was returning to the movement of bands of sound (as in the first and last movements of the First Symphony), 'using solely the sequence of complex groups and exploiting the tensions that then

---

[4] Bohdan Pociej's assertion, in his otherwise perceptive entry on Górecki in *The New Grove Dictionary of Music and Musicians*, ed. Stanley Sadie (London, 1980), vii. 539, that Górecki 'had lessons in Paris with Messiaen' is erroneous and has misled many subsequent writers, including the present author.

[5] Górecki returned to Paris between June and Aug. 1963, this time with his wife. Like his first visit, this too was a composition prize, on this occasion from UNESCO for the First Symphony. They stayed with Spisak and his wife; Górecki took off for a few days for his only visit to Darmstadt, where his Symphony was given its first complete performance on 15 July.

[6] At various stages between 1962 and 1964, Górecki had other ideas for the cycle. In his interview with Leon Markiewicz (p. 6), given after the composition of Op. 19 Nos. 1 and 2, he cited future projects in it, including *Monologhi II* (eventually *Monodramma*), Symphony No. 2 for strings (eventually *Choros I*, Op. 20), and other untitled pieces. In Górecki's list of works in the programme book for the 1964 Warsaw Autumn, *Choros I* is cited as Op. 19 No. 4, alongside two unrealized projects in the cycle: *Choros II*, Op. 19 No. 5, for wind instruments and percussion, and *Kantata w formie postludium* (Cantata in the Form of a Postlude), Op. 19 No. 6, for orchestra.

arise. Because *Elementi* begins the whole cycle, what is happening in the work should be regarded as the initial movement of something like nucleae, individual atoms'.[7] *Elementi* does indeed act as a rugged sequence of combative modes of attack, dynamics, and timbres. And while it is possible to discern its expressive rationale, the underlying structure is much more obscure. It comes as something of a surprise to learn that 'the foundation of the construction of the entire piece is the set of intervals of the Prime and Retrograde series', but not that 'as for the sound phenomena, their sequence, duration, dynamics, these I regulate purely by ear. . . . As soon as I draw formal consequences from a series, I no longer stick to the initial sequence of sounds in the series. I choose what I consider most appropriate at a given moment.'[8]

The twelve-note series at the root of *Elementi* is all but obliterated in the score. The only real evidence for its existence is the sequence of twelve open fifths at $\boxed{25}$, but this is an aural fiction as all three instruments have been detuned since $\boxed{20}$. And the twelve violin pitches linked by an extended glissando between $\boxed{17}$ and $\boxed{18}$ form a series so unlike any other in Górecki's work in its preponderance of whole tones that it seems, even at its most definable, to be a distant relative of the series from *Monologhi*. If the textural feel of *Elementi* is comparable to that of an oil canvas much worked over and scraped down with a palette-knife, it follows that the intervallic ramifications of the series on its construction are also likely to be inaudible. The listener will perceive that the second half (from $\boxed{15}$) is generally much quieter than the first, but not that in concept it has the same number of fragment groups as the first half (eleven). The number of events (or substructures) within these fragment groups is determined by the intervallic sequence of Po and then Ro, giving the work a notional mirror design. Górecki linked his twenty-two fragment groups into six larger sequences (cf. *Scontri*): I (to $\boxed{8}$), II ($\boxed{8}$–$\boxed{11}$), III ($\boxed{11}$–$\boxed{15}$), IV ($\boxed{15}$–$\boxed{18}$), V ($\boxed{18}$–$\boxed{23}$), VI (from $\boxed{23}$). Their definition is less than clear-cut, with many cross-currents, and such are Górecki's varying criteria for defining individual events within the fragment groups that it is the expressive and not the technical aspect of the work which takes aural precedence, despite the latter's generative significance.

The events of the first four fragment groups (Sequence I) are based structurally on the opening intervals of Po (11.5.11.2, the retrograde of the cello intervals between $\boxed{25}$ and $\boxed{26}$). The eleven events of the opening fragment group (1'39", up to $\boxed{5}$) are determined consecu-

[7] Interview with Markiewicz, 6.    [8] Ibid.

tively, (*i*) by changes of pitch as a dense wedge is built up from a throbbing open D♮ (a clustered derivative of the viola ostinato in Op. 11), (*ii*) by new methods of rhythmic animation when a seven-note cluster is reached, and (*iii*) by a shift to unspecified 'highest pitches' in irregular repetition. In contrast, the five substructures of the second fragment group (24″, ⑤–⑥) are overlapped: each of the three instruments, playing simultaneously, has its own order of five different rhythmic-motivic units based on material from the end of the first fragment group. The third fragment group (32″) illustrates the impulsive nature of Górecki's invention: its eleven events consist of two consecutive events carried over from the second fragment group, followed by a high violin note (the bow pressed hard on the string to create a grating effect) which then descends through a glissando under which eight marcato 'chords' (events four to eleven) are attacked by viola and cello. And the two mini-events in the final fragment group of the sequence (4″) act as a coda. Sequence II takes further the separation between the instruments and departs wholesale from specified pitches into the world of atonal articulation which Górecki had thoroughly investigated before commencing work on *Elementi*. One of the most striking fragment groups is that beginning at ⑫. The variety of tremolandos, bow techniques, and interlocking planes of glissandos and sustained notes is a vivid example of the three instruments at work on a unified texture (Ex. III.2).

The rate of change in the second half of *Elementi* is certainly lower than in the first. And even though there is frequent carrying over of ideas from one of its eleven fragment groups to the next, the second half is carried out at a markedly slower pace. This is clear from the trills which occupy the twelfth fragment group (⑮) and from the remaining three fragment groups of this fourth sequence (up to ⑱). For all their hyperactivity, fragment groups 13 to 15 explore only five short motivic ideas in overlapping rotation, sometimes singly, sometimes in pairs with the third instrument playing a glissando, or most vehemently in threes (the start of fragment group 14). The overall impact of *Elementi* is one of ceaseless energy and movement, of coordination as well as disjunction, and of an untraditional approach to the evolution of form (shades of *Scontri*). Not for nothing is this a work for three instruments rather than for trio: with each player seated a minimum of six metres from the others in a triangular formation, Górecki wishes to forgo anything that smacks of convention.

*Elementi*'s generally high dynamic tessitura and incessant activity is taken up by both of its companion pieces. But the unified instrumental

Ex. III.2. *Elementi*, [12], bb. 7–12

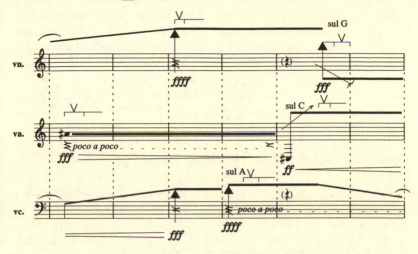

timbre of *Elementi* (which harks back to the Sonata for Two Violins) is abandoned for more colourful palettes in *Canti strumentali* (cf. the scoring in *Epitafium*) and *Monodramma*, with its timbral echoes of *Monologhi*. The instrumentation of *Canti strumentali* includes not only three violins and three violas, percussion, two pianos, and three high wind instruments, but also mandolin and guitar. This spectrum suggests what Józef Patkowski has called 'sonic hedonism', even though Górecki has lost little of his aggressive stance to his material.[9] But the intense, almost manic concentration of *Elementi* is lacking, having given way to a broader sweep in which many of the earlier work's ideas and textures now vie with exotic timbral contrasts as *Canti strumentali*'s driving forces. The reduced austerity is tellingly employed in the coda ([22]), which for the first time in the piece introduces a dynamic other than *ffff*. A gentle combination of overlapping ostinatos for flute, trumpet, and two tam-tams not only anticipates the end of *Beatus vir*, Op. 38 (1979), and a couple of later works but also

[9] In a Polish Radio broadcast, 4 Oct. 1962. Repr. in *Horyzonty muzyki*, a collection of fifty-six radio scripts on contemporary music, broadcast as introductions to relays of new music for over ten years from Oct. 1959, in Józef Patkowski's series of the same name. The scripts' authors in the first year included Lutosławski, Evangelisti, Xenakis, Nono, and Boulez. Górecki recalls 'Horyzonty muzyki' as a vital part of his radio listening. Patkowski also set up in 1957, at Polish Radio in Warsaw, the first experimental electronic studio in Eastern Europe; although many Polish composers worked in it, Górecki was not one of them.

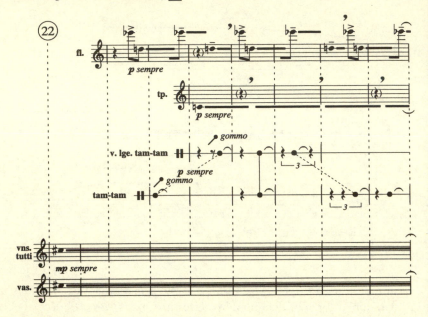

establishes the structural precedent of a quiet conclusion. It also outlines, in the parts for flute and trumpet, the intervals of Górecki's modal 'motto' (Ex. III.3).

The scoring for *Monodramma* confines the role of precise pitches to a solo soprano and a set of tubular bells. It marks a return to a more restricted instrumentation, comprising detuned double basses and a range of unpitched metal instruments played by a dozen percussionists. The ritual element is high, with plentiful ostinatos and a vocal line which consists mainly of the Polish vowel sounds A - O - U. At the final climax, the soprano manages to put consonants to her melisma, a composite word (again, the influence of Młodożeniec): LI - TO - ME - TA - LE - FO - NI - TY - GRA - NI - TY - GRAANI - TY. Górecki's neologism conflates the ancient word for solid ('lity'), granite, and metallophone, with allusions to the Polish for play ('gra'). There is an atavistic streak in Górecki which has already made its presence felt, but in *Genesis* it comes to the fore. Both *Elementi* and *Monodramma* show different aspects of this characteristic. Where *Elementi* digs deep into the rough-hewn ancestry of string instruments, *Monodramma* captures the relationship between the human voice and metal instruments, invoking primitive rites.

With one exception, the detuned double basses play a low six-voice pedal-point throughout *Monodramma*; they depart but briefly to join in at the main climax. So the burden of energy and movement is in the hands of the percussion, which is split into two groups, one placed either side of 39, which also marks off an extended coda from the body of the movement. The first part of *Monodramma* uses twelve metal blocks, eight cymbals, and four gongs laid flat on a pad of material. The resultant sound (using metal beaters) is therefore not as resonant as that in the coda, where the players shift to twelve triangles (metal beaters), eight suspended cymbals, and four tam-tams (soft sticks). Their activity in the coda is a mixture of trills and unison attacks. In the main body of the work, Górecki adds passages of highly patterned rhythmic heterophony to the repertoire of trills and unison attacks, playing off one percussion group against another. The bells perform a punctuating function, with isolated dyads (sevenths, ninths) appearing from 5 onwards. They are allowed one moment of glory, when all seven of the pitches they have so selectively sounded are grouped together in a grand decelerating flourish into the metal percussion's final *ffff* entry.

In their exposé in the opening section of *Monodramma*, the percussion had enjoyed the type of muscular hocketing heard in parts of *Scontri*. When the soprano first enters, she electrifies the percussion and then compels it to disintegrate, until the first of the main climaxes reunifies them. At this point, she unfurls an almost complete twelve-note series in hysterical yelps against tutti percussion beats. The double basses remain impervious, but within seconds launch their own assault, which is taken up by the soprano (declaiming Górecki's text) and by the percussion in the most elaborate heterophony in the piece (Ex. III.4). These superimposed patterns are gradually reduced, lessening the tension in preparation for the three-part coda. With softer dynamics and beaters, a slower rate of change, and occasional reminders of earlier textures, this is an old-fashioned coda, given more weight than the codas in the previous works in the cycle.

In his 1962 interview, Górecki spoke of 'subjecting myself to strict self-control', indicating his intention to discipline his technical and creative impulses in the service of controlled composition, an overarching desire to eschew the looseness and listlessness he observed in musical developments elsewhere.[10] In the search for his ideal of a harmonically compact and precisely worked-out piece, *Choros I*,

[10] Interview with Markiewicz, 6.

Ex. III.4. *Monodramma,* 22

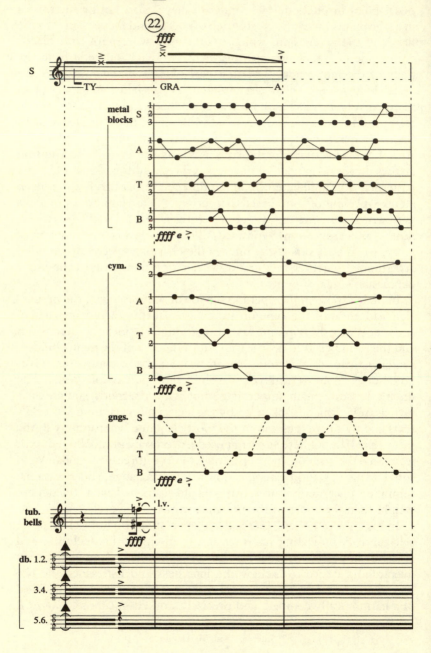

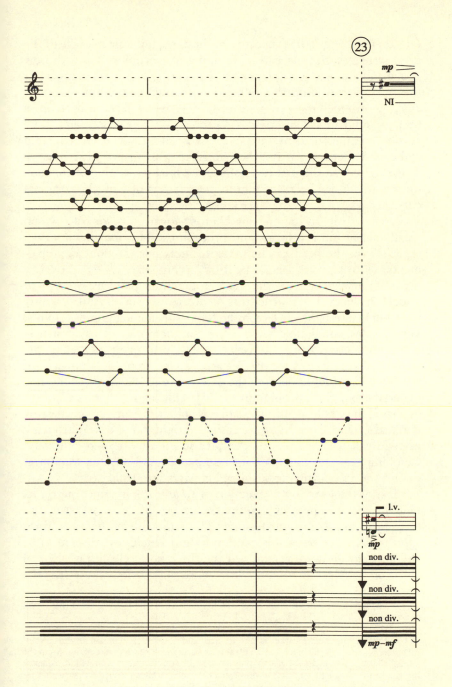

Op. 20, for strings (1964) became a milestone, not least because of the great struggles Górecki had in bringing it to fruition. He withdrew and abandoned the preliminary version shortly before its première at the 1963 Warsaw Autumn. When he returned to the score in early 1964, he dropped most of his carefully devised effects in harmonics because of notational and practical problems.[11] The subsequent 'first' version, premièred at the 1964 Warsaw Autumn, was itself renotated and edited after the festival: the published score (especially from [36]) shows further substantial revisions and a final jettisoning of the harmonics which had been such an important part of Górecki's original concept.

From early in his career, Górecki has shown a love for titles which recall ancient musical forms and procedures. This may be observed especially in the headings he gives to individual sections or movements, as in *Epitafium* and the First Symphony. *Choros I* overtly provokes expectations of the verse and refrain patterns which had underlain the evolving structures of preceding works. And certainly the 'choral' alternation between the four instrumental groups (violins, violas, cellos, and double basses) is one of the work's main rationales. The antiphonal writing, however, is far from confrontational: the music moves at a measured pace, apart from a sequence of accelerandos which constitute the emergence of the principal motivic material from the opening unison A♯. One of its most significant aspects is the wholesale return to precise pitches: from the A♯ a narrow chromatic cluster emerges, releasing a tight three-note chromatic motivic cell which stalks the texture in an almost menacing way. Combining and turning in on itself in parallel and contrary motion, it excites the accompanying sustained clusters into trills.

Most of the introductory section of *Choros I* is in triple metre, its highly structured phrases shaping the genesis of this most basic material in an almost Baroque fashion. The main body of the work (from [12]) throws off some of this caution by introducing what seem to be rhythmically aleatoric versions of the three-note cells.[12] The general level of activity increases, with more altercations between the

---

[11] For a discussion of the differences between the abandoned and the first performed version of *Choros I*, see Leon Markiewicz, 'Choros I Henryka Góreckiego', *Ruch muzyczny*, 21 (1964), 8–9.

[12] In reality, Górecki's notation is not as clear and absolute as it might be for ease of performance: although the notes look as if they are in a type of space-time notation (as in the heterophonic patterns in *Monodramma*), they are very precisely placed in regular subdivisions of the bar. And the conductor has the problem of deciding whether to have these and later heterophonic textures played loosely or as tightly co-ordinated hockets.

hocketing textures and sustained clusters, all enlivened with frequent crescendos. In a guarded criticism of *Choros I*, Leon Markiewicz wrote of the music 'having something about it of a dance on a volcano'.[13]

Several Polish critics in 1964 found *Choros I*'s obsession with limited pitch resources and repetitive motivic-rhythmic strata monotonous. That is to misunderstand the reality as well as the intention. The octave displacement of the three-note cell after $\boxed{12}$ highlights whole-tone configurations rather than the cell's constituent semitones. This anticipates the second part of the main section (from $\boxed{32}$), where Górecki begins his motivic exploration anew, this time deep in the lowest strings. This regeneration stumbles upwards until the cellos take over what is now in itself a whole-tone motif, bringing light and harmonic space into the obscurity. The reintroduction of the upper strings is co-ordinated with a recapitulatory coda based on the original three-note semitonal cell, initially in duple metre and coloured by connecting glissandos, but as the texture thins the triple metre re-emerges before the final tutti cluster. These last pages are in their way the most conventional aspect of *Choros I*, rounding off a process which somehow seems incomplete. But Górecki's intention does not seem to have been geared to a neat structure, just as it had not been in previous works, especially the *Genesis* cycle, of which *Choros I* is an honorary member. His time-scale and the severely pruned timbral and motivic resources perhaps have their closest counterparts not in the medium of music but in that of meditation or contemporary abstract painting. We may, in these works of 1962–4, find more meaningful parallels in the saturated colour of a canvas by Mark Rothko.

## Refrain

Górecki's *Genesis* project was an intense and often disturbing examination of both himself and his materials. It raised questions of the nature of continuity and contrast, of the relationship between pitch and other types of sound, and of the need or otherwise for an audibly comprehensible structure. All these matters were addressed in his next work, one of the most distinctive contributions to contemporary music in the 1960s. *Refren* (Refrain), Op. 21, for orchestra (1965) was Górecki's first foreign commission and première. And, while he him-

---

[13] Ibid. 9.

self sees it as coming out of *Choros I*, its newly confident air and pristine clarity are symptomatic of far-reaching technical and expressive decisions that he made in the aftermath of his problems with Op. 20.

*Refrain* is cast in a simple ternary form, its sequence of slow–fast–slow being an inverted image of the Piano Sonata. The outer sections are the first examples since the Grave pesante e corale in the sonata of sustained slow music (crotchet = MM 26–8). More significantly, the serial procedures used as generators of rhythm, dynamics, and durations in the works of the preceding seven years are abandoned in favour of simpler and more audible phrase structures and rhythmic patterns. And there is now not only a more distinct harmonic idiom but also an ear for the melodic line which, perhaps unknowingly, anticipates developments in Górecki's next phase.

The central section of *Refrain* is dominated by a systematically constructed mirror sequence in which woodwind and string chords are spiced by interlocking brass and timpani fusillades. The texture is a direct descendant of the woodwind and string hockets in *Scontri* (sheet 2), but here is extended over several pages (⑨–⑮). It is one of Górecki's largest mirror patterns, with the pivot coming two bars before ⑫. There are seventeen bars, each of seven crotchets' duration, and each separated by bars of 1/8 or 1/4 occupied by brass and/or timpani. The woodwind and string chords in each bar have two concurrent patterns: the rhythmic pulses are grouped in variant rotations of one, two, three, and five quavers with intervening quaver rests, a numerical procedure derived from earlier pieces, but here having almost the character of hyperventilating chant; the pitch patterns are overlaid on these pulse groups in miniature mirrors (4–3–4, 5–1–5, 3–5–3, etc.), using two whole-tone-derived twelve-note clusters moving in contrary motion (Ex. III.5). The brass and timpani begin to cut in on the quaver rests, spiking an otherwise regulated process. But even these seemingly *ad hoc* invasions are planned: their pattern on either side of the pivotal bar is based on a positive–negative mirror design, where attacks are substituted by rests and vice versa. The woodwind and string dynamics contradict this extended palindrome with an overall crescendo from *pppp* to *ffff*, leading to a brief disruption by rhythmic mayhem in the brass. This in turn is cut by a return to a less forcefully articulated hocket texture (the brass are excluded, the timpani play singly or in pairs). A new 'verse and response' process gets under way before a tam-tam stroke masks the revised da capo of *Refrain*'s opening idea.

Ex. III.5. *Refrain*, central section, 12

The first section has a quite different aura: very slow, very quiet, totally non-confrontational. It is scored for multiple divisi strings (no woodwind or percussion), acting in rhythmic unison. The strings unfold a melodic line, beginning and ending on C♮, in a series of six palindromic phrases (refrains), each developing melodically and rhythmically from its predecessor; the maximum ambit is C–E♭. Pitted against them are isolated brass quavers, which initially mark off the beginnings and ends of the string phrases with C's tritonal opposite, F♯. Occasionally the brass add a G♯ or other quiet punctuations as if trying to emancipate themselves from their subservient role (this of course they succeed in doing in the central fast section). The melodic parallels with church chanting, albeit greatly slowed down in the outer sections, are regarded by Górecki as coincidental. Nevertheless, this is the first of many instances in his music where this influence is felt: for all its chromatic turns, the line sings. This cantabile is something new and acquires a luminosity because of the way in which it is duplicated across the string registers. The first refrain (C–D♭–C outline) is played simultaneously in five different octaves. In each subsequent refrain, the line accumulates another note a whole tone higher (the C-based line remains at the top and bottom of the harmony), so that by the time of the sixth refrain the line moves in a full whole-tone cluster in each of the four octaves. It is an extraordinarily simple technique, but one which was unique in its time.

53

The opening section of *Refrain* possesses a meditative restraint of great potency, devoid of flamboyance and decorative trappings. It reveals itself like a slowly opening bud. When the third section of the ternary design emerges from under the central bombardment, it restates the sixth refrain and codetta from the first section, but this time broken up by rests. And instead of thinning the harmony back to pure octaves, Górecki simply peels away the upper layers until dense two-octave whole-tone harmony is intoned by the cellos and double basses. But C♮ is not forgotten, nor is its polar tritone. The final 'cadence' of unison G♮s, this time on woodwind as well as strings, is framed by horns returning with their familiar F♯ and, at the very end, with F♯ and C together. It symbolizes Górecki's concept of the orchestra as a single instrument.

In retrospect, *Refrain* appears to be a pivotal work, drawing from its predecessors and anticipating later compositions, sometimes at a remove of many years. In this sense, its role is fundamental. Details such as the C–D♭–C outline and the whole-tone harmonic language reappear in specific works later in the 1960s, but broader features such as mirror patterns and refrains, sustained harmonic schemes, and slowly evolving melodic lines within the ambit of a minor third, along with the familiar abrupt contrasts of texture and dynamics, are now thoroughly integrated as substantive structural components. Górecki had achieved in *Refrain* the individual and uncompromised balance between technique and expression for which he had been so diligently searching.

# IV
## OLD POLISH MUSIC

In parallel with the self-questioning that followed *Scontri*, there was another period of reflection after *Refrain*. Partly because of Górecki's ill health no works appeared for almost two years; when one did, it initiated a series of four exploratory chamber works, fulfilling much the same function in the late 1960s as the *Genesis* cycle had in the first half of the decade. The title *Muzyczka* (*La Musiquette*, or Little Music) is somewhat ironically non-committal, because all four works in the series are, according to the composer, about character (where *Genesis*, according to the composer, was concerned primarily with technical matters) and have a temperament that is anything but puny.[1] In an interview published in 1968, Górecki commented that they 'all tackle the same problem, that of putting the most stringently restricted material to maximum use'.[2] He was intent on exploring ordinary things but with unusual means, wanting 'to rehabilitate the small problems which may turn out to be the most important to a composer at a given moment', and indeed the first three pieces show evidence of this workshop approach.[3] They were composed in quick succession between April and October 1967, a year which was further marked by the birth of the Góreckis' first child, their daughter Anna Weronika, in June. *Muzyczka 1*, Op. 22, for two trumpets and guitar was written as a belated birthday present for Szabelski, who had reached 70 the previous December and with whom he had kept in close contact since his student days. Górecki withdrew *Muzyczka 1* soon after its com-

---

[1] Conversation with the author, Oct. 1993.

[2] In Tadeusz Marek, 'Composer's Workshop: Henryk Mikołaj Górecki', *Polish Music*, 2 (1968), 27. I have excised the erroneous negative in the original translation from the Polish. The interview gives an insight into Górecki's preoccupations at the time, and he talks about several pieces which never materialized. Among these were *Muzyczka 4* for orchestra (the existing *Muzyczka 4* is for four instruments), *For Three* for flute, viola, and harp, *In memoriam* for large orchestra, and *Barbaric Mass* for five soprano soloists, choir, and orchestra. A new translation of Marek's interview was reprinted in *Tempo* alongside a commentary on these unfinished works by David Drew, in 'Górecki in Interview (1968)—and 20 Years After', *Tempo*, 168 (Mar. 1989), 25–9.

[3] Ibid. 26.

pletion. There certainly is a startling acoustic discrepancy between the energetic trumpets and a rather undemonstrative guitar, whose main idea is an inversion of elements from the chromatic string line in *Refrain*, played in double octaves. There is also a stiffness in the verse–refrain alternations, and the work has the air more of an extended maquette than of a fully fledged composition.

*Muzyczka 2*, Op. 23, for trumpets, trombones, two pianos, and percussion (cymbals, tam-tams, and bass drums) is dedicated to the conductor Andrzej Markowski (1924–86), an early and constant champion of Górecki's music (he premièred no less than seven of his works). It was Markowski who instigated the composition of *Epitafium* for the 1958 Warsaw Autumn, and he conducted the première of *Muzyczka 2* at the 1967 festival.[4] It is quite small-scale, despite its instrumentation, and the motivic structure avoids strongly delineated elements of contrast and development. Górecki's loose rhythmic notation and the close-cropped semitonal motifs, both relating back to *ChorosI*, emphasize stasis rather than momentum. Although the piece starts *mp*, it is fixed in a band from *ff* to *ffff* for most of its duration. It is really only at the denouement (the appearance of pianos, tam-tams, and bass drums) that the ensemble rings out, aided by the all-too-brief emergence of a broader harmonic field (C–C♯–D♯–F♯), whose tritonal envelope relates to the opening pitches for the trumpets. In the earlier part of *Muzyczka 2*, two features are explored which have a particular bearing on Górecki's next orchestral work, *Muzyka staropolska* (Old Polish Music), Op. 24, for brass and strings (1969): the presentation of the principal motivic idea in short roulades, accruing additional instrumental layers to create a dense counterpoint, and, secondly, the separation of this motivic texture by pauses and by passages of relative inactivity (trills for tutti brass, accompanied by cymbals).

The third piece in the cycle, *Muzyczka 3*, Op. 25, for violas, also anticipates *Old Polish Music*, although it is a more structurally effective work than *Muzyczka 2*.[5] It was premièred on 20 October 1967 at the opening of the fourth annual exhibition by members of the Katowice artists' group Arkat. Górecki had joined Arkat earlier that year as the only member who was not a visual artist; he was and

[4] Górecki originally scored *Muzyczka 2* for three each of trumpets and trombones; in the event, the published score has four of each, and some of the writing for the cymbals has been thinned out.

[5] *Muzyczka 3* may be played by any multiple of three violas, although it is most regularly played by just three.

remains a great admirer of the work of one of the other members, Zygmunt Lis (b. 1931), several of whose dark-hued and 'fantastic' paintings adorn the walls of Górecki's flat in Katowice.[6] *Muzyczka 3* belongs to a significant strand in Górecki's *œuvre*, that of chamber works for strings. It has a timbral affinity particularly with *Elementi* because of 'highest-note' across-the-strings writing in the two episodes and because it employs severe scordatura. This is applied throughout, as it was to the double basses in *Monodramma*.

There was in Górecki's works from the late 1950s to the late 1960s (*Refrain* excepted) a degree of deliberate obscurity. This took a number of forms, initially focused on the relationship between the series and numerically derived patterns in various parameters. In *Muzyczka 3*, the relationship of severe detuning and the material affected by it comes to the fore. In the two episodes ('Ad libitum', *ffff*), where the three lines trade a mix of individual and ensemble across-the-strings chords, the scordatura has a marginal effect.[7] The first, third, and final sections are more tellingly scarred by the distortion. In the first and third, against low open-string drones, leisurely melodic roulades are repeated and developed in turn by each of the three violas. Their evolving refrains, ornamented by grace-notes, muse pensively in a narrower chromatic range than those used in *Muzyczka 2*. The mood is introspective, even when the central portion of the third section becomes a little more animated. The final section, prefaced by the end of the second episode when the violas suddenly shift from playing the highest to the lowest notes across the strings, looks rather new, but is closely related to the opening melodic idea. What had been implied is now stated more clearly: the melodic roulades had their origin in chant. Here the melody notes are stripped of all decoration and are stated in organum at three pitches a notional fifth apart, each instrument simultaneously sounding (as it has done previously) another open string (now the detuned equivalents of G, D, and A: Ex. IV. 1). The connection with *Refrain* is clear, as is the melodic palindrome forming this conclusion. The major element of obscurity, however, lies in the heavily disguised origins of the melodic line, a well-known Polish church chant which was to receive a clearer acknowledgement in a later orchestral work, *Canticum graduum*, Op. 27 (1969).

[6] Górecki left Arkat a year later, alongside Lis and four other members, when artistic divisions appeared in the group.

[7] The 'Ad libitum' marking is a little misleading: most of the attacks are in rhythmic unison at the start of a bar, with individual ricochets following shortly afterwards in a limited number of patterns.

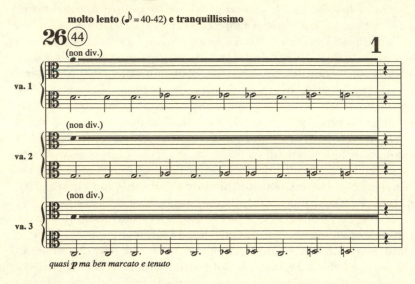

It would soon become clear that there was an alternative Górecki at work in the 1960s. To be referring, however obliquely, to old musical traditions in Poland at this time was both unusual and, with regard to church music, something of a finger in the eye of the state authorities (the most overt work in this respect was Penderecki's amalgam of several traditions in his *St Luke Passion,* completed in 1966). Górecki's interest in old Polish music dates back to before his student days, and his movement titles ('Antiphon', 'Lauda', etc.) and passing allusions to 'Bogurodzica' indicated publicly his fascination with old music in the late 1950s. What is surprising is that he composed some pieces openly based on Polish Renaissance compositions at the very time that he was at the height of his experimental period. The first of these was *Chorał w formie kanonu* (Chorale in the Form of a Canon), composed in 1961 between *Scontri* and *Diagram IV.* This was followed two years later by the final movement of *Trzy utwory w dawnym stylu* (Three Pieces in Old Style), which came between *Monodramma* and *Choros I.* The fact that neither work had an opus number was perhaps indicative of their marginality for Górecki, although in retrospect their composition appears to have been just as crucial to his long-term development as any of the other pieces of the period. The source material for both of these pieces had been highlighted in a multi-part article on Polish Renaissance music by Karol Hławiczka, published in *Muzyka* in 1958.[8] Both *Muzyka* and *Ruch muzyczny* in 1958–61 included several articles on early Polish music which Górecki later culled for inspiration during the 1960s.

*Three Pieces in Old Style* for string orchestra was written in response to a friendly taunt by the head of Polskie Wydawnictwo Muzyczne (or PWM, Polish Music Publishers), Tadeusz Ochlewski, that Górecki was not composing with tunes. All three pieces are strongly modal: the outer ones use only the seven 'white' notes, while the antique country dance of the second is written in the Aeolian mode on G. The first piece is characterized by two prescient features: a pair of background oscillating chords (formed by overlapping perfect fourths) and a melodic line with short phrases repeated in the manner of a Polish folksong. The most straightforward borrowing is in the last piece. This is introduced by a transcription, at the original pitch, of an anonymous four-part Polish song from the mid-sixteenth century, 'Pieśń o weselu Króla Zygmunta wtórego' (Song on the Wedding of King Zygmunt II).[9] As in the first piece, Górecki uses melody notes to form an harmonic aura: the first five notes of the Dorian mode provide the initial backdrop. Equally significant for future pieces (cf. *Refrain*) is another harmonic-melodic technique: the stacking of a melody—in this case, the tenor of the Wedding Song—on top of itself, creating a massive parallel statement in which each of the eight instrumental parts begins on a different note of the Dorian mode, with the original transposition appearing at both the top and the bottom of the texture (Ex. IV.2). This simple and darkly resonant technique is the descendant of the matrix deployed in the opening movement of the First Symphony, but it speaks with a clarity which twelve-note manipulations and octave transpositions obscured.

The idiom of *Three Pieces* was essentially immune from the avant-garde world around it. This was not so with *Chorale in the Form of a Canon*, composed for string quartet two years earlier, also at the request of Ochlewski.[10] The source of the canon is another tenor, this time drawn from one of the most beautiful pieces of four-part choral

[8] 'Ze studiów nad muzyką polskiego Odrodzenia' (From Studies into the Music of the Polish Renaissance), *Muzyka*, 1–2 (1958), 53–71.

[9] Górecki irons out a few dotted rhythms and ignores *musica ficta* at the cadences. These details aside, this is the first untreated citation in his music.

[10] It was destined for an 'Evening of Early Polish Music and Poetry', held in the chamber hall of the National Philharmonic in Warsaw. Górecki returned to *Chorale* in its self-contained form in 1984 as an intended tribute to the Italian composer Goffredo Petrassi, but it surfaced publicly in a different context when he released his first string quartet in 1989.

music from the Polish Renaissance (published *c*.1556) by Wacław z Szamotuł (Ex. IV.3).[11] His evening hymn 'Już się zmierzcha' (Already Dusk is Falling), also known as 'Modlitwa gdy dziatki spać idą' (Prayer for Children Going to Sleep), appealed to Górecki for several reasons, not least the symmetry of its design in modern barred edi-

[11] Hławiczka, 'Ze studiów nad muzyką', part III, 65–8, put forward an intriguing argument that z Szamotuł's tenor might have been derived from the melody of 'Vater unser', contained in the Schumann hymn-book of 1539. Górecki was also familiar with Adolf Chybiński's major study, 'Wacław z Szamotuł' (*Kwartalnik muzyczny* (1948), nos. 21–2, 11–34; no. 23, 7–22; no. 24, 100–31; see esp. the third part of the study) and with the transposition of this song, down a tone, in *Muzyka polskiego Odrodzenia* (Music of the Polish Renaissance), ed. Jósef Michał Chomiński and Zofia Lissa (Kraków, 1953).

Ex. IV.3. Wacław z Szamotuł, tenor from 'Już się zmierzcha'

tions: six five-bar phrases grouped in three ten-bar sections, with a common note (A♮) linking one ten-bar section to the next. Unlike the later *Three Pieces*, the *Chorale* employs a basic serial technique, each instrument having one version of the tenor (P, viola; R, cello; I, first violin; RI, second violin), all playing *sul ponticello*.[12] The result of filtering z Szamotuł's tenor in this way is to isolate it, as if to empha-

---

[12] Details from a lecture that Górecki gave on 'Old Polish Music' in Warsaw and Kraków in the late 1960s.

size its disembodied quality. Eight years later, the tenor reappeared as a major component in *Old Polish Music*.

The compositional history of *Old Polish Music* shows the effect of somewhat disparate trends in Górecki's music. It was begun shortly after the completion of *Muzyczka 2*, and the intensifying fanfares for trumpets and trombones with which it opens clearly hark back to the earlier work. But Górecki soon put the project aside for *Muzyczka 3* and other pieces and did not even mention it in his 1968 interview. He then composed *Cantata*, Op. 26, for organ, in which his predilection for pedal-points, refrains, and choruses found a traditional home (it also shares several motivic and harmonic features with *Muzyczka 2*). Górecki's other composition in 1968 was a brief fanfare, *Wratislaviae gloria*, for brass and strings, whose instrumentation, if not its material, anticipates *Old Polish Music*.[13] When he eventually returned to Op. 24 in 1969, Górecki refocused his ideas into one of his most sophisticated structures, advancing the thematic and formal clarity of *Refrain*. He also openly recognized his indebtedness to Polish music of the past, anticipating even simpler and more harmonious treatments of early music in works of the next decade.

There are three principal ideas, sharply characterized by instrumental timbre, texture, tonality, and dynamics. Initially, *Old Polish Music* is dominated by trumpets and trombones, one of each instrument in four pairs. It opens with the first duet, in which a two-voice fanfare, in rhythmic unison, is created out of contrary motion appoggiaturas around a perfect fifth, E–B (cf. *Muzyczka 3*). This is Górecki's distillation of a medieval organum, 'Benedicamus Domino' (*c.*1300), one of the earliest polyphonic compositions surviving in Poland.[14] This modal organum caught his fancy because he could draw from its range of a major ninth an eight-note symmetrical pitch field around a (non-sounded) G♮. When this first fanfare stops, its four central notes are left resonating in the strings, enhancing the implied

---

[13] It was at this time that Górecki made a brief foray into the world of the feature film: he wrote the music for *Jędrek*, a short film by Jadwiga Kędzierzawska (1969), plus a new signature tune for 'Polska kronika filmowa' (Polish Film Chronicle), although he had withdrawn from a project to write the music for Krzysztof Zanussi's *Struktura kryształu* (The Structure of Crystal, 1969), which was taken over by Górecki's colleague from Katowice, Wojciech Kilar (b. 1932).

[14] The organum from the convent of Stary Sącz was discussed in Adam Sutkowski, '"Benedicamus Domino"—nieznany zabytek wczesno-średniowiecznej polifonii' ('"Benedicamus Domino"—an Unknown Monument of Early Medieval Polyphony'), *Ruch muzyczny* (1960), no. 18, 16–17, and 'Początki polifonii średniowiecznej w Polsce w świetle nowych źródeł' (The Beginnings of Medieval Polyphony in Poland in the Light of New Sources), *Muzyka*, 1 (1961), 3–22. It was later published in Heironym Feicht (ed.), *Muzyka staropolska* (Old Polish Music), (Kraków, 1966), 7–8.

echo of time. The process is repeated, with variation and extension, until all four brass pairs are participating, each passage being separated by a string 'aura'. Stage by stage all eight appoggiatura pitches are also assigned longer note values, bringing increasing robustness to the texture (Ex. IV.4). By 25, the trumpet-trombone texture has reached its full form; subsequent appearances act as recollections and as interjections to the two remaining ideas.

It is now the turn of the strings to begin their process of accumulation, which Górecki accomplishes in a comparable manner, although the various stages are spread over a longer time-span and with interruptions from the brass (these include the third texture, an amorphous burbling for five horns, centred on the G♮ omitted from the symmetrical pitch field of the trumpets and trombones). The string texture is in total contrast: a very quiet, almost paralysingly impassive chorale. It is here that Górecki re-employs the tenor from z Szamotuł's evening hymn, given out *sul ponticello* (as in *Chorale in the Form of a Canon*) but homophonically rather than contrapuntally.

Each string part plays a different version of the tenor, creating a dissonant texture that is quite removed from the euphony of z Szamotuł's original prayer (the technique of superimposing serially varied versions of one line harks back to the First Symphony's Invocation).[15] Like the expanding fanfares, the string chorale also develops on successive appearances, moving from the initial pairing of violins and violas (playing just a third of the tenor), through a quartet (two thirds), to complete statements for sextet and the final full matrix of twelve simultaneous voices. The choice of transpositions is determined by their initial notes, fanning out from the duet's D and D♯ at 25 (a cousin of the symmetrical pitch design for trumpets and trombones; Ex. IV.5).

On the structural level, the string passages act as cushions against the brass sections. The string duet comes at the culmination of the trumpet-trombone fanfares, the quartet (49) marks the end of the juxtaposition of the fanfares with the new horn figurations, and the sextet (71) concludes the superimposition of the two brass ideas, where the complementarity of their pitch patterns is finally acknowledged. When the brass combination tries to reassert itself after the string sextet, the full twelve-part string matrix enters, and for the first time the strings move up from their accustomed quiet dynamic level towards the maximum *ffff*. At this climactic point, in symbolic synthesis, Górecki unites the instruments in chords built from the notes of the organum.

*Old Polish Music* is a particularly austere, granitic sculpturing of the blocks of sound in which Górecki finds such strength. Argument is engaged less through the minute details than through the structural design, where the three ideas are played off against one another in different stages of their individual development. The accumulated tension is resolved in the coda, whose harmony is based on the G♮ at the centre of the brass pitch symmetry. In a manner strongly reminiscent of the opening section in *Refrain*, G♮s (spread over six octaves) are surreptitiously joined by the other notes of the mode from A up to F. The melodic release, set against this harmonic after-image, comes in the iconographic quotation of the original 'Benedicamus Domino', intoned by two trumpets *sotto voce*, 'absolutely without shading'.

A similar, if less directly attributable atmosphere pervades the conclusion of Górecki's next orchestral work, *Canticum graduum*,

---

[15] The I and RI versions are not straight intervallic complements of P and R: Górecki consistently alters one pitch (the equivalent of the second note, F♮, in the original tenor), effectively transposing the line into a different mode.

Ex. IV.5. *Old Polish Music*, chart of tenor transpositions

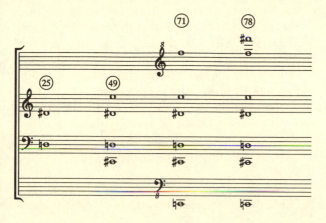

commissioned by West German Radio and premièred in Düsseldorf in December 1969. Its coda—by now becoming a Górecki hallmark— is a slow, quiet reflection. Atop its Dorian-mode chordal repetition (the six notes from A to F) can be heard a melodic outline which relates to one of the Polish chants for the 'prefacja' of the mass, a much clearer reference than in the coda of *Muzyczka 3*, but far from a direct citation. *Canticum graduum* is one of Górecki's forgotten works, and yet its simple outline, containing many familiar elements, conceals some masterful details. Its orchestration is large, including quadruple woodwind (no oboes but saxophones as well as clarinets) but, like that of *Old Polish Music*, no percussion. It shares with Op. 24 a subtle progression of interlocking ideas, although Górecki subdues the timbral aspects to concentrate upon the harmonic design. This has origins in the single-pitch openings of works such as *Elementi* and *Choros I*, and in the slow palindromic unfolding of melodic motifs and treatment of the orchestra as a single instrument in *Refrain*. More particularly, *Refrain* is the model for its harmonic intensity and whole-tone ambience. The deliberate chant rhythm articulates a single giant wedge from the initial D♮ to a four-octave chord. In two alternating chordal combinations, each whole-tone scale occupies its own register on either side of a central overlap cluster, but the inexorable registral (and dynamic) expansion is temporarily halted by returns to an eight-note core, first heard at ⑥ (Ex. IV.6). The melodic surface of this eight-note core (mirrored symmetrically by the bass of

Ex. IV.6. *Canticum graduum*, pitch structure

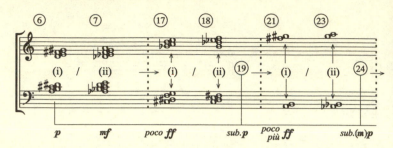

the texture) is a *majore* version of the minor mode 'prefacja' allusion in the coda, although it independently bears a strong resemblance to the 'Pater noster' chant.[16]

There remained, at the end of the 1960s, one further constituent of the *Muzyczka* cycle, which seemed to have run its short course in 1967. *Muzyczka 4*, Op. 28 (1970), was commissioned by the Warsaw-based ensemble Warsztat Muzyczny (Music Workshop), led by the indefatigable pianist and composer Zygmunt Krauze (b. 1938). He was responsible for encouraging a host of composers, not just from Poland, to write works for his idiosyncratic instrumental line-up of clarinet, trombone, cello, and piano. At a time when Górecki was definitively moving in the direction of large instrumental groups where individual timbres were consciously being lost in the crowd, it was something of a departure for him to consider such a proposal. And he went further, subtitling the work 'Koncert puzonowy' (Trombone Concerto): the trombonist is responsible for 'conducting' *Muzyczka 4* as it has no full score, just a set of co-ordinated performing parts.

[16] Górecki pointed out the allusions to the two chants in conversations with the author (Oct. 1993 and July 1994).

Ex. IV.7. *Muzyczka 4*, first movement, clarinet part

(repeat until the trombonist gives the signal
for a break; after a VERY SHORT caesura, begin,
at his next signal, section B)

Until the blossoming of his international reputation in the late 1980s, this unusually scored chamber piece was Górecki's most frequently performed work both at home and abroad.

*Muzyczka 4* is a seminal nine-minute composition whose brevity is belied by the powerful antithesis between unmitigated aggression in the first movement and the almost total passivity of the second, although this latter movement is really one of Górecki's reflective codas. In a comment that reflects on Górecki's wider perception of the relationship between the brutal and the humane, David Drew observes that 'the static modality of its coda clearly represents a transcendence of the previous events and a critique of the violence that informs them'.[17] The structure of the highly charged first movement is a short exposition of four harmonic-motivic ideas, played tutti *ffff* in fast tempos, with a registral approach to texture, the clarinet being generally the most active, the piano the least so (Ex. IV.7). Contrast is provided partly by the ideas' differing pitch content but more stunningly by huge silent pauses, a drastic alternative to the ruminative passages or string haloes which provided a comparable function in earlier pieces.

The second movement is a ternary exposition of a three-note chant which, like the melody in the coda of *Canticum graduum*, is another instance of Górecki's 'motto', first identified in *Songs of Joy and Rhythm* (see Ex. V.5). The comparative calm of the double-octave intoning on the three melody instruments (the piano plays pentatonic 'black-note' chords throughout the movement) is disrupted briefly by

---

[17] 'Górecki in Interview', 28–9.

a loud and dissonant treatment of the chant in which the clarinet doubles the trombone at a minor ninth, a technique which was to resurface in the chamber music of the 1980s and 1990s. But perhaps the more striking gesture occurs at the very end, where the second pitch of the chant is flattened, a premonition of an identical moment at the end of the first movement of the work which brought Górecki's name to the attention of a world-wide audience, the Third Symphony (1976).

# V

# SACRED SONGS

THE 1960s were years of maturation for many Polish composers, as their individual styles and outlooks crystallized. Lutosławski and Penderecki were seen abroad as the symbols of the Polish avant-garde, of the so-called 'Polish school'. This tag held a grain of truth, but like most labels it undervalued diversity in trying to quantify a new phenomenon: the emergence of vital new music from an unexpected source. The Poles were challenging the domination of composers of other nationalities, many of whom were perceived in the West as holding the key to the future of music. As unexpected newcomers, Polish composers had played briefly in the late 1950s and early 1960s with new idioms and technical ploys from the West before discarding or dismantling them as they sought their own path. By and large they concentrated on expressive contact with their listeners rather than investing in complex technical means. Their vigorous compositions met enthusiasm, puzzlement, and occasional hostility: their music was regarded in some quarters as shallow, mere sound for sound's sake. Cultural blinkers are nothing new, but there really was no denying that by 1970 there was a wealth and variety of music coming from Poland, with a dozen or more composers beginning to make headway abroad. Górecki's situation was not untypical.

He was accorded early recognition by the issue of a commercial recording in 1968 (*Epitafium*, *Scontri*, *Canti strumentali*, *Refrain*), although its limited run and poor distribution meant that few people outside Poland came across it. His music had been published by PWM since 1960 (beginning with *Epitafium*), and by the late 1960s his scores were appearing in music shops within a year or so of composition, frequently in facsimile editions of his own bold hand. Although he was taken up by Schott in a co-publishing venture at the start of the 1970s, only *Old Polish Music*, *Canticum graduum*, and *Muzyczka 4* appeared in the West. His foreign commissions were patchy, but the level of state support was characteristic of socialist countries in general, and like many other composers he got by.

Górecki is very much his own man in his dealings with the outside world, and his compositional career has shown the same single-minded purpose. Although he is not given to theoretical or philosophical musings, he is passionately concerned with musical materials and how his ear moulds them. So the shift of his attention in the 1970s away from the previous decade's objective explorations of instrumental textures, horizontal and vertical symmetries, and detailed parametric concerns was made in his own time and for his own reasons: to harness his discoveries to overtly expressive and sometimes highly personal compositions. An integral part of this new focus was Górecki's wish to return to the human voice.

## Ad matrem

The 1972 Warsaw Autumn provided the platform for his next work, which stood out, like so many in previous festivals, for its provoking individuality. *Do matki* (Ad matrem), Op. 29, for soprano solo, mixed choir, and orchestra (1971) is Górecki's first 'sacred' work in that its brief text is a fragment from the *Stabat mater* sequence: 'Mater mea, lacrimosa dolorosa'. While its primary focus may be the Virgin Mary, it is simultaneously dedicated to the memory of Górecki's mother.[1] *Ad matrem* is one of his most sharply etched compositions. This is mainly because Górecki has stripped away the massiveness of earlier works in favour of a fundamentally linear approach. The development of structure through the juxtaposition of blocks of sound is still there, but sometimes, as in the strikingly simple opening, a block may be laid horizontally rather than vertically.

One of the reasons why *Ad matrem* made such an impression at its première was the unabashed directness of its musical imagery. It begins with solitary pulsating bass drum semiquavers, moving from the imperceptible (and joined in stages by timpani and side drum) to a climactic *ffff*, where a stark tritone is intoned by woodwind and brass. A second run at this emotive idea extends the wind tritones into a chant-like insistence capped by the first of just two interjections by the choir, an anguished upper mordent on the words 'Mater mea'.[2]

[1] Górecki has always been fascinated by numbers, hence his use of simple and complex numerical manipulations during the late 1950s and early 1960s. During the last thirty years he has occasionally encrypted symbolic numbers (and even letters) into his pieces. In *Ad matrem*, several bar-lengths in the opening bass drum pulses are derived from dates connected with his mother's life and death.

[2] The choir's E–F–E outline is but the latest in a series of such semitonal kernels, heard previously in *Refrain*, *Muzyczka 2*, *Muzyczka 3*, and *Canticum graduum*; it was also to appear

70

The effect is electric, not least because Górecki delineates his colours and ideas with such deftness, no unnecessary detail obstructing his central aim. This spareness is further emphasized by what follows: a quite new side to Górecki's musical personality, warm, gentle, affecting. And where the opening section has a typically vigorous marking ('ritmico–marcatissimo–energico–furioso–con massima passione e grande tensione'), the second has the complete opposite: 'tranquillissimo–cantabillissimo–dolcissimo–affettuoso e ben tenuto e LEGATISSIMO'.[3]

The surprise element in the second section is the luminous diatonic harmony, an elaboration of a single dominant thirteenth on A♭ which reaches its fullest state only at the end of its second appearance (Ex. V.1). The sighing melody (flutes and violins) incorporates the choir's E and F and, with the soft-toned orchestral support, emerges as a song without words. Where the choir's 'Mater mea' encapsulated public grief, this section articulates something more private. Its composition gave Górecki some trouble. In 1977, he commented during a wide-ranging talk on his music:

If for instance I am stuck at some point, and the composition does not come, a week passes, a month, and I cannot find any solution, then Bach comes to my rescue. There was such a place in *Ad matrem* . . . I had a rough outline, but I was not able to make that lyrical moment on the strings on a unison of E♭–G♭–B♭–F. The trumpets played B♭–E♭ [actually B♭–E♮], the percussion was also there, but the strings were still missing. I had the vocal ending, but that lyrical fragment still evaded me. So I abandoned my work for some time and later, by chance, I opened Bach's Prelude in E flat minor [Book I, No. 8]. I played it and instantly, as by the touch of a magic wand, I moved forward.[4]

What Górecki borrowed from Bach was simply the E♭–G♭ dyad, but in effect, as the dyad was already present in his plans, the connection is more akin to the meeting of like minds. And, as has been seen in works as diverse as *Songs of Joy and Rhythm*, the First Symphony, *Three Pieces in Old Style*, and *Old Polish Music*, as often as not Górecki latches on to pre-existing material at the original pitch, giving his use of it an iconographic significance that goes beyond the mere act of quotation.

frequently in subsequent compositions. The difference here is that it is nakedly self-contained, without further elaboration.

   [3] Górecki's markings habitually underline the extremes of dynamics and expression. Those in *Ad matrem* are among the most extensive.

   [4] 'Powiem państwu szczerze . . .' (I shall Tell you Frankly . . .), *ViVO*, 1 (Kraków, 1994), 44–5.

Ex. V.1. *Ad matrem,* [17]

The central part of *Ad matrem* alternates this 'lyrical fragment' with a sombrely scored dirge, a reinterpretation of the principal melodic idea from *Muzyczka 3* (scored here for violas, with bassoons, piano, and lower strings). Lest this reverie become too settled, Górecki savagely recalls the first section, now on full wind, piano, and percussion, without the preparatory pulsations. They smash in on the heels of the second choral 'Mater mea'. Many would consider such an infrequent use of a choir to be a squandering of resources, but this was not the last occasion on which Górecki chose when and how often he uses his performers, regardless of convention or cost. The same applies to the coda, where a new harmonic backdrop (an unresolved Hypoaeolian chord for piano and strings, eventually multiplied through five octaves) releases the voice of the solo soprano.[5] Her seven-bar lament ('Mater mea, lacrimosa dolorosa') concludes *Ad matrem* with a contemplation on the notes of Górecki's 'motto', the harmonic aura more pungent than its close counterpart in *Canticum graduum*. Górecki's restraint is masterful, the expressive impact almost shocking.

If *Ad matrem* remains one of Górecki's forgotten compositions, despite the award of first prize at the 1973 UNESCO Rostrum, its successor, written just a month later, is even more in the shadow. *Dwie pieśni sakralne* (Two Sacred Songs) exists in two versions: Op. 30b for baritone and piano, and the later orchestration Op. 30 for quadruple woodwind (without flutes and oboes), brass, and strings. The texts, by a contemporary Polish poet, Marek Skwarnicki, were first published

[5] Górecki derived this harmony (C–D♭–F–G–A♭) from his knowledge of Podhalian folk music (conversation with the author, Nov. 1991). The lower three notes (C–D♭–F) also recall the central 'lyrical fragment'.

in the Catholic journal *Tygodnik powszechny* (Universal Weekly). *Tygodnik powszechny* had a long and honourable tradition as an anti-Communist focus throughout the troubled post-war decades, and during the 1940s and 1950s played a vital part in social and cultural dissent. Times were less stressed but still difficult in 1971, and *Tygodnik powszechny* was required reading for anyone interested in information other than that provided by the state-run media.[6] The editorial in the issue of 13 June 1971 revealed that Skwarnicki had been specially commissioned to write four poems in response to the success of popularized worship in the shape of a 'beat' mass by Katarzyna Gaertner. Górecki's response had nothing to do with this chain of events: he simply identified with Skwarnicki's poetry and selected two of the four published poems (No. 1, 'Offertorium', and No. 2, 'Introit'):

> The lyrical subject of Skwarnicki's verses uses phrases taken from prayer books, uses ordinary words taken from the popular language of the church, from Polish liturgies, litanies. Such prose-like language, used colloquially, makes his utterance free of poetical embellishment, of literary conventions, of cross-references to any cultural code. It is authentic, personal poetry.[7]

In the quiet seclusion of the Podhale village of Witów, Górecki wrote music of comparable straightforwardness, although his response is more robustly insistent than lyrical. The first song has a ternary design whose joyful central section (setting the fourth of Skwarnicki's five couplets) is a paean to God: the baritone peals away on a high F♮ against chords made up of the notes of the D flat major scale. In fact, the song's outer sections are cast in the Hypophrygian mode on C, and the semitonal alternation of C–D♭ informs both vocal and instrumental parts. The second couplet, where the supplicant promises to disclose his grief to the Lord, is a latter-day recollection of the contrary-motion fanfares at the start of *Old Polish Music*, although the harmonic inflections here are more subtle. The baritone line in the second song is more active than that in the first and, closely anticipating the baritone solo in *Beatus vir*, wends its way to a climactic oscillation on a top E♭–F (Górecki likes vocal extremes too). The message here is anguished: 'I am coming to Your house | A man tired

---

[6] Dec. 1970 had seen the fatal riots outside the Gdańsk shipyards which led to the supplanting of Gomułka by Gierek, events which were memorably recalled at another critical juncture by Andrzej Wajda's film *Człowiek z żelaza* (Man of Iron, 1981).

[7] Krzysztof Droba, 'Dwie pieśni sakralne' (Two Sacred Songs), *Zeszyty naukowe zespołu analizy i interpretacji muzyki* (Academic Notebook of the Group for the Analysis and Interpretation of Music (at the Higher School of Music)), 2 (Kraków, 1977), 187.

with hunger'. The chordal oscillations beneath the vocal line reinforce the prayerfully obstinate attitude, melodically stressing the C–D♭ alternation but progressing beyond the initial pairing to include other chordal complexes, including one consisting of whole tones. But the overall impression is one of heavyweight, modal harmonies in contrast to the delicate linear aspects of the first song.

## Symphony No. 2

Nothing in Górecki's works hitherto had quite prepared his audiences for what was to come next. And yet all the seeds were there. It is simply that he had found a theme with which he could fulfil one of his abiding passions: the contemplation of the cosmos. He had broached it laterally through Tuwim's poem in *Songs of Joy and Rhythm*, spatially in *Scontri*, and more directly in *Refrain*, which he once likened to how he imagined the experience of flying at high altitude between the sea and the stratosphere.[8] When he was commissioned by the Kościuszko Foundation in New York to write a work to celebrate the 500th anniversary of the birth of the Polish astronomer Mikołaj Kopernik (1473–1543), he was simultaneously honoured and challenged. Typically, he did a great deal of background research for what emerged as his Second Symphony, 'Kopernikowska' (Copernican), Op. 31 (1972), scored for soprano and baritone soloists, large choir, and orchestra. He was especially concerned to find texts that fitted his understanding of Copernicus's main achievement. As Norman Davies has commented: 'His discovery, of the earth's motion round the sun, caused the most fundamental revolution possible in the prevailing concepts of the human predicament'.[9] Górecki was very much aware of the associated minuses: 'It was not an optimistic discovery'.[10] But he did not know how to reflect the complexity of the project: 'What can you write about Copernicus—that he stopped the sun and moved the earth? That's banal.'[11] Discussions with the film director Krzysztof Zanussi helped to crystallize Górecki's thoughts:

Zanussi said that, in fact, Copernicus . . . was one of the greatest tragedies in the history of the human spirit: an entire system of thought, the way of thinking on which man's attitude to the reality out there was based, was in ruins. We were no longer the centre of the universe, we became nothing. It

---

[8] Conversation with the author, Sept. 1984.
[9] *God's Playground: A History of Poland* (Oxford, 1981), i ('The Origins to 1795'), 150.
[10] Conversation with the author, Oct. 1993.
[11] Górecki, 'Powiem państwu szczerze . . .', 45.

was then that the entire subject became clear to me and obvious in its musical form. Hence the duality of the two-movement Symphony: first the whole mechanism, let us say, of the world, followed by contemplation.[12]

The musical realization of this duality, rather than the chosen texts, constitutes Górecki's response to Zanussi's view of Copernicus's discovery. The texts of the Symphony are in Latin, and those selected to represent the 'mechanism of the world' are well-known excerpts from the Book of Psalms that reflect God's role: 'Deus. Qui fecit caelum et terram . . . Qui fecit luminaria magna . . .'. There is nothing exceptional in these biblically factual words, although by confining them to the very end of the movement Górecki puts the spotlight on the unscripted instrumental imagery conjured up by the huge orchestra and, as David Drew has keenly pointed out, on 'the gigantic orbital progressions of its forms and harmonies'.[13] The opening wall of orchestral sound is deafening. Instead of a gradual chordal accumulation (cf. *Refrain* or *Canticum graduum*), the Symphony begins *en masse*, with a violent report on percussion and a deafening six-octave whole-tone chord. An instrumental chant thunders out. Its rhythm, galvanized by three different registers of hocketing timpani and bass drums, is drawn from the choral setting of phrases from the Psalms with which the movement ends. The part-writing, like that in *Canticum graduum*, moves in contrary motion on either side of a central pivot. The melody's four-note ambit (the initial descending semitone seems all-pervasive) causes a savoury combination of linear chromaticism and shifting whole-tone agglomerations. This monstrous and violent 'mechanism of the world' turns and parades itself in a manner that is both awesome and apocalyptic. After a substantial pause (cf. the first movement of *Muzyczka 4*), a respite is provided by what is in effect a quiet slow-motion cousin of the opening. The strings, now moving in parallel, unveil a melodic line that is an inversion of the intervals in the first section, gently supported by punctuating whole-tone chords in the wind. The soothing nature of this passage is disturbed by a significant harmonic change: whenever the melody moves from its root note C onto D♭ or E♭, the underlying lines shift not in exact parallel but onto notes of the 'black-note' pentatonic scale. This change brings a shaft of light and air, all too quickly obliterated by an extended return of the pounding chant. What at first hearing might have been taken for exultation now seems fatalistic.

[12] Ibid.
[13] Liner notes to the Elektra Nonesuch CD recording of the Third Symphony.

Before the final reappearance of the first section at the end of the movement, this time with full choir, Górecki unsettles the rhythmically and harmonically purposeful design by interpolating a series of less deliberate ideas. There are brass fanfares on tritones (maintaining the whole-tone connection) and ad libitum rhythmic scurrying for brass, whose tight chromatic cells give way eventually to a hyperactive version of the opening chant. This narrows inwards to intone a new variation, now in an octave-wide semitonal cluster. The choral recapitulation of the main chant, whose climax is curiously abbreviated, leaves the argument unresolved. Just as in *Muzyczka 4*, these tense, passionate outpourings need to be resolved in the second half of the bipartite structure. Here, the overpowering turmoil that Górecki has engendered needs to be transcended and humanized.

Since the 1960s, a standard feature of Górecki's long-term planning has been some element of pitch stability. In *Diagram IV*, this took the form of a series of interlocking pitch fields; in *Refrain*, it was the use of a root note for melodic and harmonic digressions; from *Ad matrem* onwards, it has ranged from a single pitch to a mode, arpeggio, or triad. Where, as in the Second Symphony, there is a polarization of material, there may be more than one tonal centre. The brief but telling incursion in the first movement of a pentatonic element now takes its rightful place as the embodiment of the second movement's contemplation. The same D♭-based 'black-note' chording, now only in the low register (cf. *Muzyczka 4*), accompanies the solo baritone while the soprano, who appears later, is accompanied by three chords of which the first inversion of A flat major is a principal structural component.

It soon becomes clear that this second movement is not a mere coda to the first: it has outgrown this function, taking further the process already observed in *Muzyczka 4*. The dissonance between the baritone's sighing incantation, with its descending semitones borrowed from the first movement, and the passivity of the accompanying pentatonic drone promises something more diverse. As he struggles slowly and painfully to comprehend the work of the Lord, the baritone rises triumphantly to a high-toned climax, where his role is imperceptibly taken over by the soprano (her effortless ascent to a top G♭ anticipates the Third Symphony). The soloists join in quiet wonder at the 'luminaria magna'. After an abbreviated repeat of this progression, the pair extol the Lord with the text 'Solem in potestatem diei . . . Lunam et stellas in potestatem noctis . . .'. This is the central climax of the movement, with a partial resolution provided by the return of the soprano's rising scale and another pensive duet for the soloists. But the concluding semitonal sighs on 'Deus' from the baritone are cowed rather than joyous.

If Górecki is aiming to show both sides of the Copernican discovery, as indicated in his conversations with Zanussi, the coda of the second movement dispels the negative aspects. Characteristically, it provides resolution through the contrast of modality and with material totally at peace with itself. The first part of the coda is a direct transcript at pitch of a mid-fifteenth-century vocal fragment which had captured his attention years earlier, an anonymous 'Laude digna prole'.[14] Although this short piece of four-part Dorian homophony is nothing special in itself, Górecki acknowledges that he chooses such fragments for incorporation at key moments because they affect him personally: 'Tradition fascinates me greatly, sometimes it may be just a single phrase which will not let me alone'.[15] In this instance, he had already used the fragment for the short orchestral fanfare *Wratislaviae gloria*, composed for Andrzej Markowski to conduct at the 7th Festival of Contemporary Polish Music in Wrocław in 1969. His approach on that occasion was to state 'Laude digna prole' three times, also at original pitch, first on trombones and tuba (crescendo from *p*), then on full brass without tuba (*ffff*), and finally on a concertino of lower strings (*mp*, *sans nuance*, a marking which recurred in *Old Polish Music* at the citation of 'Benedicamus Domino'). The link with the coda of the Second Symphony is that in both works the measured statements of the fragment are accompanied by the same steady 'black-note' pentatonic drone. In the symphony, of course, this links back to the second section of the first movement and to the baritone's harmonic support. The uniting of the pentatonic orchestral chord with the choir's Dorian mode fittingly provides a fully chromatic setting for the empyreal sentiment Górecki chose (as a substitute for the original text) from the first book of Copernicus's *De revolutionibus orbium coelestium*: 'Quid autem caelo pulcrius, nempe quod continet pulcra

---

[14] 'Laude digna prole' was found in the antiphonary of a minor monastic order called the Bożogrobcy, which had guarded Christ's tomb in the Holy Land in the 12th cent. and which had later settled in the town of Miechów, north of Kraków. Górecki came across it in one of two articles by Adam Sutkowski, 'Nieznane zabytki muzyki wielogłosowej z polskich rękopisów chorałowych XIII i XV wieku' (Unknown Monuments of Polyphonic Music from Thirteenth- and Fifteenth-Century Polish Chorale Manuscripts), *Muzyka*, 3 (1958), 28–36, and 'Organum "Surrexit Cristus hodie" i inne zabytki średniowiecznej muzyki wielogłosowej' ('The Organum "Surrexit Cristus hodie" and Other Monuments of Medieval Polyphonic Music', *Ruch muzyczny* (1958), no. 19, 2–6.
[15] 'Powiem państwu szczerze . . .', 45.

omnia?' (What indeed is more beautiful than heaven, which of course contains all things of beauty?).[16]

The purifying effect of this Renaissance homophony, the quotation from Copernicus, and the tonal polarity and interdependence of the Dorian and pentatonic modes all combine to bring a quiet awed reflection after the preceding exertions. But Górecki is not yet finished. In a gesture of extraordinary faith in the simplest of ideas, very slowly he extends the low pentatonic harmony into the upper registers, in a sustained crescendo, as if to embrace the universe and bathe it in light. Eventually, the image fades, and the cadence of the symphony comes in with three soft iterations of the first-inversion chord of A flat major which accompanied the soprano's first entry. The second movement symbolizes the progress of Górecki's conversion to modal and diatonic language since *Old Polish Music*. It was to dominate his thinking hereafter, because he was now prepared to let this new idiom speak for itself, to discard yet again what he perceived as any unnecessary ornamentation.

As a breather from the monumental scale of the symphony, Górecki composed three short works for a cappella choir, two of which had sacred connections and one in which Górecki returned to the poetry of Julian Tuwim. *Dwie piosenki* (Two Little Songs), Op. 33 (1972), for a choir of four equal voices, is dedicated to his daughter, then aged 5. The first, 'Rok i bieda' (The year and hardship), a riddle on the seasonal cycle, is a slow mazurka whose Aeolian modality on D grows out of Górecki's three-note 'motto' (see Ex. V.5). The second, in a striking anticipation of the bipartite key scheme of the Harpsichord Concerto he was to write in 1980, is in D major. 'Ptasie plotki' (Bird gossip) is a lively tongue-twister, a patter song in the rhythm of the krakowiak.[17]

While composing the Second Symphony, Górecki wrote the first of his sacred works for a cappella choir, *Euntes ibant et flebant* (They who Go Forth and Weep), Op. 32. It seems probable that, in perusing his beloved Book of Psalms for the Second Symphony, he had come across the two psalm texts which he proceeded to interleave in *Euntes ibant et flebant*. The work marks the beginning of a separate strand in his music: not only is the choir his favourite medium because of the

---

[16] The original syllabic text reads: 'Laude digna prole cum matre procreata sine patre laudent omnes cum iubilo'.

[17] The theme of 'Bird gossip' bears a generic relationship to one of the best-known krakowiaks, 'Albośmy to jacy tacy chłopcy krakowiacy' (freely translated as 'We're just Cracow boys'), which many Polish composers, Chopin included, have appropriated more directly.

wholeness of its sound-quality, but the composition of unaccompanied choral pieces also became an increasingly private activity to the extent that many choral works of the 1980s remain unpublished and unperformed. Once again, Górecki returns to his 'motto' on the notes D–E–F, whose pervasive reiteration and resultant harmonic halo give the melodic line an other-worldly presence, as if recreating chant in a church acoustic (chanting proper, exceptional in his music, occurs part-way through the work, sung by the basses against a resonant backdrop).

Górecki's approach to harmony is revealingly uncomplicated, entrusting everything to modality coloured by a few discreet touches, such as a harmonic shift onto the chord of B flat, against which the motto's E♮ acquires a folk-like tint, suggesting the composer's continuing although sublimated interest in Polish folk music. The conclusion of *Euntes ibant et flebant* has a few surprises too, small inflections like the solitary Phrygian E♭ in the melodic line. But the juxtaposition of weeping and adoration which Górecki has fashioned out of the two psalm fragments is summarized by the closing bars: a shaft of sunlight on three chords of D major, a brief recall of the B flat chord, and a final resting-point in the modality with which the work began. The overriding meditative character of this work is carried over into *Amen*, Op. 35, completed in 1975. This is accentuated by the use of just the one-word title as its text. The harmonic kernel of *Amen* is identical with the contrary-motion pitches of the trumpets and trombones in *Old Polish Music*. The tone here is contrastingly sustained, the effect like that of slow breathing, and Górecki expands the range of the concertina patterns beyond the confines of Op. 24's brass fanfares. There is a conscious brightening of the harmonic spectrum towards the A major climax but, like *Euntes ibant et flebant*, the piece returns to a quiet reflection in the minor mode at the end. For the next ten years, these two a cappella works seemed to be isolated tributes to the traditions of Polish church songs, an unusual constituency for contemporary Polish music. But Górecki was to be drawn irresistibly again to this environment in 1985.

The first half of the 1970s had brought some changes in the Górecki household. The family had moved in 1969 into a large rented apartment, a stone's throw from the flat that Henryk and Jadwiga occupied for the first nine years of their married life. A second child, Mikołaj Piotr, was born in February 1971, and Górecki decided to take up a long-standing offer of a scholarship from the Deutsche Akademische Austausch Dienst in what was then West Berlin. But, as his limited output indicates, Górecki was hampered yet again by ill health. The one orchestral work he completed, in 1973, was *Trzy tańce* (Three Dances), Op. 34, dedicated to Antoni Szafranek and the Rybnik Philharmonic Orchestra. Together with his brother Karol, Antoni Szafranek was the leading spirit at the Rybnik Intermediate School of Music when Górecki began his first proper music studies there in the early 1950s. As a student, Górecki played the violin in the Philharmonic Orchestra, and this work is an affectionate tribute. Its melodic and rhythmic countenance is evidently folk-related (sharpened fourths, ostinatos, juxtapositions of duple and triple metre), particularly in the rumbustious outer dances. There are no real counterparts in his previous music, except in the central movement of the *Three Pieces* written a decade earlier, because stylistically these dances look back to Polish music composed in the late 1940s and early 1950s.[18]

Together with his wife and children, Górecki eventually arrived in Berlin in the autumn of 1973, only to fall seriously ill with kidney problems at New Year. He then had to spend the remaining six months recuperating. On their return, the family considered moving to Warsaw, but Górecki is rooted in Silesia and they decided to stay. Given his recent ill health and his distaste for bureaucracy and for anything that might take him away from composition, it was all the more surprising that he agreed to become Rector of the Higher School of Music in Katowice in 1975. He nevertheless had a sense of duty to his school and the students. Górecki was an exacting teacher, and several of Poland's most talented young composers had the benefit of his critical gaze. These included three of the precocious generation born in 1951: Rafał Augustyn, Eugeniusz Knapik, and Andrzej Krzanowski (d. 1990). The prospects of time for Górecki's own composing did not look bright. There were a couple of minor pieces: two short bugle-calls for the World Ice Hockey Championships, held in Katowice in 1976 (one of them spices up C major with a sharpened fourth), and *Trzy małe utworki* (Three Little Pieces), Op. 37, for violin and piano (1977), tiny teaching pieces for his 6-year-old son.[19] And yet, for all the distractions, Górecki produced arguably his two most

---

[18] For a formal analysis of *Three Dances*, see Martina Homma; 'Das Minimale und das Absolute': Die Musik Henryk Mikołaj Goreckis von der Mitte der sechsiger Jahre bis 1985', *MusikTexte—Zeitschrift für neue Musik*, 44 (1992), 51–2.

[19] They were written in exasperation at the low quality of the music his son was being given to play by his violin teacher. There was also at this time a large orchestral project, commissioned by the city of Nuremberg. Górecki began work in 1976 on what he has called a 'concerto giocoso' entitled *Siedem dni tygodnia* (Seven Days of the Week). He wrote three movements, but finally abandoned the project in 1980.

important large-scale compositions, successors to the momentous Second Symphony: the Third Symphony, Op. 36 (1976), and *Beatus vir*, Op. 38 (1979).

## Symphony No. 3

Some months before he left for Berlin, Górecki asked the Polish folklorist, Dr Adolf Dygacz, if he had any particularly interesting old melodies in his collection. Dygacz responded with four songs from Silesia, one of which was a folksong from the region around the town of Opole, to the north-west of Katowice. 'Kajze mi sie podzioł mój synocek miły' (Where has he gone, my dear young son) describes a mother's mourning for her son, killed during an uprising. Although the melody may be nineteenth-century, the text is almost certainly from the time of the three Silesian Uprisings against the Germans in 1919–21.[20] From this one song began the long journey to the conception and completion of the Third Symphony, 'Symfonia pieśni żałosnych' (Symphony of Sorrowful Songs), Op. 36, for soprano solo and orchestra in 1976.[21]

Górecki had heard 'Kajze mi sie podzioł' in the 1960s, but had loathed the arrangement.[22] Now, in the version from Dygacz, not only the melody but also the words made an unforgettable impression:

For me, it is a wonderfully poetic text. I do not know if a 'professional' poet would create such a powerful entity out of such terse, simple words. It is not sorrow, despair or resignation, or the wringing of hands: it is just the great grief and lamenting of a mother who has lost her son.[23]

[20] This lament was sung by a solo female folksinger at the conclusion of Kazimierz Kutz's much-praised feature film, *Sól ziemi czarnej* (Salt of the Black Earth, 1970). An ensemble version of the song (vv. 1, 2, and 4) has been recorded by Śląsk (Silesian folk and dance group), vol. 7, on Polskie Nagrania PN 1332. Górecki altered the fourth line of the song because he did not like the Germanized vocabulary: 'grenzszuce zabiły' (the border guards killed him) became 'złe wrogi zabiły' (the evil enemy killed him).

[21] The English translation of the Polish 'pieśni żałosnych' has now settled on 'sorrowful songs'. It has also been translated as 'sad songs' and 'songs of lamentation'. The Polish word 'żal' is rich with connotations of grief, as is the adjective 'żałosny' (piteous, plaintive, wretched).

[22] Its melodic characteristics are very different from Górecki's own predilections: where this is notable for its expressive intervallic range (triadic beginning, a later upward leap of a minor seventh), Górecki's tendency is to go for stepwise motion.

[23] Górecki, 'Powiem państwu szczerze . . .', 46. This article is a tape transcript of the first part of a talk that Górecki gave on his music (concentrating on the Third Symphony) at the 1977 music conference held at Baranów, near Sandomierz in south-east Poland. In 1976–80, this venue provided an important rendezvous for composers and musicians to talk about a wide range of topics. Górecki talked in 1978 on *Scontri*, and a year later on *Beatus vir*. The proceedings from 1976 and 1977 were published in book form, but Górecki was unwilling to have his 1977 talk included. The surviving tape fragment was discovered fifteen years later and published in 1994

Górecki began work on his setting, but came up against insuperable problems in designing an increasingly dense harmonic wedge related to similar patterns in earlier works (e.g. *Canticum graduum*). He put the material aside and began to cast around for new texts which would match its spirit and sense of humanity.

He looked for inspiration (in vain on this occasion) in the collected volumes of the nineteenth-century ethnographer Oskar Kolberg (1814–90). Quite by chance, he came across an account of the horrific atrocities committed by the Gestapo in the Zakopane area in the Tatra mountains. In their book *'Palace': Katownia Podhala* ('Palace': Place of Torture in Podhale), published in 1970, Alfons Filar and Michał Leyko record how a guest-house called 'Palace' was appropriated early in the Second World War and its cellars used to imprison and torture local Polish suspects. After the war, the Poles found inscriptions scratched on many of the cell walls and doors. Most of these are just names, some with and some without the victim's dates, age, or home village. Górecki chose what is undoubtedly the most moving graffito, a short sentence illustrated in one of the book's photographs. It was in the hand of a highland woman, Helena Wanda Błażusiakówna, aged 18, from Szczawnica, a town to the north-east of Zakopane. She had been incarcerated since 25 September 1944. It is a simple supplication to her mother and to the Mother of God: 'O Mamo nie płacz nie—Niebios Przeczysta Królowo Ty zawsze wspieraj mnie' (Oh Mama do not cry—Immaculate Queen of Heaven support me always). And just above this, by her name, she added a cross and the words: 'Zdrowaś Mario' (Hail Mary).

In 1977, Górecki said:

I have to admit that I have always been irritated by grand words, by calls for revenge. Perhaps in the face of death I would shout out in this way. But the sentence I found is different, almost an apology or explanation for having got herself into such trouble; she is seeking comfort and support in simple, short but such meaningful words. I like such texts: short and simple.[24]

Little did he realize that this particular text had a history of its own. After the symphony's first performances and broadcasts on Polish Radio, Górecki received a number of letters from former inhabitants of Lwów, which until shortly after the First World War was part of Poland (it is now in Ukraine). In the bitter, but unsuccessful fighting

(unfortunately with mistranscriptions of some names and dates), although without the composer's sanction.

[24] 'Powiem państwu szczerze . . .', 47.

to remain in Poland, many inhabitants of Lwów were killed. Among the most famous heroes was a 14-year-old volunteer, Jurek Bitschan, who in death became a symbol of patriotism to the city's defenders. A resistance song of 1918, 'Mamo najdroższa, bądź zdrowa' (Dearest Mama, Goodbye), lauds his memory, and lines 2–4 of the fourth verse apparently quote him as he fell fatally wounded: they are replicated almost word for word in the 'Palace' inscription. Although nothing is known about Helena's background (or whether she survived her incarceration), it is clear that she recalled this song about Jurek as she, in her turn, faced up to the ordeal of war.

With two texts, one from a mother to her son, the other from a daughter to her mother, Górecki looked for a third with the same atmosphere. He finally selected the fourth verse of 'Lament świętokrzyski' (Holy Cross Lament), a mid-fifteenth-century Polish manuscript in which the Virgin Mary speaks to her Son dying on the Cross: 'Synku miły i wybrany, Rozdziel z matką swoje rany . . .' (O my son, beloved and chosen, Share your wounds with your mother . . .).[25]

This text was folk-like, anonymous. So now I had three acts, three persons. . . . Originally, I wanted to frame these texts with an introduction and a conclusion. I even chose two verses (5 and 6) from Psalm 93/94 in the translation by Wujek: 'They humiliated Your people, O Lord, and afflicted Your heritage, they killed the widow and the passer-by, murdered the orphans.'[26]

This intended preface would have given a definitive context to the main body of the symphony: its fairly explicit reference to (twentieth-century) war traumas would have highlighted the oblique references in two of the main texts. It would appear that its exclusion from the final plan had as much to do with Górecki's wish to transcend such specifics as to clarify the musical structure. To round off the symphony, Górecki had chosen a conciliatory text by Piotr Skarga from his *Żywoty świętych* (The Lives of the Saints): 'Happy your labours, for which you were rewarded with rest. Happy your fasting, your torment and poverty, for which you have eternal bliss. And blessed are your martyrdoms for which you are given such rewards.'[27] As with the preface from the Psalms, Górecki decided to abandon Skarga's text in order to concentrate solely on his three moving laments.

---

[25] The MS was discovered in the library of the Benedictine Holy Cross Abbey in south-east Poland but the original was lost during World War II.
[26] Ibid. 47.    [27] Ibid.

Ex. V.2. 'Oto Jezus umiera'

O - to Je - zus u - mie - ra,        u - wa - żaj  grze - szni - ku,
Śmierć Mu o - czy za - wie - ra,     za-płacz nie- wdzię - czni - ku.

O - grze - chy  lu-dzkie,        wy-ście to  spra - wi - ły,

Pa - na  swo - je - go      zło - śli - wie za - bi - ły

When it came to composing the music of the Third Symphony, Górecki found himself toying over and over again with the three notes of his 'motto', this time E–F♯–G. He already had in mind the first movement's main feature: 'I knew it would be a canon with a long theme. . . . but what sort of material should be used in the theme? Should I compose it myself or should I look for authentic material and quote?'[28] Eventually he did both. He found a Lenten beggar's song, 'Oto Jezus umiera' (Lo, Jesus is dying), in his much-thumbed copy of Father Jan Siedlecki's *Śpiewnik kościelny* (Church Songbook).[29] To his delight, it began with the notes E–F♯–G, although it was too short for his purposes (Ex. V.2). He found his solution in a study by Antonina Wozaczyńska (1956) of the folksongs from the Kurpie lowlands near the Mazurian lakes north of Warsaw. Her discussion centred on the massive unpublished collection made in the inter-war years by Father Władysław Skierkowski, whose *Puszcza Kurpiowska w pieśni* (The Kurpian Forest in Song, 1928–34) had been immediately raided by Szymanowski for his two volumes of Kurpian songs. In her section on modalism, Górecki found a religious song, 'Niechaj bendzie

[28] Powiem państwu szczerze . . .', 47.
[29] The text of 'Oto Jezus umiera', although not used, is a powerful complement to the Holy Cross Lament. The first verse reads: 'Lo, Jesus is dying, be aware, sinner. Death closes His eyes—shed tears, ingrate. O human sins, you are to blame for this: you maliciously killed your Lord.'

Ex. V.3. 'Niechaj bendzie pochwalony'

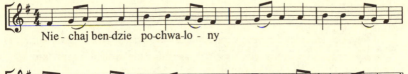

Nie - chaj ben-dzie po-chwa-lo - ny

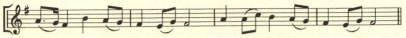

pochwalony' (Let Him be praised), which Skierkowski had notated in a church in Myszyniec on 9 August 1934 (Ex. V.3).[30] Miraculously, it too was in the Aeolian mode on E. Górecki extrapolated elements of the first eight bars of the Lenten song (changing its metre from triple to duple and developing the centre of his theme to form the apex of the melodic arch) and then overlapped it with the final four bars of Skierkowski's hymn. From these fragments, Górecki created his long theme (it lasts the best part of a minute), in the process composing what effectively is his own 'church song' (Ex. V.4).

The opening of the Third Symphony lies in that expressive Slavonic tradition which includes the beginnings of Tchaikovsky's Sixth Symphony and Rachmaninov's Third Piano Concerto. Górecki's theme evolves with a natural ease, without any sense of being presented as a theme, the composer's art subsumed within a melodic span that ebbs and flows. Each phrase is distinct and memorable, contributing effortlessly to the totality. One motivic idea, however, places the theme firmly in the Polish tradition. The final cadential phrase comprises a melody with a feature characteristic of the regional folk-music: the 'turn' of a rising minor third followed by a descending semitone occurs twice. It cannot go unnoticed that the pitch contents of both the 'motto' and the 'turn' are identical. Their presence pervades many of Górecki's compositions (a selection is given in Exx. V.5&6). It is this same 'turn' that Szymanowski uses to climax the opening soprano line in the concluding movement of his *Stabat mater*. Górecki had already subconsciously referred to this melodic outline in the fourth of the Op. 4 Variations (see Ex. I.1), but here the convergence of his creative impulses with Szymanowski's were of inesti-

---

[30] Antonina Wozaczyńska, *Pieśni Kurpiowskie: Ich struktura i charakterystyka w świetle zbiorów W. Skierkowskiego* (Kurpian Songs: Their Structure and Characteristics in the Light of W. Skierkowski's Collections) (Wrocław, 1956), 80.

Ex. V.4. Third Symphony, first movement, opening theme

Key: x: derived from 'Oto Jezus umiera' (Ex. V.2)

⌣: derived from 'Niechaj bendzie pochwalony' (Ex. V.3)

mable significance for him: as he once said, 'Where Szymanowski went, I went too.'[31]

Rigorous counterpoint had not hitherto been a noticeable component of Górecki's compositional armoury. Certainly, there are many examples of looser contrapuntal sections in earlier pieces, mostly in the serial period, but the only thoroughgoing canon was in the little *Chorale* for string quartet (1961). What makes the canon in the Third Symphony work is a combination of features: a carefully graded structure of entries, a straightforward (and familiar) build-up of texture, and a steadfast use of a single modal scale (Aeolian on E). The structure for almost the first half of this twenty-five minute movement consists of a blossoming arch structure, each new voice entering a fifth

[31] Quoted in Christiane Galeski-Wild, 'Henryk M. Górecki et ses œuvres symphoniques', MA thesis (University of Strasburg, 1986). Górecki's teacher Szabelski had himself culled from Siedlecki and Skierkowski and, with the example of Szymanowski's *Stabat mater* in mind, had composed his Second Symphony (1933), later withdrawn. For an analysis of this work, see Leon Markiewicz, 'II Symfonia Bolesława Szabelskiego: Inspiracje—warsztat—stylistyka' (Bolesław Szabelski's Second Symphony: Inspirations—Workshop—Stylistics), *Górnośląski almanach muzyczny* (Upper Silesian Musical Almanac) (Katowice, 1988), 7–32.

Ex. V.5. 'motto' chart

Songs of Joy and Rhythm,
first movement

[Tranquillissimo, ben tenuto, molto cantabile]

tbn. *mp (mf)*

Muzyczka 4,
second movement

[Molto lento] *cantabile*

Cztery bie-dy na tym świe-cie Pierw-sza bie-da wios-ną,

Bie - bie-dy na świe-cie bie - bie-da wios-ną,
*(p - mp)*

Two Little Songs,
Op. 33, No. 1

[Lento] *imploringly*
*p*

Do - mi-ne De - us

Miserere

A [*sempre staccato assai ma non troppo*]

Nie piej, kur-ku, nie piej, nie budź mi Ma-ry-się.
T.B.

*mp*

Three Lullabies,
No. 3

[Allegro molto]
str.

*f*

Harpsichord
Concerto,
first movement

Ex. V.6. 'turn' chart

Symphony No. 3,
second movement

*Beatus vir*

*Beatus vir*

*Miserere*

*Good Night*,
third movement

*Kleines Requiem*, first movement

higher than its predecessor at a distance of the theme plus one bar. There are seven different entries, starting with the second double basses, until the eighth entry, on first violins, comes back via the circle of 'modal' fifths to the original starting-point on E (Ex. V.7). Two further lines are added in the violins to double the top entries at an octave. The echoing of melodic phrases from one voice to another is remarkably rich and supple, principally because each line, without diverging from the pitches of the original theme, plays it as if in its own mode (Aeolian on E, Phrygian on B, Hypophrygian on F♯, Lydian on C, etc.), each time endowing the theme with different sequences of intervals and therefore giving it new character.

Once a full eight-part canon has been achieved, Górecki draws in the outer voices, merging them stage by stage with the inner lines until only the entries on G and D are left.[32] They in turn resolve onto a unison E in preparation for the entry of the solo soprano. Her role is similar to those of her counterparts in *Ad matrem* and the Second Symphony: to render human what has hitherto been only instrumentally implied. Her short appearance embraces new tonalities and orchestral sonorities (including selected woodwind and brass) to heighten a number of different emotions. These are also indicated by expressive markings, beginning with 'dolcissimo', where her simple scalic ascent on the first four notes of the mode ('Synku') is given a magical halo by sustained flutes, harp, and strings. This is the most evocative example of this technique in Górecki's music. Her fragments echo the canon's 'turn', until she darkens the tone ('doloroso') by flattening the second degree of the mode. The cumulative harmony supporting her ascent up the Phrygian scale is a sophisticated version of that accompanying the solo soprano in the Second Symphony. The third phrase, 'appassionato' ('Have I not borne you, beloved Son, in my heart'), becomes a brief lullaby, alternating different inversions of C and G major chords (chordal oscillations go back a long way in Górecki's music). The fourth and fifth phrases continue this musical cradling, the 'affettuoso' employing the Aeolian mode on B♭ (some considerable modal distance from E), the 'lamentoso' pairing D and G major chords over a pedal D. Melodically, both of these phrases are based on the three-note 'motto'. The soprano concludes her lament ('For you are already going from me, my dearest hope') with a repeat of the rising Phrygian scale. At the climax of her phrase, the full eight-part canon returns, fortissimo. In a manner reminiscent of the

[32] Górecki elaborates on the canonic procedures in 'Powiem państu szczerze . . .', 47–8.

Ex. V.7. Third Symphony, first movement, 7

ternary structure of *Refrain*, Górecki pares the texture down over the next nine minutes to the solitary statement for double basses with which the movement began. Once the unison E has been reached, he twists it with a Phrygian F♮, recalling not only the soprano's inflections but also identical procedures in *Muzyczka 4* and *Euntes ibant et flebant*.

I wanted the second movement to be of a highland character, not in the sense of pure folklore, but the climate of Podhale. . . . I wanted the girl's mono-logue as if hummed . . . on the one hand almost unreal, on the other towering over the orchestra. . . . It cannot be a poster, drama, or tragedy, but it should be a reference to the contemplation of the first movement.[33]

The first of the two main ideas incorporates both a folk drone A–E and a *majore* version of Skierkowski's characteristic 'turn', E–G♯–F♯ (see Ex. V.6). The scoring (strings, triggered by harp and piano) is trans-lucent, as if to suggest the bright open air of the mountains. The sudden plunge onto a low B♭–D♭ dyad, scored for clarinets, horns, piano, and strings, is almost cinematic in its impact.[34] This lugubrious pedal elicits a pitiful 'Mamo' from the soprano: once again, Górecki returns to the semitonal drop (D♭–C) which characterized both the first of the *Sacred Songs* and the Second Symphony, as well as refer-ring back to the B♭ Aeolian of the first movement. In a masterful sequence of undulating phrases, matching the prayer's plea to the Queen of Heaven, the soprano reaches up eventually to a top A♭, her line tracked and cradled by inversions of primary and secondary seventh chords. Even when she sinks down again, this string harmony of thirds and seconds somehow manages to evoke a peace born of inner faith. The return of the bright opening idea, with 'Mamo' sung to the adapted 'turn' motif, is electrifying, and there is an exquisite enharmonic shift into the return of the second idea. The coda, main-taining the B♭ Aeolian harmony, is a simple chanting repetition on D♭ of 'Zdrowaś Mario łaskiś pełna' (Hail Mary full of grace).[35] In this starkly drawn musical structure, reticent but expressive, Górecki demonstrates a powerful empathy with the plight of his compatriot. It is one of his most sharply focused designs, where he seems, without

[33] Ibid. 48.
[34] Wilfrid Mellers compares these two textures as 'tingling' and 'sepulchral', adding that B flat minor is traditionally a 'dark' key ('Round and About in Górecki's Symphony No. 3' (*Tempo* 168 (Mar. 1989), 23).
[35] Górecki added the last two words himself, and chose the archaic 'łaskiś' instead of 'łaski' because it is an older form, more commonly used in country churches (conversation with the author, Oct. 1993).

pre-existing material, to have articulated the essence of his musical language.

If the second movement is closely argued, the third is more loose-limbed. In fact, Górecki was so frustrated by the intractability of his treatment of Dygacz's Opole melody that he considered ending the work with the second movement. He persisted, however, deciding to leave the text intact, but devising a short set of variations for the melody. After the original melody is sung for the first verse, the second and third verses are cast in duple metre with new versions of the cradling motifs that have already played a major role in the symphony (inversions of seventh chords and plain triads, multiplied as usual through several octaves).

Finally, there came that unvarying, persistent, obstinate 'walczyk' (on the chord of A major), sounding well when played piano, so that all the notes were audible. For the soprano I used a device characteristic of highland singing: suspending the melody on the third [C♯] and descending from the fifth to the third while the ensemble moves stepwise downwards [in sixths].[36]

The most memorable part of the third movement is the opening first verse and the fragment of it which is recalled in the coda. In simplifying his original concept, Górecki came across two coincidences which contributed significantly to the success of the final version. His almost obsessive preoccupation with cradling motifs is given its simplest form here, two chords with an outer span of a minor sixth (A–F) between which oscillate B and C. Against this duple harmonic rhythm, the triple-metre melody achieves an appropriate feeling of disorientation. But there is an iconographic significance in these two chords. They are taken, at pitch, from the opening of Chopin's Mazurka Op. 17 No. 4 (1832–3), where they are part of a three-chord introduction to one of that composer's most melancholic mazurkas.[37] The fact that Chopin had recently gone into exile as a result of the 1830–1 insurrections would not have been lost on Górecki. And his substantive use of an A major drone parallels Chopin's example in the central section of the mazurka.[38] A second

---

[36] Górecki, 'Powiem państu szczerze . . .', 48. The is the last part of the surviving tape. The section described occurs after ⑨ and is an elaborated echo of the opening idea from the second movement.

[37] Górecki had, in fact, already been haunted by the first of these Chopin chords (A–B–F) and had included it in the harmonic underpinning of the coda of *Canticum graduum* (conversation with the author, Oct. 1993).

[38] Wilfrid Mellers sees Górecki's use of these A major chords as 'ecstatic elevation', which perhaps is to ascribe more to Górecki's setting of the mother's simple prayer than the composer intended (the text reads: 'Oh, sing for him, | God's little birds, | Because his poor mother |

symbolic touch, further removed from its original, is the violin E♮ that is touched off by the piano over Chopin's two chords. This is a reference, again using the original pitches, to Beethoven's Third Symphony, to the crunching dissonance that marks the central climax of the first movement's development.[39] Drawn miraculously together, these three elements, the Opole folksong, Chopin's mazurka, and Beethoven's symphony, symbolize some of the strongest influences on Górecki's musical persona. As Wilfrid Mellers has put it: '[they] build bridges between the universality of folk song and liturgy and the terrors in historical time and in the world as-it-is.'[40] In this movement, as in the whole symphony, Górecki has synthesized a range of his techniques and creative impulses to compose one of the most outstanding and individual works of the twentieth century.

As always, his only guide was his own instinct. He was not overly concerned about what others might think, although he must have been aware that his new symphony—three slow movements with solo soprano—was quite different from anything else being written in Poland, if not elsewhere, in 1976. It made its controversial débuts the following year at the avant-garde festivals in Royan (April) and Warsaw (September).[41] Despite the symphony's release on a Polish LP, the work remained forgotten for many years, except by a few enthusiasts (mostly professional musicians) who would pass around their hard-found copies of the Woytowicz–Katlewicz recording. Performances in 1987–8 in the United Kingdom by the BBC Symphony Orchestra and City of Birmingham Symphony Orchestra, with Margaret Field conducted by David Atherton, began the slow process of public recognition. But no one foresaw the unprecedented wave of popularity that the fourth commercial recording (by Dawn Upshaw, the London Sinfonietta, and David Zinman) has created since 1992. The recording made an immediate mark in the United Kingdom and in the United States; worldwide, its sales are now on their way towards the

Cannot find him. | And you, God's flowers, | Bloom all around him, | So that my poor little son | May rest happily'). But Mellers is surely right in pointing out that 'the eternal seeming repetitions of the A major triad . . . are, in their very different way, as remarkable as the infinitely repeated C major triads at the end of Beethoven's Fifth. In both cases there is neither a chord too many nor too few; that is genius' ('Round and About', 24).

[39] Górecki pointed out this Beethovenian allusion in Aug. 1984, while in conversation with the author about the citation from Chopin.

[40] Ibid. 24.

[41] The Polish critics after the Warsaw Autumn performance were divided down the middle. Their reviews in *Ruch muzyczny* (1977), no. 23, were reproduced in the Polish CD magazine *Studio*, 8 (1993), 12–13.

million mark.[42] This is not the occasion to examine in detail this extraordinary affair, which raises many questions about the relationship between the creative artist and the forces of dissemination (publishing, radio and television, record companies, and marketing).[43] Perhaps it is sufficient to observe, in the context of this study, that the Third Symphony was composed back in 1976 because Górecki needed to write it for himself. It was a ground-breaking work, not part of any wider movement at the time (understandable because of his creative isolation from much of contemporary culture), and it is mischievous to lump the symphony indiscriminately with social, political, and cultural currents of the 1990s. Górecki is very touched by the impact it has made on many people's lives: its phenomenal appeal, however complex the reasons, undoubtedly indicates that it speaks to a wide public from every background, and those who dismiss it for its success are in reality commenting on today's society.[44] The integrity of Górecki's transcendental vision remains unaffected.


Beatus vir

The commissioning of Górecki's next major work, *Beatus vir*, Op. 38, for baritone solo, choir, and orchestra (1979), was partly responsible for his resignation from his post as Rector at the Higher School of Music in Katowice. Taking on this onerous job had been a mistake: at

---

[42] A sample of informed British perspectives on the 'Górecki phenomenon' of 1993 would include articles by Robert Neville (*Sunday Telegraph*, 17 Jan.), Alan Rusbridger (*Guardian*, 13 Feb.), and Andrew Billen (*Observer*, 11 Apr.).

[43] Music from the symphony has appeared in countless television programmes and several films. The first film, Maurice Pialat's *Police* (1985), starring Gerard Depardieu, used a snippet just over the closing credits, and yet marketed an LP of the entire symphony on this basis. The most recent feature film is Peter Weir's *Fearless* (1994), which fully incorporates the first movement. Films directly based on the Third Symphony include *Requiem* (first movement only), directed by Bent Staalhøj (DOK film, Denmark, 1989, *c*.22′), a re-edited version of which (entitled *Songs of Sorrow*) was released in 1994, and *The Symphony of Sorrowful Songs*, directed by Tony Palmer (London Weekend Television, 1993, 51′). The films by Staalhøj and Palmer (first part) focus on an equation involving the Third Symphony and the concentration camp at Oświęcim (Auschwitz), which *Songs of Sorrow* updates by overlaying images of neo-Nazi skinheads from the film *Nazinigger*. But only the middle movement has specific links with World War II (and there it relates to solitary suffering in Zakopane and not to mass extermination in Auschwitz). Such overt parallels are anathema to the ethos of both the music and the texts (as witnessed by Górecki's abandonment of the explicitly narrative verse from the Psalms). The symphony is concerned with inner sorrow and compassion and is, in itself, no more connected with Auschwitz that it is with more recent barbarities elsewhere.

[44] For a polemical overview of the reception of the Third Symphony, see David Drew, 'Górecki's Millions', *London Review of Books*, 16/19 (6 Oct. 1994), 9–10. See also Brian Morton's discussion of the Third Symphony in his *The Blackwell Guide to Recorded Contemporary Music* (Oxford, 1966), 238–44.

every turn Górecki found himself in confrontation with the Party, which infiltrated all major institutions. His phone calls, meetings, and correspondence were subject to direct or secret scrutiny at any moment. He was prevented from appointing to the teaching staff the brightest of the younger generation of composers, like Knapik, Krzanowski, and Aleksander Lasoń (also born in 1951). Without a coterie of trusted and musical colleagues, he was isolated and unable to neutralize the intrigues of party members on his staff. At the celebration of an important Higher School of Music anniversary in 1979, he was 'airbrushed' out of all the records, his name omitted from the list of distinguished graduands, his position as Rector ignored in a television film. All of a sudden, the school seemingly had no rector: officially, he no longer existed. The particular catalyst for this classic isolation by the Party of an awkward customer was the news, which leaked out in 1978, that Górecki had been commissioned by Cardinal Wojtyła of Kraków to write a work to commemorate the 900th anniversary of the assassination of Bishop (later Saint) Stanislaus of Kraków in 1079. This was too much for the Party bosses in Katowice, and Górecki was effectively ostracized. He had already completed his first three-year term in 1978 and had reluctantly agreed to continue for a second term. But, in 1979, he decided that enough was enough and resigned from the nightmare, severing all links with the Higher School of Music.[45]

Although Górecki had carried out his usual meticulous precompositional research on the new work, by the autumn of 1978 he still had not begun the composition itself. Suddenly, with the elevation of Cardinal Wojtyła to the papal throne on 16 October, the pressure was on, and within months the première was fixed for 9 June 1979, in Kraków, on the occasion of John Paul II's first pilgrimage to Poland since becoming Pope. It was bound to be a momentous occasion, but Wojtyła's commission was problematic as well as important: St Stanislaus had long been a symbol of the Church at odds with the State. In an address to foreign dignitaries in Kraków on the day of the première, the Pope commented on his distant predecessor: 'For centuries he has been considered an illustrious witness of genuine freedom and to the fruitful synthesis which is brought about in a believer between loyalty to an earthly fatherland and fidelity to the Church.'[46]

[45] He was later invited to set up a new Higher School of Music in Bydgoszcz in northern Poland, where he could have picked his own staff, but he decided to stay in Katowice, nearer to Podhale.
[46] *The Pope in Poland* (Radio Free Europe Research, 1979), 80–1.

The facts that over the centuries a cult had grown up around Stanislaus (by the fifteenth century he was regarded as Poland's patron saint), that a valuable collection of medieval music centred on the saint has survived to today, and that a host of paintings and sculptures were made in his honour meant that Górecki worked even harder to reach his own understanding of a complex situation.[47]

Górecki was well aware, as he had been in his consideration of Copernicus for the Second Symphony, of the potential for different interpretations of the life and death of the Kraków bishop. History records that in 1079 Stanislaus Szczepanowski, who had already had disagreements with his king, joined a rebellion against Boleslaus II, 'The Bold', for which treason he was summarily executed and dismembered on 11 April.[48] The parallels between this eleventh-century confrontation of Church and State and the situation in the Poland of the 1970s are not hard to see (in a macabre way, the story also anticipates the fate of Father Jerzy Popiełuszko, the Warsaw priest murdered by state police a mere five years later, in 1984). History also suggests that there was good and bad on both sides of the conflict, something which Górecki wished to reflect in his composition. He turned once more to the Book of Psalms, and his selection of verses is correspondingly ambivalent, even noncommittal given the circumstances of the commission. It was not in his nature to sensationalize a historical event; instead he chose to emphasize doubts and supplications in composing this sustained meditation, whose essential message is directed at the spiritual and moral aspects of the tragedy of St Stanislaus and Boleslaus II rather than any sort of representational drama.

The baritone in *Beatus vir* is not identified specifically with either of the historical figures. Consequently, the listener may identify personally with this prayer, in both its inner torment and moments of exultation. From the outset, Górecki stresses the role of common

[47] For examples of the musical repertoire, see *Gaude, mater Polonia: St Stanislaus in Polish Music and Mediaeval Poetry* (Warsaw, 1993), a comprehensive transcription and edn. by Tadeusz Maciejewski, and the CD 'Wincenty z Kielc: *Historia gloriosissimi Stanislai*', Pro Musica Camerata PMC 005. Among more recent figures who were fascinated by the story of the saint were Franz Liszt (whose setting of Ps. 129 and a pair of polonaises were intended for his long-planned but unrealized oratorio, *Stanislaus*), the inspired Cracovian dramatist and artist Stanisław Wyspiański (1869–1907), and Szymanowski's fellow composer in the group Young Poland in Music in the early years of this century, Ludomir Różycki (1884–1953). Różycki wrote two works based on Wyspiański, a symphonic poem (1906) and an opera (1908), both with the title *Bolesław Śmiały* (Boleslaus the Bold).

[48] Within two months of the bishop's death, Boleslaus was forced into exile. Coincidentally, Stanislaus' murder presaged by ninety-one years a similar conflict in England between Henry II and Thomas à Becket. For a full historical account of the Polish confrontation, see Tadeusz Grudziński, *Boleslaus the Bold and Bishop Stanislaus* (Warsaw, 1985).

humanity by giving the opening section to the chorus: its octave-unison texture persists for most of the work, emphasizing its ritualistic function. The initial insistence on a descending semitone (C–B) has many precedents in his music, but the starkness of its melodically evolving utterances brings memories of the apocalyptic opening of the 'Copernican' Symphony. Whereas the earlier work made play at the outset with all chromatic pitches in its two whole-tone configurations, in *Beatus vir* Górecki has furthered his search for ultimate tonal clarity by using only four pitches in the entire section. While the choir (instrumentally doubled) evolves its repetitive chant of 'Domine' on C, B, and D, the orchestra also maintains E♭. The C minor tonality (with some emphasis on the potent diminished fourth B–E♭) is the first key in an unusually classical scheme in which C minor gives way to its relative, E flat major, for the central body of the piece, with a return to C minor superseded by C major in the coda.

As soon as the desperate choral cries of 'Domine' broach their own E♭, they drop away to make way for the baritone. At once, parallels can be drawn with both the spirit and the substance of *Two Sacred Songs*, the second movement of the 'Copernican' Symphony, and the Third Symphony. But different subtleties are at work here: the suggestion that the tonality has already moved to the relative major is tellingly disabused before the baritone has uttered a note. His own gloss on the continuing C minor tonality is initially to recall the expressive 'turn' from the Third Symphony (see Ex. V.6), but he soon begins to reach upwards ('exaudi orationem meam') as his counterpart had done in the second of the *Two Sacred Songs* and in the Second Symphony. A varied repetition of this prayer, with choral echoes, does finally achieve the goal of E flat major, significantly at the conclusion of the phrase 'exaudi me in tua justitia' (Ex. V.8).

The key of E flat dominates the climactic central section of *Beatus vir*. The *Angst* of the C minor sections is replaced by a rosier outlook, and the psalm texts (not in themselves noticeably different) are supported by Górecki's now characteristic two-chord cradling. Three separate phases are initiated by the soloist, the second of these introducing something of a rarity in his music, an accelerando, appropriately on the words 'Velociter exaudi me'. This marks the beginning of the intensification towards the culmination of the baritone's third phase, where the chorus joins him (still in unison). At this moment Górecki introduces an alternative tonal area (C major coloured by an F♯) and uses the brief alternation of the E flat and C polarities to engender more momentum towards the grand restatement of the first

Ex. V.8. *Beatus vir*, 23

two-chord cradle in E flat ('Deus meus es tu'). To stress the substance of this tonality, Górecki even introduces some emphatic second-inversion dominant chords, and the section climaxes in a glorious affirmation of the two alternating chords (sixteen bars) followed by plain tonic chords (ten bars) on full orchestra, including for the first time the jubilant sounds of glockenspiel and tubular bells.

The ensuing return to C minor seems to question if not negate this unalloyed optimism. The baritone hesitantly recreates the obsessive pitches of the choir's first section in a manner reminiscent of Mussorgsky's treatment of Boris Godounov (given Górecki's admiration for Mussorgsky, this is not as far-fetched as it might seem). Although the baritone recovers some of his poise at 'Domine Deus salutis meae', we are left with a distinct sense of an inner conflict unresolved (just as in the 'Copernican' Symphony). And, in a striking parallel with the earlier work, Górecki introduces a moment later a two-part coda, the first part principally choral, the second orchestral.

98

In both works the resolution is as much to do with the text as with the change of harmony and tonality.

The final psalm verse—'Gustate, et videte, quoniam suavis est Dominus'—is sung by the choir, for the first time unaccompanied and singing in four real parts (in familiar contrary-motion homophony), as if to acknowledge the transition from uncertain supplication to unqualified acceptance. Its chorale is centred on the coda's root chord, a first inversion of C major, which is also played quietly by the strings and horns to frame each choral phrase. The strings then cushion the choir in the final part of the psalm text ('Beatus vir, qui sperat in eo') before preparing for the last phase of the coda. These concluding pages are rich with internal and external associations: the coda of *Canti strumentali*, the C major drone in first inversion (a favourite harmonic device, embracing tonal clarity but not finality) which recalls the end of the Second Symphony, the cross-reference of the E–G–F♯ melodic ostinato not only to the baritone's first entries but also to the 'turn' of the Third Symphony's canon (see Ex. V.6) and to the opening theme of Szymanowski's Second Violin Concerto, plus the overall folk ambience of the C–F♯ tritone.[49] These echoes also reinforce the maxim that Górecki had uttered with regard to his aims in the *Muzyczka* cycle: putting the most stringently restricted material to maximum use.

More particularly, in *Beatus vir* Górecki realized his wish to write a major choral and orchestral work which drew upon and related audibly to the church traditions he knew and loved.[50] It is shot through with harmonic patterns, melodic turns of phrase, and reiterative textual chanting that would have been immediately intelligible to his Polish audience. The première was a personal triumph, because Górecki conducted the performance himself (a rare occurrence). He conveyed with the emphatic enthusiasm that comes with his every gesture the depth of feeling contained within its straightforward sounds, from the seriousness of the opening to the yearning of the

[49] And, in a matter of incidental symbolism (cf. *Ad matrem*), it contains in its eleven repetitions of the four-beat ostinato the day and month of Stanislaus' death in 1079, in the same way that the climactic orchestral pealing in E flat ([38]–[40]) contains in the lengths of its two phases the day and month of Wojtyła's election as Pope in 1978.

[50] *Beatus vir* was intended as the first of several pieces to be grouped under the title *Sancti Tui Domine florebunt sicut lilium* (Górecki has a love of connected cycles, as in *Genesis* and *Muzyczka 1–4*). To date, no further compositions have emerged, although in 1984 he mentioned to the author that the next in the cycle would be *Offertorium*, dedicated to the famous Polish martyr Father Maximilian Kolbe, who gave his life for another prisoner in Auschwitz during World War II.

final pages. His music requires that extra power and intensity that a committed performance will bring. Afterwards, huge crowds gathered outside the *Curia* to hear the Pope's final words (it was his last night in Poland). He was home again, so the atmosphere was relaxed: the visit had been an overwhelming success, despite the obstacles put in its way by the authorities. The Pope singled out *Beatus vir* for special praise, thanking Górecki publicly for providing such a 'profound experience'. It must have been galling for the Party bosses in Katowice, if they were paying any attention. If they were not, then they misread the situation to their cost. Górecki's battles against the Party were symptomatic of a prolonged malaise in Polish society and culture. The Pope brought a ray of optimism to millions of ordinary citizens and was quite consciously stoking the fires of rebellion. Such was the impact of his visit that within months Solidarność (Solidarity) became a force to be reckoned with and, without denying the significance of the events of 1956 or 1970, the socialist state apparatus became seriously imperilled for the first time since the war.

# VI

# BROAD WATERS

GÓRECKI has described himself as an 'odludek' (recluse), unsure whether this has been good or bad for his life as a composer.[1] Although he had travelled abroad on a number of occasions in the late 1970s, for much of the 1980s he seemed to disappear from public view.[2] The 'stan wojenny' (state of war), which followed the imposition of martial law by General Jaruzelski on 13 December 1981, curtailed everyone's mobility, and Górecki was not to travel abroad again until a visit to Denmark in 1984. More crucially, he had a serious hip operation in 1982, and general ill health kept him at home for a considerable time thereafter. His compositional attention began to split in different directions, partly occasioned by the enforced isolation. He totally abandoned the large-scale orchestral medium with voice(s) and concentrated on two more intimate genres: music for unaccompanied choir, and chamber music (for the latter, see Chapter VII). His first pieces for a cappella choir had been composed in 1972–5 (*Euntes ibant et flebant*, *Two Little Songs*, and *Amen*), and their successors of 1979–88 show a similar division between the sacred and the secular. And in both cases Górecki moved directly to pre-existing source material for inspiration. There is one major exception to this, a free-standing work whose dimensions and ambitions matched those of the three symphonic compositions of the previous decade: *Miserere*, Op. 44 (1981).

The inscription in the score of *Miserere*—'I dedicate this to Bydgoszcz'—needs a little explanation. For once in his life, Górecki was making an overtly political gesture, even though composition on this work began before the event in question. Since 1980, Solidarity had become an extraordinarily powerful and popular focus of opposi-

[1] Conversation with the author, Mar. 1994.

[2] In addition to attending the première of the Third Symphony in Royan in 1977, he visited Bolzano and Kremsmünster for a congress of musicologists and composers, was on a composers' competition jury in Ancona in 1980, and visited, among other cities, Paris, Baden-Baden, and Berlin (like many Poles, he went to West Berlin from time to time to purchase goods unavailable in Poland in the 1970s).

tion to the Communist government. By 1981, over a third of the population had joined either Solidarity or its sister organization, Rural Solidarity. On 19 March 1981, there was a confrontation in the city of Bydgoszcz between representatives of Rural Solidarity and some 200 members of the militia, called in to evict them from protracted negotiation with the Provincial Council. The occasion was recorded on tape. In the ensuing violence, when some of the protestors were forced to run the gauntlet of militia batons (the so-called 'path of health'), over twenty union members were injured, several of them very seriously.[3] News of this provocation spread rapidly throughout Poland, and suddenly there was a dangerous national crisis. The world looked on in concern (the Soviet Union and other socialist countries from one perspective, the West from another), and within nine months Jaruzelski had outlawed Solidarity and put the country under martial law. But Górecki had already responded with his new piece in personal protest at the outrage of the Bydgoszcz incident. Not surprisingly, with heavy governmental restrictions in force, no immediate performance of *Miserere* was possible or planned, and the score was put in the bottom drawer. Like other principled members of the artistic community, Górecki refused to have anything to do with any activity or event which would, however obliquely, bring credit to the regime. Only in 1987 did an appropriate moment come for the première. After working again on the piece in the spring of that year, Górecki gave the score to the Bydgoszcz Music Festival, and it received its first performance on 10 September in nearby Włocławek, where the body of Jerzy Popiełuszko had been found in 1984.

The ground-plan of *Miserere* is daringly and typically blunt, geared entirely to the coda. In this sense, it relates back to the works of the late 1960s, but more self-evidently to *Ad matrem*, because in both cases the textual punch-line is left till last. There are more specific connections with the canonic sections of the Third Symphony's first movement. On the tonal plane, *Miserere* maintains a single harmonic field from start to finish, as did the symphony's canon. Such a unifying device is typical: the backbone of *Miserere* is a 'white-note' ladder of thirds, from the bass A to soprano middle-register A, of which the initial A minor triad is the most evident feature. Quite apart from its powerful expressive impact, it is a technical *tour de force* (unlike in *Euntes ibant et flebant* and *Amen*, there is not the slightest digression from the white-note modality). The subtleties of the opening twenty-

---

[3] One of the most detailed accounts of this incident is in Timothy Garton Ash's *The Polish Revolution* (London, 1983).

eight minutes or so do not stem from the text (only three words are sung—'Domine Deus noster') but from a new, flexible approach to building a texture that is at once contrapuntal and homophonic. Whereas in the opening of the symphony each of the string parts enters in sequence with essentially the same melodic line (a canon refracted through different notes of a single mode), in *Miserere* each voice has a different melody as it enters. From the second basses' first A♮, each subsequent voice is more or less anchored on the next note of the ladder of thirds.

Giving each of the eight voices its own melodic identity gave Górecki some considerable headaches along the way, but he was insistent that this was a crucial part of the musical and symbolic design. After two unsatisfactory attempts at the opening sections, he decided not to stick rigidly to one reiterated line for each voice but to mould the lower voices to the upper ones as the musical need arose. The result is a finely controlled sequence of expressive 'paragraphs', each building on its predecessor(s) and yet having a distinctive character. The initial monody for the second basses places *Miserere* unequivocally in the tradition of Polish chant. Its overall ambit of a perfect fifth, its not unexpected basis in the Aeolian mode, its incorporation of the Górecki 'motto' (see Ex. V.5), and its progress through a series of phrases involving straight and altered repetition constitute the most extended and direct acknowledgement of this aspect of Górecki's background (he would have heard the same reiterated 'motto' phrases every time he was in church). And the element of the massed choralism typical of a church congregation is underlined by Górecki's insistence that there be a minimum of 120 voices in all.

With the entry of the first basses, Górecki recalls the genre of the two-voice church song prevalent in Poland. In the third paragraph, the second tenors open up the intervals and the melodic range and, like most of the entries, their line is marked 'błagalnie' (imploringly). Their increasing concentration on G rather than their E anchor-note anticipates what becomes in later paragraphs a gravitation towards C major (paralleling the tonal scheme in *Beatus vir*). But before this gets too strong a hold, there is a resonant shift at the seventh paragraph to the chord of F major, taking the second basses down below their original A♮ for the first time. This simple but effective change (some twenty minutes into the piece) is prefaced by the fullest statement of the background chord (Ex. VI.1). The seventh paragraph also introduces predominantly simple triads, rather than configurations of seconds and thirds. It is a moment of resonance which clears the air for

Ex. VI.1. *Miserere*, seventh paragraph

what Górecki has called a 'cadenza': the second sopranos sing a variation of their melody over a pedal E, a reduced texture on the modal dominant which acts as both preparation for and a foil to the fortissimo eighth paragraph and its full eight-voice homophony.

From the fifth bar of this first tutti, the Skierkowski 'turn' asserts itself in the first soprano line (see Ex. V.6), but the more fundamental feature is the increasing presence of G major as the dominant of C. Both in the quiet four-part passage that follows and in the ensuing dominant-based harmonies with their obsessive repetitions, decreasing note values and increasing dynamics, expectations are raised for a climactic statement of this sustained prayer. For over twenty-five minutes—Górecki's longest span—the listener not only has absorbed a gathering sequence of melodic and harmonic variation but has also become very sensitive to the slightest change in the underlying modality. So when the dynamic and rhythmic climax is not matched by any harmonic change (Górecki effectively cadences onto his own dominant), the lack of fulfilment is palpable. Why has he sidestepped the expectation of a significant tonal or harmonic change? The answer lies in the underlying sentiment: this is not a triumphalist piece, hence Górecki's unwillingness to cadence even in the relative major. *Miserere*'s unassuming focal point steals in at a later stage. At what is therefore only the dynamic and textural climax, the same three words which have been present since the beginning are hammered out, but in short decrescendos and a narrowing vocal range. Their function rapidly becomes cadential until the final 'noster' is sung pianissimo with a descending semitone (C–B) over A♮, returning to the three notes and Aeolian mode with which the work began.

Quietly, but still 'błagalnie', the choir sings 'MISERERE NOBIS' (the capital letters are Górecki's). This focal coda is the culmination of more than twenty years' exploration of this crucial structural and expressive component (cf. one of the earliest examples of the elision of climax and coda, the final section of *Scontri*). Its modal integration, its newly resonant chordal spacings, and the extension of the bass register in the central phrases down to low D give the coda, for all its brevity, the weight necessary to counterbalance the massiveness with which it has been preceded. But it is also true that the daring formal evolution of *Miserere* requires expert handling in performance if the full emotional impact, particularly of the concluding sections, is to be achieved. As Ivan Moody has commented, it is music 'with an almost unparalleled physical immediacy . . . possessed of the most astonishing tension, precisely built up to an almost unbearable pitch and then released at "miserere nobis" into a post-penitential meditative calm'.[4]

Despite differences in design and performing forces, *Miserere* may be seen as a companion piece to *Beatus vir* and also to *O Domina nostra*, Op. 55, for soprano and organ (1985). This latter work is dedicated to the soprano Stefania Woytowicz, who gave the première of the Third Symphony. Woytowicz and her husband gave invaluable assistance to Górecki and his family when he was struck down in 1982 with a life-threatening deterioration to his damaged hip. *O Domina nostra* was conceived in 1982 as a meditation, with a Latin text compiled by the composer, for the 600th anniversary of the Black Madonna in Częstochowa. Its salient characteristics are all drawn from chant—the

---

[4] 'Górecki: The Path to the *Miserere*', *Musical Times*, 133 (1992), 284. The recent CD première conducted by John Nelson succeeds movingly in bringing out *Miserere*'s subtle qualities and the strength of its unique architecture.

quiet Dorian entry for soprano as well as her exultant D flat major, the organ's interlaced passages in first- and second-inversion triads, the pedal-notes on the polar opposites of D♮ and A♭. The tonal shift at the conclusion to a first-inversion A major chord with added D♯ and G♯ not only gives the work a folk tinge (the 'turn' reappears) but is the first of several instances where a work's coda moves away from rather than reasserts the fundamental tonality.

Between 1985 and 1988, Górecki moved even closer to the musical and spiritual world of the Church by returning to the source from which he had borrowed 'Oto Jezus umiera' for the Third Symphony. The *Church Songbook*, first compiled by Jan Siedlecki in 1878, has become one of Poland's principal sources of hymns and chants. Many of the tunes were originally collected by earlier nineteenth-century compilers, such as Michał Marcin Mioduszewski and Teofil Klonowski, and rank with the folksong collections of Oskar Kolberg in their antiquity and rich repertoire. Some editions are for single voice, some are for two voices, and the contents vary somewhat from edition to edition.[5] Four of the five *Pieśni Maryjne* (Marian Songs), Op. 54 (1985), twenty of the twenty-one songs collected in *Pieśni kościelne* (Church Songs, 1986), and *Pod Twoją obronę* (Under Your Protection), Op. 56 (1985), take both texts and melodies from Siedlecki. One of the *Marian Songs* and *Przybądź Duchu Święty* (Come Holy Spirit), Op. 61 (1988) share just their texts with Siedlecki. Only four of these twenty-eight settings have to date been performed and recorded, and none has been published. Despite the composer's hesitancy about preparing them for public performance, they constitute a vital part of Górecki's musical ethos of the period. It is equally important to emphasize that neither in these songs nor in any of his compositions does Górecki consider that he is writing religious music.

The description of some of Górecki's works as sacred must be taken in the broadest artistic and spiritual sense and not as indicating any functional or liturgical dimension. The relationship of his religious beliefs to his artistic credo was summed up by the composer himself in the acceptance speech he gave on being awarded an honorary doctorate at the Catholic University of America in Washington, DC, on 28 February 1995. And, not untypically on such occasions, he used words by someone else to speak for him; in this instance, he turned to fragments abstracted from a homily given by Pope John Paul II during a Mass for Artists held in Brussels on 20 May 1985:

---

[5] The most recent edn. is the 39th (Kraków, 1900). Górecki's personal copy dates from the time of the jubilee edns. of 1928.

Each authentic work of art interprets the reality beyond sensory perception. It is born of silence, admiration, or the protest of an honest heart. It tries to bring closer the mystery of reality. So what constitutes the essence of art is found deep within each person. It is there where the aspiration to give meaning to one's life is accompanied by the fleeting sense of beauty and the mysterious unison of things. Authentic and humble artists are perfectly well aware, no matter what kind of beauty characterizes their handiwork, that their paintings, sculptures or creations are nothing else but the reflection of God's Beauty. No matter how strong the charm of their music and words, they know that their works are only a distant echo of God's Word.[6]

Górecki concluded his speech with the quiet observation: 'Those words are perfect: you can neither add to them nor take anything away. Just think deeply about the sense of those words.' It is in this reverential context that Górecki sees all his creative output, from the largest orchestral works to the most modest church song.

For the most part, the settings in *Marian Songs* and *Church Songs* are very faithful to the original melodies. Normally, Górecki uses them at pitch, in the same metre, harmonizing them as homophonic hymns, with phrasal repeats. Slight variations include extra repeats, particularly of the concluding phrase (cf. this habit in larger works, such as *Miserere*), and the occasional transposition of a melody or the eliding of elements from different versions. Harmonically, they conform to expectations aroused by preceding works, with their use of internal or bass pedal-points, first-inversion triadic drones, parallel-fifth movement in the lower parts, or descending bass-lines at the start. Parallel melodic movement, often in thirds, is also a feature. The larger of the two sets, *Church Songs*, has a correspondingly wider range of melodies and compositional approaches. Górecki has selected the twenty-one songs from across the Church calendar, with a number of Marian hymns mixed with songs from Lent (including one of the famous *Gorzkie żale*—Bitter Laments), Easter, Corpus Christi, and a couple associated with St Nicholas and St Joseph. Their moods consequently embrace the pensive (e.g. No. 4, 'Ludu, mój ludu') as well as the triumphant (No. 13, 'Krzyknijmy wszyscy').

Musically, they range from the chant to the genre of the folk-dance. Chant is present in the repeated four bars of No. 11 ('Pozdrawiajmy wychwalajmy') and in No. 6 ('Zawitaj Pani świata'), where the metre

[6] A transcript of this homily is included in: Jarmila Sobiepan, *Jan Paweł II w krajach Beneluksu i w Liechtensteinie* [John Paul II in the Benelux Countries and Lichtenstein] (Warsaw, 1987), 320–6. I am grateful to Beata Paszyc for furnishing me with a copy of Górecki's Washington speech.

is dictated by the shifts between five- and four-beat phrases. Irregular groupings occur in No. 9 ('Dobranoc, Głowo święta') and No. 10 ('O Matko miłościwa'), which are both constructed from two phrases of four and five bars. One of the oldest is the Polish version of the Easter hymn 'Surrexit Christus hodie' (No. 16, 'Wstał Pan Chrystus z martwych ninie'), which shares in common with many Polish folkmelodies a bipartite division into 2/4 (four bars) and 3/4 (six bars). Characteristically, Górecki repeats the first section and, sequentially, the three two-bar phrases of the second. The link with folk patterns is carried through in Górecki's rare treatment of the melody as tune with accompaniment (No. 21, 'Ciebie wzywamy, Ciebie błagamy', and No. 15, 'Witaj, Jutrzenko'). This latter song is one of several based on folk-dance rhythms: No. 5 ('Witaj Pani, Matko Matki Jezusa Pana') is a mazurka in da capo form, while No. 2 ('Idźmy, tulmy się, jak dziatki') uses a melody from Podhale strikingly reminiscent of the accompanimental figure from the Wet-Nurses' Dance in Stravinsky's *Petrushka*.

The two church songs to have been performed and recorded, No. 12 ('Święty, Święty, Święty') and No. 18 ('Twoja cześć chwała'), are both Eucharistic hymns. No. 12 is unusual in transposing the original melody (down a minor third) and having a constant tonic pedal-point in the bass, although its slight decoration of the melody (a little turn at its apex) and the upper movement in thirds are more common features. One of its most expressive moments is in the second phrase, where the semitonal sighing in the inner parts of a flat sixth onto the dominant gives it a poignancy which Mussorgsky would have recognized (cf. the Simpleton's aria in *Boris Godounov*). The melodic variation in No. 18 brings greater movement, and chromatic inflection (yet another reference to the 'turn' motif), to Mioduszewski's solemn melody, whose incipit is nearly identical with that of 'Bogurodzica' (Ex. VI.2).

The two independent hymns (*Under Your Protection* and *Come Holy Spirit*), along with the anthem *Totus Tuus*, Op. 60 (1987), are on a larger scale. *Under Your Protection* is a setting of the antiphon 'Sub Tuum praesidium'; and although Górecki stays close to the incantatory interlocking of phrases, both textually and melodically, the melody itself moves beyond the original's limited ambit for a greater expressivity which harks back to *Beatus vir*.[7] The best-known of Górecki's a cappella choral works from the 1980s is *Totus Tuus*, a

---

[7] It seems also to draw on the preceding melody published in Siedlecki's collection, 'Litanja do Matki Boskiej' (Litany to the Mother of God).

Ex. VI.2. 'Twoja cześć, chwała', Mioduszewski's nineteenth-century version with Górecki's variations

Górecki

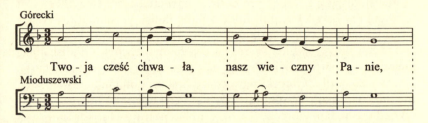

Two - ja cześć chwa - ła,      nasz wie - czny   Pa - nie,

Mioduszewski

Na wie - czne   cza - sy   niech nie u - sta - nie.

tribute, based on the Pope's motto, written by the contemporary writer Maria Bogusławska and composed by Górecki for performance during John Paul II's third pilgrimage home in 1987. It returns to the simplicity of the straightforward homophony characteristic of the earlier *Marian Songs*, although there is an expansive gentleness in this setting which captures Bogusławska's poetry in a way which the Siedlecki-based works are not always in a position to achieve.

*Come Holy Spirit*, the most recent of his sacred works, is notable for its amalgam of chant-derived idioms and of unusually sumptuous harmonic shifts, particularly the use of the dominant ninth (cf. *Ad matrem*). It underlines the bond between Górecki's choral works of the 1980s and the model presented by Szymanowski's *Stabat mater*, particularly its unaccompanied fourth movement. The reiteration of the additional words 'Amen, Alleluja' in the coda of *Come Holy Spirit* reflects Górecki's admiration for the poet Jan Kasprowicz (1860–1926), one of whose final poems, 'Wstał Pan Jezus z martwych' (Lord Jesus is risen from the dead), is an Easter hymn whose verses each end with 'Aleluję'. There are, in fact, facets of character, temperament, and background in and love of the Tatra region which unite Górecki and Kasprowicz. 'If the term "expressionism" has any meaning,' wrote Czesław Miłosz of the Polish poet, 'it can designate a will to find artistic means for violent emotions, and in this sense,

Kasprowicz's hymns could be called expressionistic. At the same time, they are rooted in a typically Polish, religious, peasant sensibility.[8] The same observation rings true for Górecki.

There remains one other work which, although unpublished and unperformed, is regarded by Górecki as his best for a cappella choir: *Na Anioł Pański biją dzwony* (The bells ring out for the Angelus Domini), Op. 57 (1986). It is one of three works of the period (the others are for voice and piano) which explore sacred poetry by Polish writers. The poet in this instance is Kazimierz Przerwa Tetmajer (1865–1940), another literary figure engrossed by the culture of the Tatras. Tetmajer had originally been interred in Warsaw, and Górecki composed *Angelus Domini* for his reburial in June 1986 in Zakopane, although its performance never materialized. It shares with *Miserere* not only a tonal basis in a ladder of thirds (this time realized in a funereally persistent alternation of the open fifths F-C and A-E) but also melodic ideas derived from the pentatonic mode. What marks *Angelus Domini* out is the extensive coda (some four minutes) and its exotic triadic progressions. Some of these are folk-based, like the root-position chordal sequence C major–B flat major–F major–G major–A minor (Szymanowski again), others more colourfully impressionistic, in keeping with Tetmajer's lyrical poetry. *Angelus Domini* develops the idea, mooted in *O Domina nostra*, of abandoning modal stability in the coda, crowning one of Górecki's most passionately expressed a cappella compositions.

The two works for voice and piano are settings of poetry by Cyprian Kamil Norwid (1821–83) and Juliusz Słowacki respectively: *Błogosławione pieśni malinowe* (Blessed Raspberry Songs), Op. 43 (1980), and *Śpiewy do słów J. Słowackiego* (Songs to Words by J. Słowacki), Op. 48 (1983).[9] In *Blessed Raspberry Songs*, Górecki takes a markedly sombre view of the world. Using the same ladder of thirds as in *Angelus Domini* as his unifying chord (emphasizing the first inversion of A minor), he constructs a series of funeral marches to match Norwid's raw and majestic verse. All of the four songs are

[8] *The History of Polish Literature* (Berkeley and Los Angeles, 1983), 339.

[9] Norwid is generally regarded as the forerunner of modern Polish poetry and often wrote on Christian, national, and cultural themes. He was befriended in Paris by Chopin, whose name crops up in Norwid's writings, as in his poems 'Promethidion' (1851) and 'Chopin's Piano' (1863). Two poems by Słowacki had appeared in Górecki's earliest acknowledged songs (Op. 3). Only rarely has Górecki departed from his attachment to Polish poetry or to the Book of Psalms in Latin, as in his setting of two poems by Lorca, in Polish translations. 'Nokturn' (Nocturne) was composed at the same time as Op. 3 and was later grouped with 'Malagueña' (1980) as Op. 42.

settings of poetic fragments, and their melancholically unresolved sentiments are matched by the obsessive tread of alternating chords. The second song, for example, ends tonally adrift from the A minor chord, while elsewhere Górecki counterpoints it with dissonant motivic oscillations in the bass (D♭–B♭ in the first song, F♯–D♯–F♯–C in the third). The third song is an astonishing upward struggle of escape ('when the *spirit* emerges under pressure'), its strain of chromaticism looking back to Szymanowski's *Three Songs to Poems by Kasprowicz*, Op. 5 (1902), especially 'Jestem i płaczę' (Here I am, weeping). The final fragment is cast as a contemplative and lugubrious recitando, recalling Górecki's early fascination with recitative (cf. the first of his own *Three Songs*).

Górecki's proximity to Szymanowski has been a recurrent feature of his career. Nor should there be any surprise, particularly given Szymanowski's example, that Górecki's music demonstrates that sacred and folk influences are essentially one and the same. While to non-Poles the modality he employs may seem more generally sacred than secular, Górecki identifies his fingerprints of the 'motto' and the 'turn' as being recognizably of folk origin and particularly characteristic of Podhale.[10] The closest Górecki has moved towards folksong has been in his several sets of songs for a cappella choir composed 1979–84 (i.e. written ahead of his *Church Songs*).[11] His sources ranged from three children's story-books to the massive nineteenth-century collections of Oskar Kolberg. Only three of the six works with opus numbers have been published. The first, and arguably the most important, is *Szeroka woda* (Broad Waters), Op. 39, composed in December 1979. Its five songs, with the exception of No. 3, are concerned with rivers: the Narew (No. 1) and Poland's main river, the Vistula, which runs through both Kraków and Warsaw on its way to the Baltic (Nos. 2 and 5). Górecki has also united the cycle around the tonality of G (minor/major), and his treatment of the melodies, to which he remains completely faithful, is typical in many respects of his general approach in all the six works.

The tempos are predominantly slow, the tone serious rather than light-hearted, reflecting the verses' melancholic or solemn sentiments. The most straightforward is the title song with which the set ends: the hymnic chordal style ('maestoso, espressivo') is found frequently in other songs, as is its total avoidance of the root-position tonic chord (cf. the oblique cadences in No. 3 (modal) and No. 1 (minor) and the

---

[10] Conversation with the author, Nov. 1991.
[11] Górecki's ideal complement for most of his a cappella works is around sixty voices.

Ex. VI.3. 'Polne róże rwała', bb. 1–8

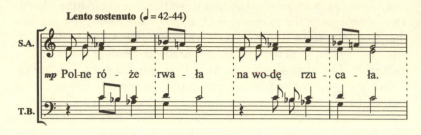

persistence of second-inversion dominant chords in the latter). The mazurka rhythm of No. 1 is typical of these sets of songs, as it is of the church songs, and No. 2 is in the faster tempo of its cousin, the oberek. Here, Górecki has selected the melody-and-accompaniment texture which, along with the hymnic style, accounts for almost all of his songs (contrapuntal or thematic elaborations are notable for their absence). The original melody (four repeats of a four-bar phrase) is the simplest of the set although, in the later *Ach, mój wianku lewandowy* (O, my Garland of Lavender), Op. 50 (1984), there is a nonsense rhyming lullaby, 'Bzi, bzi, bzibziana', which consists only of the semitonal alternations of the mediant and subdominant notes. Occasionally, Górecki essays a more chromatic idiom, as in Nos. 1 and 4, which also share a very similar opening phrase. Such colorations are drawn from Górecki's intimate understanding of Polish folk-music (Ex. VI.3).

*Wisło moja, Wisło szara* (My Vistula, Grey Vistula), Op. 46 (1981), is a solitary folksong, with a text very familiar to Poles. In its metre and constant mediant pedal, it anticipates *Trzy kołysanki* (Three Lullabies), Op. 49 (1984). These lullabies, along with the unpublished

*Kołysanki i tańce* (Lullabies and Dances), Op. 47, for violin and piano (1982), are a specific manifestation of the deeply rooted attachment Górecki evidently has to the genre (cf. Op. 9 and his abiding admiration for z Szamotuł's evening hymn). His music is informed by the idea of departure and return, be it structural, or minutely melodic, or harmonic. The rocking 'to and fro' may privately have symbolic or more fundamental meaning, but its musical origins lie in the Polish vernacular traditions. The third lullaby, as distinct from the hymnic style of the first two, is an example (rare in the choral songs) of a slow-breathed modal melody accompanied by pattering quavers, which combine the melody notes with some of their tritonal equivalents (see Ex. V.5). What may look dissonant is in fact a harmonic and rhythmic ostinato which merges a minor mode (on D) with a minor scale (on F), one consequence being an emphasis on whole-tone harmony. The *Three Lullabies* is the only group of songs for which Górecki did not draw on existing musical sources, and yet such is his mastery of this deceptively simple idiom that this is never apparent.

The other three sets of a cappella folksongs remain unpublished. *Wieczór ciemny się uniża* (Dark Evening is Falling), Op. 45 (1981), is based on material from the same story-book from which Górecki borrowed two songs for *Broad Waters*. More interesting, and certainly more significant, are the two cycles of songs from Kolberg's collection made in Pomorze: *O, my Garland of Lavender* and *Idzie chmura, pada deszcz* (Cloud Comes, Rain Falls), Op. 51, both composed in 1984. Oskar Kolberg was a phenomenon whose reputation inexplicably remains restricted to Poland. Without doubt, he was the most significant nineteenth-century European ethnographer, and many would argue that his achievements have never been surpassed. He criss-crossed the country, noting down not only folksongs and folk-dances but customs, ceremonies, architecture, and aspects of everyday life. Over sixty volumes of his collections, arrangements, original compositions, and correspondence have now been published. Kolberg's work is central to Górecki: 'For me, this is the entire history of Poland, all of Poland, not the history of royalty—that's fine and good—but this, this is without peer. I could not live without it. It is everything. For me, it is like a bible.'[12]

Pomorze is a region below the Baltic, not particularly famed for its contribution to Polish folk-music. Górecki was unexpectedly captivated by this volume in Kolberg's collection:

---

[12] Conversation with the author, Nov. 1991.

What could be interesting about Pomorze—Kurpie, Podhale, yes, but Pomorze? And yet I wrote out such beautiful Pomeranian melodies and texts. Take this one from *Cloud Comes, Rain Falls*, 'Szła sierotka po wsi':

> An orphan girl walked through a village,
> three dogs set upon her,
> Nobody turned round
> to rescue the little orphan girl.
>
> Lord Jesus came down
> himself from heaven,
> to take the little orphan girl
> with him to heaven.

It is a beautiful text, such as no poet could write: highly religious, highly Christian.[13]

Górecki sets as much store by the words as by the music, as has been evident in earlier and larger pieces. Those in the first of the Kolberg cycles, *O, my Garland of Lavender*, are grouped to show aspects of life from the female point of view: courtship, wedding, marriage, and childhood, concluding with a bonnet song from harvest time. For the most part, the cycle is characteristically understated. From time to time, Górecki spices the harmonic language, as in No. 3, 'Taiłam się' (I have kept silent), where he places a C major harmony against a rising E major seventh arpeggio, a neat parallel to the marital friction in the text. 'Bzi, bzi, bzibziana' follows the tradition of the terrifying nursery rhyme ('the wolves ate a lamb, the dogs ate a sheep, you child sleep'), its simple alternation of F♯ and G suitably menacing. The variety of mood is continued in the fifth and sixth songs, one a pious religious tale for children, with an atmosphere akin to the title song of *Broad Waters*, and a wistful mazurka in which a young woman complains to her mother that she has been married off to the first available man, 'to get rid of a nuisance . . . nothing good will come to a wife, only sorrow and slavery'.

*Cloud Comes, Rain Falls* is a shorter cycle of five songs. Except in the central fast mazurka ('When it will be sunny and warm, do come, Johnny, to me in the garden'), the mood is pensive. There is some element of the Third Symphony in this cycle: the combination in the fast mazurka of a melody in triple time with a rocking pair of chords in duple and the harmonic inflections of the story of the orphan girl (No. 4) both recall Górecki's treatment of the Opole lament. The metrical treatment of the original melodies is also more varied than in

<hr>

[13] Conversation with the author, Nov. 1991.

earlier sets, although in contrary ways: No. 1 irons out a pair of duple bars to conform to the triple metre elsewhere in the song, whereas the pauses in No. 5 are realized in creating 4/4 bars in an otherwise 3/4 context. There is no doubt in Górecki's mind that his favourite song from all these sets is No. 2, 'Gdzie to jedziesz, Jaszu?' (Where are you going, Johnny?). This is a very well-known song, common to many regions of Poland: Szymanowski included it as the ninth of his *Polish Songs* (1926), and Lutosławski incorporated it as the seventh of his *Ten Polish Folksongs on Soldiers' Themes* (1951).[14]

The attraction for Górecki was twofold. The text is a poignant verse-and-refrain conversation between a young woman and her beloved:

> Where are you going, Johnny?
> To the war, Kasia,
> to the distant war.
> Take me with you, Johnny,
> I will go with you
> To the distant war.
>
> What will you do there
> Kasia, little Kasia
> at the distant war?
> I'll wash my scarves,
> embroider them with gold
> at the distant war.[15]

Again, the private human cost of war evoked strong emotions in the composer, and it is matched by what is indubitably the most expressive version of the melody that Kolberg ever collected (Ex. VI.4). Where, for example, Szymanowski's and Lutosławski's versions are in a plain duple metre, the Pomorze version has that bipartite division into 2/4 and 3/4 which Górecki was to find again in the sixteenth of his *Church Songs*. Here, its function in separating the question and answer of the two lovers is a folksong's equivalent of high drama, particularly when it is coupled with the decisive change in modality. Górecki captures the sweet sorrow of their parting with an extraordinary harmonic sensitivity (see Ex. VI.4 for summary of underpin-

[14] The source of Szymanowski's version ('Gdzież to jedziesz, Jasiu') is unclear; Lutosławski drew his melody ('Gdzie to jedziesz, Jasiu') from Kolberg, *Dzieło wszystkie* (Complete Works), xxvi: 'Mazowsze III' (Kraków, 1887; repr. Poznań, 1963), No. 419.
[15] Górecki took his second verse from another Kolberg transcription, even though the Mazurian dialect brings different refrains (Kolberg, *Dzieło wszystkie*, xxvii: 'Mazowsze IV' (Kraków, 1888; repr. Poznań, 1964), No. 383).

Ex. VI.4. 'Gdzie to jedziesz, Jaszu'

ning): the saving of the *musica ficta* C♯ until the third appearance (the F♯ in the key signature has been ignored until this point), the move from D to first-inversion F over the metrical break and the semitonal F–E shift that immediately takes the harmony onto A minor, the sequence of inverted triads in the succeeding bars, and particularly the progression in bars 11 and 12 of second-inversion major triads B flat–C–D bring out all the tenderness of this nineteenth-century war-time love song. If only for this, one hopes that Górecki will relent and release these cycles for the enjoyment of the wider public.

# VII
# QUASI UNA FANTASIA

GÓRECKI'S use in the choral music of the 1980s of folksongs from Pomorze, rather than from his spiritual home of Podhale, was perhaps a little surprising. But his devotion to the area around Zakopane remained absolute. Since 1978, the family had rented a log house and barn on the banks of the Czarny (Black) Dunajec river on the outskirts of Chochołów, and it was with considerable regret that they lost their tenancy in 1989. They had made many friends since their first holiday there in 1966, pre-eminently the sculptor, violin-maker, and musician Wojciech ('Waszek') Blaszak (d. 1974), several of whose instruments and folk sculptures Górecki now proudly owns. Other local craftsmen included Władysław Gromada, one of the last hand-embroiderers of the traditional Góral (mountaineers') coats and trousers. Górecki feels totally at home in these surroundings, a throwback perhaps to his childhood in Czernica and his time with Hajduga. Undoubtedly, contact with local musicians brought him the greatest joy, folk groups such as Oficerki in Dzianisz and individual players like Blaszak, from whom he learnt folk-fiddling. Arguably the most significant musicians were from the Obrochta family, whose earlier generation (particularly Bartek) had been great friends with Szymanowski when he had rented the villa 'Atma' in Zakopane from them in the 1920s. Górecki himself played from the early 1960s onwards with Władek Obrochta (d. 1993), who was captured on film, shortly before his death, with Górecki and a long-standing friend and musical colleague, the baritone Andrzej Bachleda, a member of another distinguished Góral family.[1]

The chamber and orchestral music written since 1980 is as identifiable with instrumental folk traditions as the choral pieces are with

---

[1] Bachleda gave the première with Górecki, in Zakopane, of *Śpiewy do słów J. Słowackiego* (Songs to words by J. Słowacki), Op. 48. The film including Władek Obrochta is *Autoportret* (Self-Portrait), directed by Krzysztof Bukowski (Polish Television, 1993, *c.*45′). With the purchase in 1995 of a house in a Podhale village looking out on the Tatra mountains, Górecki has finally realized his long-held desire to live and work in an environment imbued with those elements of Polish culture he holds most dear.

their vocal counterparts. This period began in 1979 with *Broad Waters*, which Górecki has said is a more important work for him than the first instrumental composition of the period, describing the *Koncert na klawesyn—lub fortepian—i orkiestrę smyczkową* (Concerto for Harpsichord—or Piano—and String Orchestra), Op. 40 (1980), as a 'wybryk' (frolic, caprice).[2] And yet it is equally significant as his first mainstream instrumental work since *Canticum graduum* and *Muzyczka 4*. It is one of his most exuberant pieces, in which Góral influences are a strong but less overt element than in the works of his fellow Silesian Kilar, whose folk-inspired orchestral pieces include *Krzesany* (Sparking Dance, 1974) and *Orawa* for strings (1986). Its two fast movements and overall duration of only nine minutes are a salutory reminder that the large-scale works of the 1970s represent just one part of Górecki's musical personality. The title, usually shortened to 'Harpsichord Concerto', allows for performances using the piano with a larger complement of strings, and the piano's different weight and articulation enable, for example, some dissonant harmonic details to emerge more tellingly (e.g. the soloist's low F♯s in the central section of the first movement). But it is as a harpsichord concerto that it has become well known, with the Baroque instrumental combination being invested with the sort of rhythmic zest which so characterizes the early *Songs of Joy and Rhythm*.

Not untypically, Górecki rejected the initial draft of the first movement, but the final version's bipartite structure gave him quiet satisfaction in its simplicity: 'The first movement is a constant two-voiced superimposition of cantus firmus (strings) and figuration (solo), while the second turns the duality around to create juxtaposed tutti–solo contrasts. Often a simple idea lies behind a major decision.'[3] In the first movement, the duet stratifies the melodic and harmonic functions to the extent that, as Teresa Malecka has suggested, the roles of tutti and solo seem to have been inverted.[4] While the soloist provides a running harmonic commentary using the Aeolian mode on D, it is the strings which unfold a chant-based melody in slow sustained phrases (see Ex. V.5), using just the first four notes of the same mode (the 12/8-6/4 superimposition of these two lines recalls the duple-triple superimpositions of the Third Symphony's finale). The sudden interruption of the brief central section (4/4) chromaticizes the solo-

---

[2] Conversation with the author, Mar. 1994.      [3] Ibid.
[4] 'O Koncercie klawesynowym Góreckiego' (On Górecki's Harpsichord Concerto), in Teresa Malecka (ed.), *Mieczysławowi Tomaszewskiemu w 60-lecie urodzin* (For Mieczysław Tomaszewski on his 60th Birthday) (Kraków, 1984), III.

ist's harmonic palette, just as the strings leave the chant-based material for something new (the mode is retained). This new idea, in descending thirds with a rising sixth up-beat, is linked by Malecka to a phrase from a melody associated with the church song 'Ludu, mój ludu' (People, my people).[5]

At the subsequent return of the opening texture, both partners feel a new sense of freedom, maintaining their relative functions but revealing several features reminiscent of Górecki's slow-tempo works from the 1960s and 1970s. The keyboard continues its chromatic roulades while the strings extend the range of their triple-octave unison line until it coalesces on an alternating tritone E–B♭, by which time the soloist has reverted to the opening Aeolian runs. A stuttering reiteration of the 1/4 up-beats which have ushered in the chant phrases since the beginning is halted by an unexpected *tierce de Picardie* chord of D major. This marks the dividing-point as well as the link between what might be called the sacred chorale prelude of the first movement and the secular round dance of the second. The structural dualism is emphasized by the shift from minor to major as well as the concertante nature of the dialogue in the finale. Its origins in folk-dance are evident in melodic decorations, syncopated cross-rhythms, harmonic configurations, and strong cadential phrasing. Although it shares superficially some features with material in the first movement, the finale has its own vivacity and character which fully realize the composer's intention to provide two movements at right angles, as it were, to one another. It is a uniquely constructed composition, itself at a tangent to the more sombre masterpieces which immediately preceded it.

The hiatus in Górecki's instrumental composition after 1980 has been largely explained with regard to the advent of martial law, his poor health, and his private focus on choral music. He did consider a couple of instrumental projects directly connected with folk-music: the partly composed *Mazurki* (Mazurkas), Op. 41, for piano (1980), the *Lullabies and Dances*, and the unrealized *Pieśni i tańce* (Songs and Dances) for soprano and string quartet. The mazurkas were to be modelled on cycles such as Messiaen's *Vingt regards sur l'enfant Jésus*, not in the grandeur of the Frenchman's vision but in the idea of multipartite sequences of musical structures. Górecki completed only two of these manifold mazurkas, whose style is commensurate with the unadorned nature of the choral songs rather than with the ternary

---

[5] Ibid. (Górecki's setting of this text in his later *Church Songs* uses an alternative melody.)

structures and melodic-harmonic detail of Szymanowski's outstanding contributions to the genre. In truth, Górecki seemed by 1983 to have lost heart and confidence in his plans for large-scale compositions. It took a telephone call from Denmark to break his isolation.

## Recitatives and Ariosos 'Lerchenmusik'

The Danish composer Poul Rovsing Olsen had visited the Warsaw Autumn on a number of occasions, and his *Patet* for instrumental ensemble was premièred at the 1966 festival. After his death in 1982, his widow Louise Lerche-Lerchenborg found some of Górecki's scores in her husband's library and, at the suggestion of the composer Ib Nørholm, she telephoned Górecki in December 1983 with a commission proposal. Out of the blue, Górecki received the stimulus he needed to set to work on a major piece, and he credits Louise Lerche-Lerchenborg with initiating a new creative phase. She has proved to be a true friend and patron, with several later works also commissioned and/or premièred at the annual Lerchenborg Music Days.[6] In the event, the première of *Recitativa i Ariosa 'Lerchenmusik'* (Recitatives and Ariosos 'Lerchenmusik'), Op. 53, for clarinet, cello, and piano was rather fraught. Górecki had not completed the work when he arrived in Denmark in July 1984, and withdrew the first movement and part of the second from the hurriedly prepared performance. The following year, the finished trio was premièred at the Warsaw Autumn, only to be revised again, mainly in respect of extensions and repetitions of certain phrases in all three movements. The final version was premièred in April 1986.

The scoring of *Lerchenmusik* was an integral part of the commission, one to which Górecki agreed despite his avowed preference for the unified ensembles of voices or strings (although he points to his own student compositions as exceptions and cites Schubert's Octet as a work he admires). He had not ventured into the realm of chamber music since the multi-timbred *Muzyczka 4* of 1970. At the time, of course, he could not have foreseen that this trio would initiate a chain of works for chamber forces with which much of his international

---

[6] Louise Lerche-Lerchenborg was the first of only a handful of visitors to be invited to Górecki's composition studio in a house in the suburbs of Katowice. He had bought it some months previously in order to gain some peace and quiet away from the family flat—his two children, then in their teens, were proving to be highly musical (Anna is now a professional concert pianist, and Mikołaj a composer). This is where his mother's piano is located and where he continues to spend much of his time, until such time as he relocates to his new house in Podhale.

reputation would be made. Back in 1984, his situation was still that of a recluse, and it is not surprising that he took great pains with a composition that potentially held the key to his future. In the event, he produced a chamber work lasting some forty minutes, placing it on a par with the tonal and thematic breadth of *Beatus vir*. It also reverts to the pattern of the Third Symphony, with three predominantly slow movements; even where the rhythmic pulse is fast (as in the main body of the first movement), the harmonic rhythm is very measured (cf. *Muzyczka 4*). As is his wont, Górecki uses the instruments to highlight structural levels and divisions and, in the process, turns to advantage his wariness about mixed ensembles. The character of each movement is sculpted partly through a different instrumental focus (cello in the first, clarinet in the second, and piano in the third) as well as through a carefully graded mix of individual and shared motivic cells.

The lento–largo frame of the first movement is a solo for cello on the C string with octave C chimes on the piano. Its lineage of chromatic meditation may be traced back to the 1960s, although here it is shorn of decoration and from the outset incorporates intervals wider than semitones and tones. In the second half of the opening section, the motivic outline C–E–F♯ emerges: while in the ensuing fast episodes this same motif relates overtly to the folk-music tradition, here it bears more than a passing resemblance to the opening of the Fourth Symphony by Sibelius, a composer with whom Górecki shares many basic musical tenets. But whereas in his orchestral music he is able to develop his textures almost by stealth, with only three instruments at his disposal Górecki chooses different means of exploring his material. In the central portion of the first movement, an insistent and exhilarating ritual develops from the repetition and contrast of small melodic motifs and punctuating chords. Here are to be found the 1/4 up-beats from the Harpsichord Concerto, sequences of repeated phrases creating larger paragraphs, the entry of the clarinet giving a high-profile folk character to the C–E–F♯ motif against a C major base, and a sequence for solo piano in which shifting balances between repeated bitonal chords and melodic fragments create music reminiscent of Messiaen. For all its appearance as a movement of block juxtapositions of relatively static material, it has a developmental rondo structure, whose textural climax is the superimposition of the C–E–F♯ motif and the piano solo's bitonal material (Ex. VII.1). From this high point, Górecki does a volte-face, retreating to the low C♮ of the beginning.

Ex. VII.1. *Lerchenmusik*, first movement (p. 14)

If the first movement may be regarded as a sophisticated distillation of some of the brutal elements in its predecessors in the *Muzyczka* series, the second movement is a quite new phenomenon in Górecki's instrumental music. It is an extended arioso for clarinet (later doubled in thirds and minor ninths by the cello) against dispassionate piano chords modelled on, although not identical with, their bitonal cousins in the first movement. There are other links, such as the clarinet's initial F♯–E and punchy motivic concentration in its high register. Although again there is a hint of Messiaen in this texture, it is unmistakably abstracted from Polish folk-music. The tantalizing aspect is the tonal design. The piano part consists almost entirely of a prosaic shifting from one combination of first-inversion triads—G and B major—to the same a tone lower (the preponderance in this movement and the finale of first- and second-inversion triads is directly related to Górecki's harmonic practices in his recent choral works). This is not his accustomed chordal 'cradling' but a predictable quasi-cadential movement from the lower bitonal chord (which quickly becomes dominant in both senses of the word) to the upper whenever the melody rests on D♯. The piano's stepwise motions are one instance of a subliminal intervallic design in the trio which simply but effectively helps to give it a symphonic dimension. This is the pervasive use of alternating notes a tone apart. The whole tone is one of the two prime intervals in the first movement (the other being the tritone), and it is the generative melodic interval and the bass interval of harmonic progressions in this second movement. In contrast to the limited activity of the piano, the melodic line of the clarinet remains determinedly evasive, focusing for some time on C♯ and playing on the 'motto' intervals until it reaches a full seven-note complement on A. At this moment, the melody relocates as a major scale with a sharp fourth and a perpetually unresolving leading-note, both of which give the clarinet line much of its bite. There is a brief softening of the harmonic-melodic idiom when the clarinet reaches up to a high B and a new bitonal chord makes an appearance, a combination of two minor triads (E and G sharp) a 'relative' minor third below the G–B major combination.

The cello rejoins the clarinet for the recapitulation of the opening arioso. Their parallel movement in minor and major thirds is typical of melody instruments in Góral folk ensembles, and soon they settle into a rumbustious compound metre that bears all the hallmarks of village music-making. When thirds become minor ninths, the angularity increases sharply, and the music is at once closest to its folk sources and so abstracted from them that it moves onto quite another plane. The relationship between the figurative and the abstract becomes a central consideration in many of Górecki's subsequent works. In *Lerchenmusik*, it serves both a local and a long-term function. So the coda of the second movement, a piano version of the 'melody in thirds', acts as a disembodied echo of the full-blooded clarinet and

Ex. VII.2. *Lerchenmusik*, third movement, beginning

cello original. It also anticipates the focal role the piano plays in the finale.

The dynamic profile of the trio moves from high to low, emphasizing the finale's role as a quiet culmination. In this respect, it is a further development of the process already observed in *Muzyczka 4* and *Miserere*. With the exception of a violent solo piano outburst before the coda, this entails an increasing textural and dynamic serenity until the closing pages recall the C–E–F♯ motif from the opening movement. But the real magic of the finale takes place simultaneously in the presentation and transformation of its thematic material. Where, in the earlier movements, the external references were more general than specific, in the finale Górecki's attention turns to iconographic associations of a more rarefied kind. He maintains carefully the language of gentle bitonality and stepwise melodies, but there is no mistaking the chant origins of the opening sequence of second-inversion major triads (cf. their use in the second song of *Cloud Comes, Rain Falls*). It is a vespers melody whose outline and rhythmic presentation also bear a distinct resemblance to the opening solo in Beethoven's Fourth Piano Concerto (Ex. VII.2). This is deliberate: as was observed in reference to the genesis of the first movement of Górecki's Third Symphony, the composer lays some store by serendipity, and the connection between the stepwise vespers melody and the Beethoven phrase set Górecki's creative juices flowing. Unlike previous icons, neither is presented at original pitch, nor is it unadulterated by decorative dissonance. Rather than baldly stating the

Beethoven original at the outset, Górecki is uniquely intent on gradually removing the fine layers of filter; it eventually appears shortly before the coda, at pitch, in slow motion and characteristically avoiding any root-position chording. This is still a veiled reference (there are some upper grace-notes that have strayed over from the previous bars), and it is left first to the piano and then to the two orchestral instruments (again in thirds) to cite the original theme more accurately, but nevertheless transposed. By this stage, Górecki is embarked on a prolonged coda which is based cyclically on melodic and harmonic motifs from the first and second movements.

This allusory process is intercut by two unrelated ideas, although both have iconographic import of a more private nature. The first is the more significant (it appears three times to the other's once), but it is likely that both were being referred to, rather than any more general point about ornamentation in high registers, when Górecki commented in 1985 that 'the "Lark" material pushed its own way onto the paper'.[7] Both are derived from the letters of the commissioner's surname, Lerchenborg: E–C–H(B♮) and B(B♭)–G. Such encryptions may be identified in a number of Górecki's works and are publicly important in so far as they create musical ideas which he then moulds to his own will.[8] The first is particularly poignant, especially since it is set against each of four second-inversion major triads descending by whole tone, a variant of an idea at the end of the youthful Piano Sonata (Ex. VII.3). Whatever their private import, these two ideas interwoven with the unveiling of the Beethoven citation are indicative of Górecki's continuing fascination with block structures. The difference here, as in the later string quartets, is that the figurative and the abstract, the specific and the general, the narrative and the reflective, and the contrasts of content and approach that each of these pairings suggests have led to a new thematic and structural richness which is faithfully reflected in the descriptive pairing of the trio's title: *Recitatives and Ariosos*.

---

[7] In the 1985 Warsaw Autumn programme book.

[8] This is one of the more musically significant examples of ciphers in Górecki's music. The phenomenon appears to be concentrated in the works of the 1980s and 1990s and, being usually a private matter, normally remains undetected. There have been suggestions that *O Domina nostra* includes cryptic or numerical references (cf. *Beatus vir*), and there are acknowledged examples in later works, as in the coda of the third movement of *Good Night* and in occasional pieces composed as gifts for friends. Two recent examples include *Lento cantabile* for flute, violin, and cello (30 Jan. 1994, *c*.30″) written for his colleagues at Boosey & Hawkes, and *Moment musical* for piano (27 Feb. 1994, *c*.2′) written for the wedding of Ruth Williams and Stephen Gieser.

Ex. VII.3. *Lerchenmusik*, third movement (p. 52)

Another use of descending second-inversion triads occurs in *Dla ciebie, Anne-Lill* (For you, Anne-Lill), Op. 58, for flute and piano (1986), written for the Norwegian flautist Anne-Lill Ree, whom Górecki had heard during his visit to Lerchenborg in 1984.[9] After a gap of twenty-three years, it picks up his initial fascination with the flute in *Three Diagrams* and *Diagram IV*, and anticipates both *Good Night*, Op. 63 (1990), and Górecki's major work for the instrument, *Concerto-Cantata*, Op. 65 (1992). It is a challenging work for the flautist, particularly in the obsessive flurries of the central section. The character of these snippets at the very top of the register and their furioso repetitions again emphasize the crucial influence of *Muzyczka 4*. They form a modern equivalent of an operatic mad scene, whose derangement is all the more set in relief by the totally unrelated and unmoved ostinato in the piano. This dysfunctional combination of melodic line and accompaniment may be traced as far back as *Epitafium* and *Monodramma*, and it has even closer parallels in *Lerchenmusik* and *Good Night*.

*For you, Anne-Lill* opens with a slow cantabile for the flute, its intervals more open than is customary. Set against the piano's unvaried tolling on high E♮s, it seems to be revisiting the opening of *Lerchenmusik*, transforming the trio's dark musings into a lighter, less portentous affair. But as the flute dwells on the tritone C–F♯ (which, combined with the piano's reiterations, evokes both internal and external comparisons), it is clear that this is no pastoral idyll. On its return after the central duo, the flute melody acquires another of Górecki's sequences of descending second-inversion major triads.

[9] Its working title was *Albumblätter* (Album Leaves); it was the second commission from Louise Lerche-Lerchenborg.

126

Where Messiaen was only hinted at in *Lerchenmusik*, here the French composer's harmonic language is explicit, if coincidental. Górecki's use of triads becomes increasingly structural during the instrumental music of this period (their clarifying effect at the start of *Lerchenmusik*'s finale is a noble precedent). In this instance, it gives the flute active support, compared with the nominal relationship between the instruments in the opening section. In essence, Górecki views triadic formations as substantive, stable, and reliable even though he almost always uses them in supposedly unstable inversions and not root positions. Because he normally concludes his compositions with a sense of return or consolidation, this is where he calls upon the unique properties of the triad to provide a resolution to preceding pitch conflicts or tonal uncertainties.

One of the oddest episodes in Górecki's career came in 1987. He was approached by the Belgian director Jan Fabre to write the music for an opera. Designed as a prologue and seven scenes, with a small cast and chorus, the libretto consisted of a series of symbolist tableaux in four different languages (English, French, German, and Italian). On the surface, there were some similarities between the style of the scenario and some of Górecki's own preoccupations, although he hardly ever considers setting anything other than the Polish language. After several months of contemplation on the proposal, he turned it down, and it was taken up by his former pupil Eugeniusz Knapik. But this uncharacteristic operatic venture was not entirely without results, because, as a preliminary sortie, Górecki composed an 'operatic scene' for tuba, piano, tam-tam, and bass drum in April 1987. *Aria* is a sustained and physically demanding monologue for tuba, a greatly extended version of the rising cantabile line heard first in the music for baritone in the Second Symphony. In *Aria*, the range stretches two and a half octaves from low B♮ to high F♯, with the tolling octaves in the piano (C♮) familiar from its two immediate instrumental predecessors. After a climax on three triads formed around the dyad B♭–D, the F♯ from the pre-eminent augmented triad provides the ultimate tritonal contrast with the piano's earlier C pedal. And it is at this moment that Górecki introduces the percussion, once again using a new timbre to point up an important structural moment. The tam-tam and bass drum reappear in the short recapitulatory coda as the initial low sonorities are tinged with the ubiquitous motif C–E–F♯.

Infinitely more significant in 1987 was Górecki's signature on a publishing contract with the London music house Boosey & Hawkes. For the first time since his limited connection with Schott in the early

1970s, and distinct from his long-term contract with PWM (whose remit was in the socialist 'bloc'), Górecki had a Western publisher who was not only prepared but eager to promote a composer deserving of international recognition. By this time, the Third Symphony was beginning to make its mark and articles on his music had appeared outside Poland. Immediately, Boosey & Hawkes set about winning commissions and exposure for Górecki. The first major survey of Górecki's music was two years later, in the spring of 1989, when eight works were performed at a London Sinfonietta 'Response' weekend (the programme was shared with Schnittke).[10] The prime mover at Boosey & Hawkes was David Drew, who early on had persuaded Górecki to turn his interest in chamber music in the direction of the string quartet. The subsequent link-up with the Kronos Quartet from San Francisco was to prove immensely fruitful, and in January 1989 Kronos premièred Górecki's first quartet, Op. 62 (1988), in Minneapolis.

### Already it is Dusk

Both of Górecki's first two quartets have titles. That of the first is *Już się zmierzcha*, which in Polish suggests a state of transience rather than completion, and a more accurate English rendering would be 'Already Dusk is Falling'. This was the third time that Górecki had turned to Wacław z Szamotuł's evening hymn, following *Chorale in the Form of a Canon* for string quartet (1961, revisited in 1984) and *Old Polish Music* (1969). The extramusical associations are important for Górecki: this 'prayer for children going to sleep', by the sixteenth-century Protestant poet Andrzej Trzycieski, was just as valid in postwar Communist Poland as in the Renaissance in its warnings about the forces of evil:

> Already dusk is falling, night closes in,
> Let us beseech the Lord for help,
> To be our guardian,
> To protect us from wicked devils,
> Who especially under cover of darkness
> Profit from their cunning.

Górecki has no particular love of the night, and his reading of this text as having political overtones caused him to write some descriptive

---

[10] The following works were programmed: *Epitafium*, *Three Pieces in Old Style*, *Muzyczka 4*, *Amen*, Symphony No. 3, Harpsichord Concerto, *Lerchenmusik*, and *Totus Tuus*.

verse of his own to detail what he has called 'a picture before nightfall: what goes on in the village [Chochołów] before dusk'.[11] This suggests, in part, an intention to encapsulate symbolically the imperviousness of the Polish countryside and its people to political or military onslaught. If his description sounds too picturesque, his bird's-eye view—a reminder of his concept for *Refrain*—was just a pre-compositional idea which has been severely abstracted in the finished quartet. And, lest the image came across as too cosy, the original ending was abandoned because Górecki thought its lyricism was inappropriate.

There certainly is a tartness in the employment of Szamotuł's tenor in canonic form. In *Old Polish Music* its *sul ponticello* homophony was cool and uninvolved. In canonic form, its intervals speak more eloquently, just as the opening canon did in the more uniform context of the Third Symphony; this is 'music for string quartet' (the work's unofficial subtitle), a picture of four instrumentalists quietly and almost in slow motion going about their connected business. The four voices replicate the P, R, I, and RI allocations in the earlier *Chorale*. As in *Old Polish Music*, the P and R forms are accurate transcriptions of the tenor, but the I and RI forms (on violins) alter one and two degrees of the mode respectively, although they are different from the changes noted in Op. 24.[12] The most noticeable alteration is at the very beginning of the canonic texture, where the second violin's first two notes have been changed from a descending C–B♭ to a rising A–B♮ (this is probably to avoid an otherwise strong suggestion of a cadence in F major). As in the string sections of *Old Polish Music*, the canon is stated in three stages conforming more or less to the threefold phrasing of the original tenor. These tranquil statements are prefaced and separated by boisterous homophonic folk fifths on C♯ and D, later joined by fifths on D♯ and C, the four root notes of the intervening tenor transpositions (the central open-string D–A is the common focus). On their last and most substantial appearance, there is an attempt to break out of the savage 'vamp till ready' mode into something more melodic, loosely related to z Szamotuł, but it is only after a brief codetta (the canon's opening bars) that the static electricity produced by such violently contrasted paragraphs is released (Ex. VII.4).[13]

[11] Conversation with the author, Mar. 1994.

[12] The tenor (or cantus firmus) printed in the preface of the Boosey & Hawkes miniature score is a transposition up a minor third (the original begins on A).

[13] Cf. the structural separation and balancing of the contrapuntal and the homophonic in the Harpsichord Concerto.

Ex. VII.4. *Already it is Dusk*, bb. 116–29

**Molto lento (ancora più come prime) - tranquillissimo**
Tutti: *pochiss. vibrato (quasi senza)*

The central 'allegro' may be regarded as a composite image of the music-making that Górecki enjoyed in Zakopane, Dzianisz, and Chochołów, where the string bands (fiddles and bass) would play late into the evenings, especially when the weather was too inclement for working in the fields. Górecki's division of the instrumentalists into two pairs, one with the melodic interest, the other with the ostinato, recalls similar deployment in Bartók's quartets. In the first section, the viola and cello develop a melody in major ninths, its phrases extended by irregular metres and repeat signs, its gradually rising tessitura adding to the excitement. It is noticeable that their line keeps returning to the rhythm and pitches with which they first started, and there is a palpable anticipation of the following section where the melody is released from its bass function. When roles are exchanged, the lower instruments take on the ostinato (the viola providing the bass, the cello the upper articulation) while the violins in thirds launch into a chain of motivic ideas. The melodic-metric shifts are skilfully unpredictable, and larger paragraphs emerge as a result of subtle harmonic and more evident melodic changes. Górecki captures the whirl of the dance without becoming naïvely figurative: his angle of view is cubist.

When, in the third section, the violins revert to their initial ostinato, the viola and cello likewise take up their major-ninth organum. But instead of recapitulating their earlier material, Górecki takes most of the opening phrase of z Szamotuł's tenor (from its second note) and gives it a completely new character. This is a quite unusual compositional process for Górecki, who until *Lerchenmusik* rarely worked out his borrowed material during the course of a composition: it usually came fully formed, in a highly polished state that lent itself to statement and contrast rather than *Durchführung*. The relationship between whole-tone alternation, the vespers melody, and the Beethoven quote in *Lerchenmusik* presented Górecki with opportunities for subtle allusions and new long-term cyclic references. In the first quartet, he has taken a more obviously deliberative step to develop his material, again to create a masterfully integrated work. This becomes gradually apparent in the fourth (and final) section of the central 'allegro'.

The section is marked 'martellando-tempestuoso' and has an idiosyncratically non-melodic texture, suggesting someone hearing a folk band from a distance and being able to catch only the accompaniment. A sequence of irregularly alternating chords moving in contrary motion—how different from the calm of many of its ancestors—is its main constituent, with upper and lower pairs working in different tonalities (cf. the model of *Lerchenmusik*). As the sequence progresses, Górecki interjects repetitions of a strong widely spaced chord built of perfect fifths and tritones. Only as the chord elbows out the rough-hewn folk-dance does it become fully apparent that this is the very same chord of superimposed fifths which alternated with the canon in the opening 'molto lento'. By stealth, he has brought us back to the recapitulation-coda, a complete statement of the canon. The coda's afterthought is a combination of a bell-like repeated A♮ (the focal centre of the opening) and three second-inversion triads (marked 'ARMONIA'). These do give the work a final mellowness, but it cannot erase the vivid impression of the rough and strange music which has filtered its sources—musical and textual—in a uniquely vibrant way. Whether this exorcises Renaissance or contemporary devils or stems from Górecki's affection for his adopted social world in Chochołów is perhaps irrelevant, but *Already it is Dusk* is as much a comment on the political situation at the time as *Miserere* was at the beginning of the 1980s. It is also a major landmark in his search for the integrated expression of his cultural roots.

There followed in 1990 two works written 'in memoriam'. The first was the more substantial: *Good Night* for soprano, alto flute, three tam-tams, and piano. Although it was completed in 1990 and dedicated in memory of the artistic director of the London Sinfonietta, Michael Vyner, the main body of the work was composed in 1988, before *Already it is Dusk* and before Vyner's death in 1989. The third movement was premièred in May 1990 at a memorial concert in the Royal Opera House, Covent Garden, London, where it was one of the most distinctive tributes; the complete performance followed six months later. *Good Night* has many resonances from earlier works: three slow movements, the combination of flute and piano, and the reserving of the soprano until the finale and of the tam-tams until the coda.

The focal third meditation of *Good Night* is the culmination of a number of understated processes in the first two movements. The tonal plan of the work moves from the piano's initial tolling 'bass' A♭ (the piano part keeps entirely within a two-and-a-half-octave range from the alto flute's low A♭) to the ostinato chord of the finale, an unresolved third-inversion dominant thirteenth (D♭–E♭–G–C). Digressions along the way include a B♭ pedal for most of the first movement and a second movement whose two tonal regions are indicated by (*i*) an F minor triadic figure which soon becomes perceived as the upper notes of a dominant ninth construction and (*ii*) an overt root-position dominant ninth on C, a whole tone higher than (*i*), paralleling the Ab–Bb polarity in the first movement. That non-functional dominant chords should play such a crucial role in Górecki's harmonic and tonal design does not come as a total surprise, not least because they make a deliberate connection with the 'lyrical fragment' in Górecki's previous memorial piece, *Ad matrem*. But this design does mark a break with the environment of intervening works, not in the principle of areas based on one or two constant chords but in the change from modal or plain triadic formations to chords with quasi-cadential connotations. If the French tradition comes to mind, it does so without Górecki having expressed any particular empathy with French composers apart from Messiaen.

Aside from the harmonic language, much of the expressivity of *Good Night* comes from its melodic intervals. The characteristic evolution of the flute line in the first movement is dominated by sighing minor thirds (as are parts of the second movement), with appearances of the diminished fourths heard to effect in *Beatus vir*. The first movement's coda dramatically opens up the repertoire of intervals within a pentatonic context, anticipating the pitches prevalent in the outer sections of the central Lento tranquillissimo. Texturally, these sections of the second movement recall in subdued vein the independent counterpoint of flute and piano in *For you, Anne-Lill*. The coda cyclically recapitulates the opening piano figuration as well as an embellished version of the first movement's coda.

Of all Górecki's farewells, his unexpected setting of Horatio's eulogy to Hamlet, 'Good night . . . flights of angels sing thee to thy rest', is the most affecting. The scoring of a single chord in the piano's middle register, supported by alto flute in short descending chromatic phrases below (bringing out the whole-tone aspects of the harmony), is magical (Ex. VII.5). The flute acts as a Greek chorus to the soprano's plaintive phrases, which modulate from simple minor thirds to alternating whole tones, descending chromatic motifs, and recollections of the 'turn' from the Third Symphony (see Ex. V.5). These latter two features combine to create her major expressive phrase, doubled at the lower octave by the flute.[14] The coda brings in the three tam-tams to seal the ritual. But Górecki has personalized the ceremony at the very end by providing a musical cipher drawn from the

[14] In the première version of the piece, the piano pinpoints most of the notes for soprano and flute (it still has this prompting role in the first movement), but in the published version Górecki has excised this element in the finale, leaving the three performers in a more fluid, less conspicuously dependent relationship.

Ex. VII.5. *Good Night*, third movement, beginning

letters of Michael Vyner's name. Although the resultant first interval of a rising minor sixth—E–C (Mi–c)—relates back to part of the second movement, the gesture is somewhat remote given the cipher's quite different tonality. In that sense, it seems to stand apart from the rest of *Good Night*, and one might be forgiven for thinking that this exquisite lament, without taking away from the pathos of the personal gesture, might be equally addressed to other lost loved ones whose names would form quite different musical encryptions.

The second of the memorial pieces composed in 1990 is a short piano piece, *Intermezzo*. This is the third of Louise Lerche-Lerchenborg's commissions to Górecki, one of a celebratory series requested from a range of international composers, including Betsy Jolas, Jōji Yuasa, Paweł Szymański, Simon Bainbridge, and Vinko Globokar. The occasion was the twenty-fifth Lerchenborg Music Days in 1990. Each of nineteen composers was asked to write a short variation on a theme chosen by the Danish composer Per Nørgård from the 'Luna' movement of Poul Rovsing Olsen's suite *The Planets* for mezzo-soprano, flute, viola, and guitar (1978). Górecki responded with a delicate miniature, a sequence of interlocked refrains with strong melodic minor thirds and a harmonic palette ranging from bell-like chords of perfect fifth and tritone to superimposed and individual triads. A year later, the Music Days hosted their fourth Górecki première, this time of the *Three Lullabies*, composed seven years earlier.

## Quasi una fantasia

When trying to place Górecki in the context of the wider history of Western music, commentators rarely call to mind the music of his contemporaries, except to draw usually spurious parallels with American minimalism or to make more meaningful comparisons with the output of composers such as Arvo Pärt (b. 1935, Estonia), Giya Kancheli (b. 1935, Georgia), and John Taverner (b. 1944, England). Even these comparisons, however, need to be treated carefully, mindful of the compositional chronology and the composers' separate cultural environments. Górecki himself has a quite different list of kindred souls, including Messiaen and Ives. And from before our own century, Polish indigenous and art traditions aside, Górecki is drawn directly to the major figures in eighteenth- and nineteenth-century Europe, particularly Bach, Haydn, and Mozart. He feels a special affinity with Schubert, particularly in matters of tonal design and treatment of basic materials (these also suggest connections with Bruckner and Sibelius). Such parallels are most appropriate in those works where Górecki composes extended swathes of harmonically stable ideas. During the second half of the 1980s, he showed signs of becoming acutely aware of more intricate structural subtleties, still bound up in his habitual use of contrasting blocks (in truth, he was returning to the more complex evolving structures of the serial period). The composer who above all has been influential in this development, both technically and expressively, has been Beethoven. Along with Schubert, he lies behind *Lerchenmusik*, not only in respect of the quotation from his Fourth Piano Concerto, but also, as in subsequent chamber compositions, in the control of the large and medium structures, and in the strong textural and dynamic contrasts: 'It is thanks to Beethoven that I was able to write these quartets.'[15]

Górecki's second quartet, *Quasi una fantasia*, Op. 64 (1991), goes so far as to borrow its title from Beethoven. Its ground-plan—already used in the Concerto for Five Instruments and String Quartet, Op. 11—bears some resemblance to that of Beethoven's Piano Sonata in E flat, Op. 27 No. 1, although that seems to be the extent of the connection. There are four discrete movements: a lament, a fast folk-related dance, an Arioso, and a second dance. It was to be his most extended chamber composition since *Lerchenmusik*.[16] Several features peculiar to individual movements are worth noting. The opening lament, with its reiterated pedal E and weeping semitones above, is strongly reminiscent of the finale of *Good Night*, and several other intervallic features recall earlier works, from *Muzyczka 3* to *Lerchenmusik*. The second movement follows the pattern of multiple-bar repeats and the gradual motivic development heard in the first quartet's fast section, although the texture here is more starkly brutal, with its stamping ostinato on the minor third E–G and its arch-shaped sequence of different folk-related thematic ideas.

The Arioso is the most strident example of a type of melodic development noticed in the concluding ensemble of the central movement of *Lerchenmusik*. On the surface, it seems a rather harsh combination of almost functional diatonic chords on viola and cello with obsessively tight motivic turns on the violins, which play in rhythmic unison but create a variety of strong dissonances between themselves and the accompanying chords (cf. the second movement of *Muzyczka 4*). It is surprising to learn that some of the material has been distantly derived from the genteel world of Chopin's posthumous D minor

---

[15] Conversation with the author, Mar. 1994. It emerges, for example, that he thinks often of Beethoven's last piano sonata, Op. 111, of the use of the minor subdominant in the coda of the first movement and the ethereal trills of the finale's coda.

[16] Although Górecki's timing for the second quartet is 38'30", neither the Kronos Quartet (31'47") nor the Silesian Quartet (31'13") comes near, although both ensembles give vigorous and committed readings. The principal discrepancy lies in the duration of the finale (Górecki: 12'30"; Kronos: 9'31"; Silesian: 9'35"). In this instance, the composer's timings (although not his tempos) are on the generous side. But since much of the character of Górecki's music is contained in unusually slow speeds (however difficult the practical demands), performers disregard his tempos at their peril.

Polonaise.[17] Such manipulations are a long way from the clearly iconographic citations in the modal works of the 1960s and 1970s, although
*Lerchenmusik* and the first quartet had already demonstrated Górecki's
newly developmental approach. But there is a softer side to the stri-
dency: the quasi-cadenza for violins alone (still in parallel minor
ninths) is in lyrical contrast to the rest of the movement and in
registral relief to the rest of the quartet.

Górecki views the finale as somewhat separate from the rest of the
quartet, believing it to be almost self-standing. It unfolds independently 'quasi una fantasia' as a series of fast-moving and exhilarating
dance patterns. These are orchestrated in pairs just as in *Already it is
Dusk*, and share much of their exuberance with the second movement
of the Harpsichord Concerto (and Górecki recognizes the coincidental
kinship of the fourth dance pattern, with its C♯–E ostinato and motivic
syncopations, with the music of Bernstein, recalling that seeing the
film of *West Side Story* was one of the highlights of the Góreckis' 1963
visit to Paris). Like the second movement, the finale develops as a
loose arch structure with coda. In recapitulating the opening of the
quartet at the very end of the finale, Górecki is following the pattern
set by its predecessor and, to a more marginal extent, by *Lerchenmusik*.
But the coda's incorporation of the notes of the first half of the carol
'Silent Night' seems far less inevitable. There are works, like
*Lerchenmusik*, where a concluding quotation has been motivically integrated. The position of 'Silent Night' may seem more akin to the
imported use of 'Laude digna prole' in the Second Symphony, al-

Ex. VII.6. *Quasi una fantasia*, outline of pitch structure

(*a*)

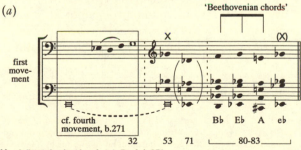

X: cf. figuration in *Already it is Dusk*, b.271

---

[17] Conversation with the author, Oct. 1993.

Ex. VII.6. *continued*

(*b*)

second move-ment

related to X

cf. fourth movement, b.160

7    41    45    64    72    ⌞84-85⌟

'Beethovenian chords'

related to X    X

86    100    129  149

(*c*)

third move-ment

(X)    'Beethovenian

3    4    7    27    48    51-53

chords'

54    62    66

138

though in fact it lies somewhere between the two types of quotation, as indicated by the way Górecki de-rhythmicizes the carol and by its deceptively casual integration (a distant echo of *Old Polish Music*). Its subtler recollections revolve around its A major tonality and specific intervals, especially the whole tone, although among its more obvious intervallic echoes are the first theme of the Arioso and, more incidentally, the Skierkowski 'turn'.[18] It points up the reality that quotation as such is of much less interest in this quartet than the subtler links provided by intervallic, tonal, and chordal cross-references (Ex. VII.6). And these are the elements that give the quartet's title its real resonance.

There are several aspects of *Quasi una fantasia*, including what Górecki calls his 'Beethovenian chords', which play a significant role as cyclic agents articulating a more complex structure than the four separate movements might otherwise imply. Thematically, the two most self-evident are (*i*) figure 'x', a 'tranquillo, mesto' back-reference to *Already it is Dusk* (cf. bars 271 ff., marked 'martellato-tempestuoso' in the earlier quartet) which introduces the codettas of both the first and the second movements (cf. the related codas of the first two movements in *Good Night*), and (*ii*) the 'Beethovenian chords' (also reminiscent of Shostakovich), an arresting but tantalizingly incomplete cadential sequence which comes in three places: at the end of the first movement, in the middle of the second (first two chords only), and during the concluding phases of the Arioso.[19] But the criss-crossing of less obvious elements gives the quartet an extraordinarily rich tapestry of allusions. This is especially noticeable in the first three movements, reinforcing Górecki's own view that the finale is something of a 'stand-alone' movement.

At the background level, the tonal structure is strongly rooted on E♮. The throbbing cello E♮s dominate the first movement, descending to E♭ during the codetta before the first appearance of the 'Beethovenian chords' (even so, as soon as the cello pitch moves downwards, E♮ appears a minor ninth higher in the viola). The second movement is likewise dominated by the bass E, now combined at a minor third with G. Its character is more forceful and parries a

[18] The quartet was begun, symbolically, on Górecki's birthday (St Nicholas' Day), and in the lead-up to Christmas the carol impinged on Górecki's musical consciousness. Górecki concluded *Quasi una fantasia*, again symbolically, on another of his name-days, St Joseph's Day (19 Mar.).

[19] It may only be coincidence, but the opening chordal flourish of Chopin's posthumous D minor Polonaise (see the discussion on the Arioso movement above) outlines the first and last of these three chords in the identical transpositions.

number of different motivic and tonal ideas in the upper voices. It loses its rhythmic pre-eminence only in the codetta, where the 'mesto' idea from the first movement resurfaces. But on this occasion, Górecki keeps the E♮ bass and creates a quasi-cadential progression into the F major chord of the Arioso. For the duration of the third movement, the harmonic attention shifts to F and subsequently to B flat minor, although E as the bass of the first inversion of C crops up at significant junctures (the lead-in to the quasi-cadenza, the beginning of the 'dolcissimo-morbido' coda, etc.). The finale largely ignores the bass E until the very end, when it recurs as part and parcel of the reference to the quartet's opening.

This recapitulatory moment also encapsulates the middle ground function of specific triads, because superimposed above the cello's E is a B flat major triad. This is the first of the 'Beethovenian chords' and assumes an increasingly important role apart from its original context: it initiates the third major idea in the second movement (b. 64), in its *minore* guise dominates the first half of the Arioso, and provides the swirling arpeggios accompanying the Lydian folk-melody in thirds and sixths in the finale (see Ex. VII.7). It also is the stable chord in the finale's 'con bravura' immediately prior to the quotation of 'Silent Night', which itself rests bitonally on the second inversion of B flat. It would be tempting to see a long ancestry of tritonal opposites in Górecki's music for the mutual interlocking of E and B♭ in this quartet, but this would not fully represent the intricacies of his pitch design.

The other two 'Beethovenian chords' have their own cross-references, although not of the same order as the B flat chord. The second chord, E flat, in its minor mode, is the substance of the recollection from *Already it is Dusk* in the first and second movements, and its lower two notes—E♭–G♭ (or D♯–F♯)—recur in the principal motif of the second movement again above E, with the B♭ (as A♯) capping the motif at its fullest extent. It also recurs more subliminally in the closing pages of the Arioso and bears a kinship with the finale's fourth dance sequence above the rocking minor third, C♯–E. The 'sharp' side of the quartet is represented by the third 'Beethovenian chord', A major. At one point, it is unashamedly presented as a second-inversion dominant seventh (end of second movement, leading into the Arioso), but the E–G reiterations of this movement have already intimated their relationship with the A major triad. In the finale, although not quoted directly, the unfulfilled cadential aspirations of these three chords are realized *en passant* in the D major violin

Ex. VII.7. *Quasi una fantasia*, fourth movement, b. 60

accompaniment of the second idea (b. 40) and in the descending chordal sequence that arises out of rapid quaver contrary motion (b. 145). By this stage, Górecki has worked up a motivic and tonal head of steam, which is released in a passage mixing dramatic gestures and an impassioned superimposition of striding triads and a densely packed version of the finale's fourth theme, which in this form also echoes motivic elements from both the second and third movements. This is the true 'fantasia', symptomatic of an uncommon delight in the quartet's myriad expressive levels and signalling a return to the methods of compositional variation and contrast which mark in particular the music of Górecki's student days. *Quasi una fantasia* is an exceptionally integrated and individual contribution to the modern string quartet.[20]

---

[20] At the time of writing, Górecki is completing work on his third string quartet for Kronos. Its planned scale is on a par with *Quasi una fantasia*.

Górecki's return to the timbre of the flute in the late 1980s reached its fullest expression in *Concerto-Cantata* (1992), his first work for large orchestra since *Canticum graduum*, composed twenty-three years earlier. Although Górecki has talked of two possible additional movements (an Intermezzo and Finale), the work's present structure of Recitativo–Arioso–Concertino–Arioso e Corale reveals a clear-cut, self-contained palindromic design (echoes here of earlier works both in titles and structure).[21] In some ways, its closest companion is *Already it is Dusk*. Both have a strongly pastoral atmosphere, created through an almost pictorial approach. If the first quartet had Brueghelian overtones, *Concerto-Cantata* is a more delicate landscape, with the flautist as the principal human figure. The Recitativo boldly highlights the solo alto flute for some five minutes, as if this were a chamber piece (Górecki had previously highlighted the solo flute at the beginning of the Concerto, Op. 11). The quality of introspection is eventually interrupted twice by the orchestra, but the alto flute pays no attention. Its groups of three repeated G♯s extend into the Arioso, where the alto flute is set aside for the 'flauto grande'. The Arioso begins with a direct citation of the opening bars of Szymanowski's mountaineers' ballet *Harnasie* (Highland Robbers, 1931). Górecki proceeds to emphasize its perfect-fifth bass drone, creating chromatic superimpositions, firstly on strings and later on horns. The effect is almost one of the flute's pastoral idyll being coloured by distant thunder.

Such potential disruption is nothing compared with the central Concertino. What starts off as a perky dance for flute, set off by punctuation on horns and pizzicato strings, becomes a whirling carousel the like of which has been hinted at in the rougher-edged string quartets, but here the instrumentation gives it an outrageously popular aspect. At first, the dance is rather dainty, but the C♯–E bass ostinato from the finale of *Quasi una fantasia* stomps in, hobnail boots flying, with a circus-like chromatic riff for unison soloist and quadruple oboes and clarinets. And fun though it may be to see parallels with other composers' use of dance or circus music (Shostakovich, for instance, not to mention more recent examples), this passage is in a direct line with the fast sections from the quartets, but also has an ancestor in the first movement of the Piano Sonata. There are additional elements of the grotesque, highlighted in this orchestral context, which may be traced back to the finale of the Sonata for Two

---

[21] Conversation with the author, Sept. 1992, in 'A Place at the Top', *Classic CD*, 32 (1992), 20–22.

Violins. And yet, tucked in quietly at the epicentre of this public cavorting, is a private, even amorous interchange between solo flute and orchestral clarinet. From this moment of close focus, Górecki retraces his steps like an observer retreating discretely from a picturesque scene of bucolic music-making. *Harnasie* makes a brief reappearance, this time fortissimo, at the very end of the Concertino, but otherwise the condensed palindrome (a direct descendant of the mirror structure in the first movement of *Lerchenmusik*) unravels straightforwardly in the Arioso e Corale. In expressive terms, *Concerto-Cantata* is Górecki's second, if occasionally more sombre 'frolic' after the Harpsichord Concerto, with which it shares a slightly unconventional attitude towards the relationship of soloist and orchestra. For Górecki, the soloist is never overtly virtuosic. In the Harpsichord Concerto, he concentrates on two types of idiomatic keyboard writing (runs and chords), while in *Concerto-Cantata* he stresses the singing quality of the flute and alto flute. But whereas in most of his works of the past thirty years it is the quiet, sustained music which captures the listener's attention, it is hard to deny the impact here of the central 'knees-up' and its distorting effect on the pastoral sections which embrace it.

### Little Requiem for a Polka

Górecki has visited a number of European and American countries in the past few years and has developed particularly close ties with those where his music has been not only performed but also commissioned. Holland is the latest country to take him up in this respect: not only was *Concerto-Cantata* premièred in Amsterdam in November 1992, but his most recent orchestral piece was commissioned by the Holland Festival and the Schönberg Ensemble. Originally titled *Nocna serenada* (Night Serenade), this work for piano and thirteen instruments was premièred in Amsterdam in June 1993 as *Kleines Requiem für eine Polka*.[22] In its combination of the serious and the seemingly light-hearted, *Kleines Requiem* follows the lead set by the quartets and *Concerto-Cantata*. Nevertheless, its central two fast movements mask

---

[22] The conductor was Reinbert de Leeuw, who features with his ensemble and Górecki in a VPRO documentary—*Toonmeesters: Henryk Górecki* (Holland, 1994, 60')—filmed in Katowice and Amsterdam in May and June 1993. Górecki has kept largely private the reasons for this curious title, although he has said that it reflects his sadness at the breakup of Czechoslovakia, where the polka is indigenous. There is also, as Polish speakers recognize, another meaning to the word 'Polka' (i.e. Polish woman), alongside a certain tension in the title's juxtaposition of German and Polish.

an inner melancholy: they may seem to derive their music and spirit from the world of the grotesque and the circus, but Górecki is the first to acknowledge that the clown is, underneath the greasepaint, ineffably sad. There is a more effective balance between the introvert and the extrovert in *Kleines Requiem* than in *Concerto-Cantata*, not least because Górecki has designed a subtler, less predictable structure (as in the two string quartets) and has achieved a happier expressive relationship between the four movements. But, going a step further than in *Quasi una fantasia*, the division into movements is increasingly notional.

The opening movement of *Kleines Requiem* is an amalgam of ternary and rondeau forms. The initial combination of tubular bells and solo piano reverts to the idea of repeated phrases, abandoning one of Górecki's favourite devices, the gradually evolving melody. The piano's motivic fragment is unostentatious, but simultaneously evokes Polish folk traditions (see Ex. V.6) with its 'turn' repetitions and Lydian modality (deliberate) and the incipit of 'Dies irae' (coincidental). The several succeeding melodic and accompanimental ideas continue the air of reflective tranquillity, with an instrumental emphasis on the two violins and piano. The parallel melodic movement in bitter-sweet sevenths and a fortissimo statement of the violins' theme seem to express both sorrow and anger, emotions first expressed in Górecki's published music in the *Three Songs*, Op. 3. The aggression so characteristic of his early music explodes in the second movement after a pair of short rising phrases on sustained strings, a deceptively quiet up-beat to the Allegro impetuoso. Employing what has become customary in his fast music since *Lerchenmusik*, Górecki exploits short phrases in irregular combinations and repetitions of duple and triple metres. In this instance, the piano's alternations between different triads (beginning with A minor and first-inversion G major) match the melodic emphases of the twisting 'choral' unison of wind and strings, dominated by the timbres of the brass (cf. the similar procedure observed in *Lerchenmusik*). This second movement is through-composed in the sense that the subsequent two sections and coda have disparate material. Furthermore, far from maintaining the gruff determination of the opening, they proceed to wind down. The second section returns to the piano's bass A minor chord, enhancing it with one of Górecki's quasi-arpeggic ideas (perfect fourth and tritone), heard previously in the *Concerto-Cantata*'s Recitativo. Its G and C♯ introduce a major–minor slant to the harmony, recalling the E major–minor chords in the third movement of *Songs of Joy and Rhythm*. The earlier work's textural and rhythmic boisterousness, hinting at Varèse, is also recalled at this moment, not least when the trumpet and clarinet produce a fanfare in a quite different tonality. But the rhythmic and harmonic machine grinds to a halt, leaving the basic A major–minor seventh to underpin a reverie for clarinet solo.

Like the folk idea with which *Kleines Requiem* began, this solo is a touching short-phrased melody with traditional origins, although it is also related to the preceding fanfare. Up to this juncture, the movement has had three largely independent sections. It is completed by a short coda for sustained strings (with tubular bells), whose melodic and harmonic identity is much more clearly formed than that of its counterpart at the end of the first movement. In fact, it bears a distinct resemblance to the vespers melody of the finale of *Lerchenmusik* as well as referring to the descending chordal sequence at the end of *Quasi una fantasia*. What Górecki appears to be saying is that *Kleines Requiem* is a much more free-flowing organism in which expectations are not all to be fulfilled. And by this stage there is little that seems predictable.

The third movement is the most rounded and self-contained of the four, but its idiom is the most irreverent. Rather like its equivalent in the second quartet, it is a sequence of melodic ideas with dancing accompaniment. The piano—which is specifically mentioned in the work's title and therefore must be assumed to have some primary role—thumps out, with little respect for decent conventionality, an 'oompah-oompah' accompaniment on A major (Ex. VII.8). After the first short section, this is supplanted by dominant sevenths on E♭ (another of Górecki's tritonal polarities). This is carefree recreation of popular music-making, be it from the village hall or the circus. But the emphatic rhythms—is this the polka of the title?—are weighed down by the static harmonies and, invigorating though it is, the passage is not a resolution of the tensions created in earlier movements. This comes in the finale, which doubles as a coda. The strings repeat their chordal progression from the coda of the second movement, and the movement gradually fades away, with a brief obbligato on the horn, and piano and bells tolling in the distance with the faintest of echoes from the very beginning of the work.

*Kleines Requiem* is something of a puzzle, its earthy atavism a confirmation of both Górecki's rural and urban background. Although its origins can be traced not only to its immediate predecessors (and it is a logical progression), they also leapfrog backwards in time to Górecki's first compositions. The future direction is unclear, because

Ex. VII.8. *Kleines Requiem für eine Polka*, third movement, beginning

the music asks serious questions about content, style, and structure. Górecki has been in this situation before, and each time he has come to an individual and fruitful solution of the compositional challenges he sets for himself. Certain things, however, are unlikely to change: they have been with him since before his studies in Katowice. On the detailed level, there are the recurrent features of cradled chords and figurations, dynamic extremes, slowly unfurling melodic lines, and harmonic stability, and the various ways in which he combines and contrasts the vertical and horizontal elements of his compositional technique. There is also the ingrained intervallic consistency drawn from his love of and total identification with chant and folksong, and Poles will hear many more subtle allusions than the 'motto' and 'turn' which are apparent to listeners from other traditions. And although much is made, rightly, of Górecki's attachment to his motherland and its native culture, that would count as nothing had he no vision and character of his own. That he has both in abundance is clear in both his music and his personality. He is a truly striking, thoughtful, and passionate individual who throughout his eventful life has single-mindedly pursued his own musical goals, remaining true to himself and his musical ethos, constantly searching for that state of body and soul so eloquently penned by Tuwim in 'Song of Joy and Rhythm':

> Slowly—inside—I am restored to myself:
> To intense joy and profound rhythm.
> . . . Enough. No need for words.

# LIST OF WORKS

Works are listed by year, in order of composition (any later changes or revisions are included in a work's main entry). There then follow details of the instrumentation, separate components of each piece (movements, songs), texts,[1] and duration. Details of commissions, precise dates and place of composition (where available), dedications, and awards form a second group.

Instrumentation is indicated when an ensemble has an unusual line-up. Where a work is based on a standard formation, the instrumentation is given in families (separated by hyphens) in abbreviated, numerical form: woodwind (fl.ob.cl.bn)—brass (hn.tpt.tbn.tba)—timpani and percussion—strings (vn1.vn2.va.vc.db).

Górecki's publishers are B&H (Boosey & Hawkes, London), Chester Music (part of Music Sales, London), and PWM (Polskie Wydawnictwo Muzyczne—Polish Music Publishers, Kraków). Currently, PWM holds the rights for indicated works in most countries of the former socialist copyright federation, while B&H and Chester Music each hold the rights, as indicated, for the rest of the world.

Première and recording details form the final group of entries for each piece (the abbreviations CO, PO, and SO stand for Chamber, Philharmonic, and Symphony Orchestra respectively). PN Muza recordings from Polskie Nagrania, Warsaw, and Veriton recordings are on LP. Those PN Muza LPs with a 'W' prefix are live recordings from Warsaw Autumn festivals.

## *Juvenilia (1954–5)*

including:

*Legenda* (Legend) for orchestra

*Five Mazurkas* for piano

*Preludium* for violin and piano

*Ten Preludes* for piano

---

[1] When employing Psalm texts, Górecki cites alternative psalm numbers (e.g. 142 or 143 at the start of *Beatus vir*); the higher number in each case is the one in more common usage. Verse numbers may likewise vary from edition to edition.

*Two Songs* for voice and piano, to texts by Maria Konopnicka
  'Przez te łąki, przez te pola' (Through these meadows, across these fields)
  'Kiedy Polska' (When Poland)
  See also under 'U okienka, u mojego' (1995)

*Terzetto quasi una fantasia* for oboe, violin, and piano

*Romans* (Romance) for piano

String Quartet

*Obrazki poetyckie* (Poetic Pictures) for piano

Piano Concerto

## Works since 1955

*Cztery preludia* (Four Preludes), Op. 1, for piano (1955)
  1. Molto agitato; 2. Lento-recitativo; 3. Allegro scherzando; 4. Molto allegro
  quasi presto
Duration: *c*.8′
Dates of composition: October–December 1955, Rydułtowy
Publishers: PWM, B&H
Première: 30 January 1970, Katowice: Kazimierz Morski
Recording: Koch International 3-7301-2, David Arden

**Toccata, Op. 2, for two pianos (1955)**
Duration: *c*.3′
Date of composition: December 1955, Rydułtowy
Publishers: PWM, B&H
Première: 27 February 1958, Katowice: Bernard Biegoń and Magdalena
  Kubzda
Recording: Veriton SXV 817 = Olympia OCD 394, Maria Nosowska and
  Barbara Halska

*Trzy pieśni* (Three Songs), Op. 3 for medium voice and piano (1956)
  1. 'Do matki' (To Mother)
Text: Juliusz Słowacki (1809–49)
  2. 'Jakiż to dzwon grobowy' (What was this funereal bell)
Text: Juliusz Słowacki, from 'Oda do wolności' (Ode to Freedom), pt. VII, v.1
  3. 'Ptak' (The Bird)
Text: Julian Tuwim (1894–1953), 26 July 1918, from *Sokrates tańczący*
  (Dancing Socrates, 1920)
Date of composition: January 1956, Rydułtowy
Duration: *c*.4′
Dedication: 'In memory of my dear mother'
Publishers: PWM, Chester

Première: 1960, Cologne: Krystyna Szostek-Radkowa (mezzo-soprano) and Magdalena Kubzda (piano)
Recording: (1. 'Do matki') Veriton SXV 897–98, A. Świątek-Matusik (soprano) and K. Waldek-Czopik (piano)

**'Nokturn' (Nocturne) for voice and piano (1956)**
Text: Federico García Lorca (1895–1936), trans. Mikołaj Bieszczadowski
Data of composition: January 1956, Rydułtowy; revised 14 June 1980, Katowice, as one of *Dwie pieśni* (Two Songs), Op. 42
Unpublished

**Variations, Op. 4, for violin and piano (1956)**
Duration: *c*.10′
Date of composition: March 1956, Rydułtowy
Publishers: PWM, B&H
Première: 27 February 1958, Katowice: Edward Cygan (violin) and Magdalena Kubzda (piano)

**Quartettino, Op. 5, for two flutes, oboe, and violin (1956)**
1. Molto allegro; 2. Lento e molto espressivo; 3. Presto
Duration: *c*.8′
Date of composition: March 1956, Rydułtowy
Publishers: PWM, B&H
Première: 27 February 1958, Katowice: members of the Silesian PO

**Piano Sonata, Op. 6 (1956)**
1. Allegro molto, con fuoco; 2. Grave pesante e corale; 3. Allegro vivace (ma non troppo)
Duration: *c*.12′
Date of composition: August 1956, Rydułtowy; revised May 1984, Chochołów, and November 1990, Katowice
Dedication: 'To J.R. [Jadwiga Rurańska]'
Publisher: B&H
Premières: (first movement only) 28 July 1984, Lerchenborg Festival: Eugeniusz Knapik; (complete) 17 March 1991, Helsinki Biennale: Paul Crossley
Recording: Koch International 3-7301-2, David Arden

**Pieśni o radości i rytmie (Songs of Joy and Rhythm), Op. 7, for two pianos and chamber orchestra (1956, 1960)**
1956 version (withdrawn):
Instrumentation: picc.1.1.1.1.–0.1.0.0 – timp.perc (3)-cel – 2pf – 8vns a4
1. Preludium and Toccata; 2. 'Recitativo–etiuda'; 3. 'Przygrywka lyriczna' (Lyric Prelude); 4. 'Mały koncert fortepianowy' (Little Piano Concerto)
Date of composition: August 1956, Rydułtowy

Duration: c.11'30"
Unpublished
Première: 27 February 1958, Katowice: Bernard Biegoń and Karol Procner,
Silesian PO, Karol Stryja (conductor)

1960 version:
Instrumentation: picc.1.0.1.1 - 0.1.1.0 - timp.perc (3) - cel - 2pf - str
(6.6.6.6.0)
1. Marcato; 2. Con moto; 3. Non troppo; 4. Ritmico
Duration: c.14'
Dates of composition: December 1959–15 January 1960, Rydułtowy
Publisher: B&H
Première: 8 July 1990, Almeida Festival, London: Andrew Ball and Julian
Jacobson, Opus 20, Scott Stroman (conductor)

### Recitativo i mazurek (Recitative and Mazurka) for piano (1956)
Date of composition: August 1956, Rydułtowy
Unpublished (currently grouped with other piano pieces under Op. 52)

### Sonatina in One Movement, Op. 8, for violin and piano (1956)
Duration: c.2'30"
Date of composition: November 1956, Rydułtowy
Publishers: PWM, B&H
Première: not known (after 1980)

### Kołysanka (Lullaby), Op. 9, for piano (1956, 1980)
Duration: c.4'
Date of composition: 26 November 1956, Rydułtowy; revised 14 June 1980,
Katowice
Dedication: 'To Jadwiga'
Unpublished

### Z ptasiego gniazda (From the Bird's Nest), Op. 9a, for piano (1956)
1. Marsz (March); 2. Piosenka ludowa (Folksong); 3. Stara melodia (Old
Melody); 4. Scherzo; 5. Druga piosenka ludowa (Second Folksong); 6.
Interludium; 7. Bagatelle; 8. Drugi marsz (Second March); 9. Finale a la
danse
Date of composition: November 1956, Rydułtowy
Unpublished

### Sonata, for Two Violins, Op. 10 (1957)
1. Allegro molto; 2. Adagio sostenuto; 3. Andante con moto–Con anima a la
danse
Duration: c.16'30"
Dates of composition: February–March 1957, Katowice
Dedication: 'To Jadwiga Rurańska'
Publishers: PWM, Chester

Première: 27 February 1958, Katowice: Edward Cygan and Henryk Gruszka
Recording: Olympia OCD 375, Marek Moś and Arkadiusz Kubica

*Dwa utwory* (Two Pieces) for piano (1957)
Date of composition: March 1957, Katowice
Unpublished (currently grouped with other piano pieces under Op. 52)

*Kopciuszek* (Cinderella), incidental music for the theatre (1957)
Text: Adolf Walewski
Dates of composition: March–April 1957, Katowice
Première: 25 May 1957, Teatr Śląski, Katowice: Mieczysław Daszewski (director)

**Concerto for Five Instruments and String Quartet, Op. 11 (1957)**
Instrumentation: fl.cl - Ctpt - xyl - mand - str (1.1.1.1.0)
1. Sostenuto; 2. Dolce; 3. Non troppo; 4. Marcato, ritmico
Duration: *c*.10′30″
Dates of composition: 19 August – 21 September 1957, Katowice
Dedication: 'To Leon Markiewicz'
Publishers: PWM, B&H
Première: 27 February 1958, Katowice: members of the Silesian PO, Karol Stryja (conductor)

*Trzy miniatury dodekafoniczne* (Three Dodecaphonic Miniatures) for piano (1957)
Dates of composition: October–November 1957, Katowice
Unpublished (currently grouped with other piano pieces under Op. 52)

*Epitafium*, Op. 12, for mixed choir and instrumental ensemble (1958)
Instrumentation: picc - Dtpt - perc (5) - va
Preludium–'Chorał' (Chorale)–'Antyfona' (Antiphon)–Postludium
Text: Julian Tuwim's last poetic fragment
Duration: *c*.5′
Commission: Andrzej Markowski
Dates of composition: 7–13 July 1958, Katowice
Dedication: 'In memory of Julian Tuwim'
Publishers: PWM, B&H
Première: 3 October 1958, 2nd Warsaw Autumn Festival, National Philharmonic Chorus, members of the Silesian PO, Andrzej Markowski (conductor)
Recording: PN Muza XL 0391 = Olympia OCD 385, National Philharmonic Choir, members of the Polish Radio SO, Katowice, Jan Krenz (conductor)

*Pięć utworów* (Five Pieces), Op. 13, for two pianos (1959)
Duration: *c*.7′30″
Dates of composition: January–November 1959, Rydułtowy and Katowice

Publishers: PWM, B&H
Première: not known

**Symphony No. 1, '1959', Op. 14, for string orchestra and percussion (1959)**
Instrumentation: timp.perc (7) – hpd – hp – str (16.16.14.12.10)
1. 'Inwokacja' (Invocation); 2. 'Antyfona' (Antiphon); 3. 'Chorał' (Chorale); 4. 'Lauda'
Duration: *c*.20′
Dates of composition: 5 January – 21 March 1959, Rydułtowy
Dedication: 'To Professor Bolesław Szabelski'
Publishers: PWM, B&H
Premières: (1st, 3rd, and 4th movements only) 14 September 1959, 3rd Warsaw Autumn Festival: Polish Radio SO, Katowice, Jan Krenz (conductor); (complete) 15 July 1963, Darmstadt: West German Radio SO, Michael Gielen (conductor)
Award: 1st Prize, UNESCO Youth Biennale, Paris, 30 September 1961
Recording: Koch Schwann 3-1041-2, Kraków PO, Roland Bader (conductor)

*Wieża samotności* (**Tower of Solitude; original play title** *Thunder Rock*), **incidental music for the theatre (1959)**
Duration: 11′
Text: Robert Ardrey (1939)
Première: 10 October 1959, Teatr Śląski, Katowice: Jerzy Jarocki (director)

*Trzy diagramy* (**Three Diagrams), Op. 15, for solo flute (1959)**
Duration: *c*.6′
Date of composition: November 1959, Katowice
Publishers: PWM, Chester
Première: 21 September 1961, 5th Warsaw Autumn Festival: Severino Gazzelloni
Recordings: PN W-774, Severino Gazzelloni; PN Muza SXL 0613, Barbara Świątek

*Akwarium* (**Aquarium), incidental music for the theatre (1959)**
Duration: 16′
Text: Andrzej Wydrzyński
Unperformed (the production planned at Teatr Śląski, Katowice, was cancelled)

**'Papierowa laleczka' (Paper Doll), song for** *Widok z mostu* (**A View from the Bridge) (1960)**
Text: Arthur Miller (1955)
Première: 18 March 1960, Teatr Śląski, Katowice: Jerzy Jarocki (director)

*Monologhi* (**Monologues), Op. 16, for soprano and three groups of instruments (1960)**

Instrumentation: 2hp – perc (3)
Text: Henryk Mikołaj Górecki, 'Monolog II', 7 April 1960
Duration: *c*.17′
Dates of composition: 14–29 April 1960, Rydułtowy
Dedication: 'To my wife'
Award: 1st Prize, Polish Composers' Union Young Composers' Competition, 15 May 1960
Publishers: PWM, B&H
Première: 26 April 1968, West Berlin: Joan Carroll, Ensemble für neue Musik Freiburg, Arghyris Kounadis (conductor)
Recording: Wergo 60058, Joan Carroll, Ensemble für neue Musik Freiburg, Arghyris Kounadis (conductor)

*Scontri* **(Zderzenia, or Collisions), Op. 17, for orchestra (1960)**
Instrumentation: 2.2picc.0.2.E♭cl.bcl.2.2dbn - 4.4.3.1 - perc (8) - 2pf - 2hp - str (30.0.12.12.8)
Duration: *c*.17′
Commission: Jan Krenz
Dates of composition: 13 May – 17 June 1960, Rydułtowy
Dedication: 'To Jan Krenz'
Publishers: PWM, B&H
Première: 21 September 1960, 4th Warsaw Autumn Festival: Polish Radio SO, Katowice, Jan Krenz (conductor)
Recordings: PN W-680, Polish Radio SO, Katowice, Jan Krenz (conductor); PN Muza XL 0391 = Olympia OCD 385, Polish Radio SO, Katowice, Jan Krenz (conductor)

*Chorał w formie kanonu* **(Chorale in the Form of a Canon) for string quartet (1961)**
Duration: *c*.3′
Commission: Tadeusz Ochlewski
Date of composition: 21 January 1961, Rydułtowy; revised 12 May 1984 (originally as Op. 52) for the 80th birthday of Goffredo Petrassi (b. 16 July 1904)
Première: 7 February 1961, Warsaw: ensemble Wywołanie

*Diagram IV*, **Op. 18, for solo flute (1961)**
Duration: *c*.7′30″–10′30″
Dates of composition: 7–12 April 1961, Rydułtowy
Unpublished
Première: not known

*Quasi walc* **(Quasi-Waltz) for piano (1961)**
Date of composition: 26 June 1961
Dedication: 'To Władysława Markiewiczówna'
Unpublished (currently grouped with other piano pieces under Op. 52)

***Genesis I: Elementi*** **(Elements), Op. 19 No. 1, for three string instruments (1962)**
Instrumentation: vn.va.vc
Duration: *c*.13′
Dates of composition: 6 February – 19 March 1962, Rydułtowy
Publishers: PWM, B&H
Première: 29 May 1962, Kraków: Henryk Gruszka (violin), Antoni Feliks (viola), and Edward Wiertelosz (cello), Henryk Mikołaj Górecki (conductor)
Recordings: PN Muza XW-570, Ensemble Instrumental Musiques Nouvelles, Bruxelles; Olympia OCD 375, Marek Moś (violin), Łukasz Syrnicki (viola), and Piotr Janosik (cello)

***Genesis II: Canti strumentali*** **(Instrumental Songs), Op. 19 No. 2, for fifteen players (1962)**
Instrumentation: picc.fl – tpt – mand – guit - pf (4 hands) – perc (2) - str (3.0.3.0.0)
Duration: *c*.8′
Dates of composition: March–April 1962, Rydułtowy
Publishers: PWM, B&H
Première: 16 September 1962, 6th Warsaw Autumn Festival. members of the Silesian PO, Karol Stryja (conductor)
Recordings: PN Muza W-825, members of the Silesian PO, Karol Stryja (conductor); PN Muza XL 0391 = Olympia OCD 385, members of the Polish Radio SO, Katowice, Jan Krenz (conductor); PN Muza SX 2314, members of the Silesian PO, Karol Stryja (conductor)

***Genesis III: Monodramma,*** **Op. 19 No. 3, for soprano, metal percussion, and six double basses (1963)**
Instrumentation: sop - perc (13) - 6db
Text: Henryk Mikołaj Górecki
Duration: *c*.10′
Date of composition: April 1963, Rydułtowy
Publishers: PWM, B&H
Première: not known

***Trzy utwory w dawnym stylu*** **(Three Pieces in Old Style) for string orchestra (1963)**
Duration: *c*.10′
Dates of composition: 28 November – 23 December 1963, Rydułtowy
Publishers: PWM, B&H
Première: 30 April 1964, Warsaw: ensemble Con Moto ma Cantabile
Recordings: PN Muza SXL 0586 = Olympia OCD 313, National Philharmonic CO, Karol Teutsch (conductor); PN Muza SX 1256 = PN CD 233 = Accord ACD 023, Polish CO, Jerzy Maksymiuk (conductor); EMI 5 65418 2, Polish CO, Jerzy Maksymiuk (conductor); Schwann CD 11615,

Warsaw CO, Karol Teutsch (conductor); Aperto APO 86 421, Polish CO, Jan Stanienda (conductor); Koch Schwann 3-1041-2, Kraków PO, Roland Bader (conductor); AMF ST-104 = Conifer CDCF 246, Amadeus CO, Agnieszka Duczmal (conductor); Telarc CD 80417, I Fiamminghi, Rudolph Werthen (conductor); Tring TRP 084, Royal PO, Yuri Simonov (conductor)

## *Choros I*, Op. 20, for strings (1964)
Instrumentation: str (24.0.12.12.8)
Duration: *c*.18′ (preliminary version: *c*.8′)
Dates of composition: (preliminary version, withdrawn) May 1963; (first version) January – 8 August 1964, Rydułtowy; revised October–December 1964, Rydułtowy
Publishers: PWM, B&H
Premières: (first version) 22 September 1964, 8th Warsaw Autumn Festival: Silesian PO, Karol Stryja (conductor); (revised version) not known
Recordings: (first version) PN Muza W-966, Silesian PO, Karol Stryja (conductor); (revised version) Koch Schwann 3-1041-2, Kraków PO, Roland Bader (conductor)

## *Refren* (Refrain), Op. 21, for orchestra (1965)
Instrumentation: 0.4.4.4-4.4.4.0 - timp (3).perc (1) - str (24.0.8.8.8)
Duration: *c*.17′
Commission: for the Centenary of the International Telecommunications Union
Dates of composition: May–June 1965, Rydułtowy
Award: 3rd Prize, UNESCO Rostrum, Paris, 1967
Publishers: PWM, B&H
Première: 27 October 1965, Geneva: Orchestre de la Suisse Romande, Piérre Colombo (conductor)
Recordings: PN Muza M-3 XW-717, Polish Radio SO, Katowice, Jan Krenz (conductor); PN Muza XL 0391 = Olympia OCD 385, Polish Radio SO, Katowice, Jan Krenz (conductor)

## *Muzyczka 1* (*La Musiquette 1*, or Little Music 1), Op. 22, for two trumpets and guitar (1967)
Duration: *c*.11′
Dates of composition: 24 April – 9 July 1967, Katowice
Dedication: 'To dear Bolesław Szabelski on his 70th birthday'
Withdrawn

## *Muzyczka 2* (*La Musiquette 2*, or Little Music 2), Op. 23, for four trumpets, four trombones, two pianos, and percussion (1967)
Instrumentation: 4tpt.4tbn - 2pf - perc (5)
Duration: *c*.7′30″
Dates of composition: 12–29 July 1967, Katowice

Dedication: 'To Andrzej Markowski'
Publishers: PWM, B&H
Première: 23 September 1967, 11th Warsaw Autumn Festival: members of French Radio PO, Andrzej Markowski (conductor)
Recording: PN Muza M-3 XW-896, members of French Radio PO, Andrzej Markowski (conductor)

*Muzyczka 3* (*La Musiquette*, **or Little Music 3), Op. 25, for violas (1967)**
Instrumentation: 3va (or multiples of 3)
Duration: *c*.14′
Dates of composition: 3–10 October 1967, Katowice
Dedication: 'To Anna and Zygmunt Lis'
Publishers: PWM, B&H
Première: 20 October 1967, Katowice: Jerzy Pyzik, Antoni Feliks, and Paweł Rajzewicz, Henryk Mikołaj Górecki (conductor)

*Cantata*, **Op. 26, for organ (1968)**
Duration: *c*.13′
Dates of composition: 6–27 May 1968, Katowice
Award: 1st Prize, Szczeciń Composers' Competition, 1968
Publishers: PWM, Chester
Première: 18 July 1969, Kamień Pomorski: Romuald Sroczyński
Recordings: Veriton SXV 882, Andrzej Chorosiński; Kontrapunkt 32223, Jens E. Christensen

*Wratislaviae gloria*, **fanfare for brass and strings (1968)**
Instrumentation: 4Ctpt.4hn.4tbn.tba – str
Duration: *c*.2′
Date of composition: 19 September 1968
Unpublished
Première: 12 February 1969, 7th Festival of Polish Contemporary Music, Wrocław: Wrocław PO, Andrzej Markowski (conductor)

*Muzyka staropolska* **(Old Polish Music), Op. 24, for brass and strings (1969)**
Instrumentation: 5hn.4tpt.4tbn – str (min. 8.8.8.8.8)
Duration: *c*.23′
Dates of composition: August 1967 and April–May 1969, Katowice
Dedication: 'To Mr Tadeusz Szarewski'
Publishers: PWM, B&H
Première: 24 September 1969, 12th Warsaw Autumn Festival: National Philharmonic SO, Andrzej Markowski (conductor)
Recordings: PN Muza M-3 XW-1184, National Philharmonic SO, Andrzej Markowski (conductor); PN Muza SXL 0547 = Olympia OCD 385, National Philharmonic SO, Andrzej Markowski (conductor); Argo 436 835–2, Czech PO, John Nelson (conductor)

*Jędrek* (Little Andy), music for black and white short feature film
  (1969)
Duration: 11'
Director: Jadwiga Kędzierzawska
Production Company: Se-MA-For (Studio Małych Form)

*Canticum graduum*, Op. 27, for orchestra (1969)
Instrumentation: 4.0.4.4sax.4 - 8.4.4.0 - str (24.0.8.8.8)
Duration: *c*.12'
Commission: West German Radio
Dates of composition: 11 October – 3 November 1969, Katowice
Dedication: 'To Otto Tomek'
Publishers: PWM, B&H
Première: 11 December 1969, Düsseldorf: West German Radio SO, Michael
  Gielen (conductor)
Recording: PN Muza XW-1894, Polish Radio SO, Kraków, Gianpiero
  Taverna (conductor)

*Muzyczka 4*, 'Koncert puzonowy' (*La Musiquette 4*, or Little Music 4,
  'Trombone Concerto'), Op. 28, for trombone, clarinet, cello, and
  piano (1970)
Duration: *c*.9'
Commission: Warsztat Muzyczny (Music Workshop)
Dates of composition: 11–19 March 1970, Katowice
Publishers: PWM, B&H
Première: 15 April 1970, Vienna: Music Workshop—Edward Borowiak
  (trombone), Czesław Pałkowski (clarinet), Witold Gałązka (cello), and
  Zygmunt Krauze (piano)

*Do matki* (*Ad matrem*), Op. 29, for soprano solo, mixed choir, and
  orchestra (1971)
Instrumentation: 4 (III+IV picc).4.4.4 (III+IV dbn) - 4.4.4.0 - timp (2).perc
  (2) - hp - pf - str
Text: Henryk Mikołaj Górecki, from the sequence *Stabat mater*
Duration: *c*.10–11'
Dates of composition: 1–5 June 1971, Katowice
Dedication: 'In memory of my mother'
Award: 1st Prize, UNESCO Rostrum, Paris, 1973
Publishers: PWM, B&H
Première: 24 September 1972, 16th Warsaw Autumn Festival: Stefania
  Woytowicz, National Philharmonic SO and Chorus, Andrzej Markowski
  (conductor)
Recording: PN Muza SX 1135 = PN CD 233, Stefania Woytowicz, National
  Philharmonic SO and Chorus, Andrzej Markowski (conductor)

*Dwie pieśni sakralne* (**Two Sacred Songs**), Op. 30b, for baritone solo
  and piano (1971)

1. Lento sostenuto; 2. Maestoso
Texts: Marek Skwarnicki (b. 1930), 'Offertorium' and 'Introit', published in
   *Tygodnik powszechny* (Universal Weekly), 1168 (13 June 1971)
Duration: *c*.5′
Dates of composition: 5–12 July 1971, Witów
Dedication: 'To my wife Jadwiga'
Publishers: PWM, Chester
Première: not known

**Dwie pieśni sakralne (Two Sacred Songs), Op. 30, for baritone solo
   and orchestra (1971): orchestration of Op. 30b (see above)**
Instrumentation: o.o.4 (IV bcl).4 (III + IV dbn) - 4.4.4.1 – str
Orchestration: July–September 1971, Witów
Publishers: PWM, B&H
Première: 6 April 1976, 16th Poznań Musical Spring Festival: Jerzy Artysz,
   Polish Radio SO, Kraków, Jacek Kasprzyk (conductor)

**Symphony No. 2, 'Kopernikowska' (Copernican), Op. 31, for soprano
   solo, baritone solo, mixed choir, and orchestra (1972)**
Instrumentation: 4 (III + IV picc).4.4 (IV bcl).4 (III + IV dbn) - 4.4.4.1 - timp
   (3).perc (3) - hp - pf (4 hands) - str (36.o.12.12.12)
Texts: Psalm 145/146 (v. 6), Psalm 135/136 (vv. 7–9), and Nicolaus
   Copernicus, *De revolutionibus orbium coelestium*, book i (excerpt)
Duration: *c*.37′
Commission: Kościuszko Foundation, New York
Dates of composition: April–December 1972, Katowice
Dedication: 'To the Kościuszko Foundation'
Publishers: PWM, B&H
Première: 22 June 1973, Warsaw: Stefania Woytowicz, Andrzej Hiolski,
   National Philharmonic SO, Andrzej Markowski (conductor)
Recording: Stradivarius STR 33324, Emese Soós, Tamás Altorjay, Bartók
   Chorus, Fricsay SO, Tamás Pál (conductor)

**Euntes ibant et flebant (They who Go Forth and Weep), Op. 32, for
   unaccompanied mixed choir (1972)**
Texts: Psalms 125/126 (v. 6) and 94/95 (v. 6)
Duration: *c*.9′
Dates of composition: 13 August 1972, Katowice, and December 1973, Berlin
Publishers: PWM, B&H
Première: 31 August 1975, 10th Wratislavia Cantans Festival, Wrocław:
   National Philharmonic Chorus, Andrzej Markowski (conductor)
Recordings: PN ECD 036, Catholic Theological Academy Choir, Warsaw,
   Kazimierz Szymonik (conductor); Proudsound PROU CD 136, Oxford
   Pro Musica Singers, Michael Smedley (conductor); Elektra Nonesuch
   79348–21, Chicago Symphony Chorus and Lyric Opera Chorus, John
   Nelson (conductor)

*Dwie piosenki* (Two Little Songs), Op. 33, for choir of four equal voices (1972)
1. 'Rok i bieda' (The year and hardship)
2. 'Ptasie plotki' (Bird gossip)
Texts: Julian Tuwim
Duration: *c*.4′30″
Dates of composition: (No. 1) 29 December 1972 and (No. 2) 31 December 1972, Katowice
Dedication: 'To dear Anusia'
Publishers: PWM, B&H
Première: not known

*Trzy tańce* (Three Dances), Op. 34, for orchestra (1973)
Instrumentation: 2 (II picc).2.2.2 - 3.4.3.1 - timp (2) - str
1. Presto, marcatissimo; 2. Andante cantabile; 3. Presto
Duration: *c*.12′
Commission: Rybnik Philharmonic Orchestra
Dates of composition: June–July 1973, Katowice and Chochołów
Dedication: 'To Antoni Szafranek and the Rybnik Philharmonic'
Publishers: PWM, B&H
Première: 24 November 1973, Rybnik: Rybnik Philharmonic SO, Antoni Szafranek (conductor)

*Amen*, Op. 35, for unaccompanied mixed choir (1975)
Duration: *c*.8′
Commission: Poznań Musical Spring Festival
Date of composition: 2 February 1975, Katowice
Dedication: 'To the 15th Poznań Musical Spring'
Publishers: PWM, B&H
Première: 5 April 1975, 15th Poznań Musical Spring Festival, Poznań Boys' Choir, Jerzy Kurczewski (conductor)
Recordings: Olympia OCD 313, Poznań Boys' Choir, Jerzy Kurczewski (conductor); Proudsound PROU CD 136, Oxford Pro Musica Singers, Michael Smedley (conductor); Elektra Nonesuch 79348–21, Chicago Symphony Chorus and Lyric Opera Chorus, John Nelson (conductor); EMI 5 55096 2, King's College Choir, Stephen Cleobury (conductor)

*Dwa hejnały* (Two Bugle-Calls), for woodwind and brass (1976)
Instrumentation: 8fl.8hn.11tpt.6tbn.2tba
Commission: World Ice Hockey Championships, Katowice
Duration: *c*.1′
Unpublished

**Symphony No. 3, 'Symfonia pieśni żałosnych' (Symphony of Sorrowful Songs), Op. 36, for soprano solo and orchestra (1976)**
Instrumentation: 4 (III+IV picc).0.4.2.2dbn - 4.0.4.0 - hp - pf - str (16.14.12.10.8)

1. LENTO, sostenuto tranquillo ma cantabile; 2. LENTO e LARGO, tranquillissimo-cantabilissimo-dolcissimo-LEGATISSIMO; 3. LENTO, cantabile-semplice

Texts: 1. anon., mid-15th century 'Lament świętokrzyski' (Holy Cross Lament), v. 4; 2. Helena Wanda Błażusiakówna, graffito, 25 September 1944, Zakopane; 3. anon. Opole folksong, *c*.1919–21

Duration: *c*.55'

Commission: South-West German Radio, Baden-Baden

Dates of composition: 30 October – 30 December 1976, Katowice

Dedication: 'To my wife'

Awards: 'Best-Selling CD in 1993', *Gramophone*; 'Recording of the Year' (1993), Classical Music Awards, London, 21 January 1994

Publishers: PWM, B&H

Première: 4 April 1977, Royan International Festival of Contemporary Art: Stefania Woytowicz, South-West German Radio SO, Ernest Bour (conductor)

Recordings: PN Muza SX 1648 = Olympia OCD 313, Stefania Woytowicz, Polish Radio SO, Katowice, Jerzy Katlewicz (conductor); Schwann VMS 1615 = Schwann CD 11615, Stefania Woytowicz, Berlin Radio SO, Włodzimierz Kamirski (conductor); Erato ERA 9275-Belart 437 964-2, Stefania Woytowicz, South-West German Radio SO, Ernest Bour (conductor)[2]; Elektra Nonesuch 9 79282-2, Dawn Upshaw, London Sinfonietta, David Zinman (conductor); Belart 450 148-2, Zofia Kilanowicz, Polish State PO, Katowice [= Silesian PO], Jerzy Swoboda (conductor); Sony SMK 64078, Theresa Erbe, Baden-Baden SO, Werner Stiefel (conductor); Naxos 8.550822, Zofia Kilanowicz, Polish Radio National SO, Antoni Wit (conductor); Philips 442 411-2, Joanna Kozłowska, Warsaw PO, Kazimierz Kord (conductor); EMI 5 55368 2, Zofia Kilanowicz, Kraków PO, Jacek Kasprzyk (conductor); Arte Nova BMG 74321-27779-2, Doreen de Feis, Gran Canaria PO, Adrian Leaper (conductor); Tring TRP 084, Susan Gritton, Royal PO, Yuri Simonov (conductor); Audiophile APC 101.040, Luisa Castellani, Slovenian SO, Anton Nanut (conductor)

*Trzy małe utworki* (Three Little Pieces), Op. 37, for violin and piano (1977)

1. Allegro ma non tanto; 2. Lento, cantabile e dolce; 3. Animato, marcato

Duration: *c*.3'

Date of composition: 27 December 1977, Katowice

Dedication: 'To darling Mikołaj'

---

[2] This performance first appeared on LP in connection with Maurice Pialat's film 'Police' (1985). In 1993 it was marketed in Germany on CD as the world première. The fact that both pressings include the same curious mis-edit in the second movement (before the soprano entry in b. 78) suggests a patched recording rather than a live performance.

Publishers: PWM, B&H
Première: 5 January 1978, Katowice: Mikołaj Górecki and Jadwiga Górecka

*Beatus vir*, Op. 38, for baritone solo, mixed choir, and large orchestra (1979)
Instrumentation: 4.4.4.4 (III+IV dbn) - 4.4.4.4 - perc (2)-2hp - pf (4 hands) - str
Texts: Psalms 142/143 (vv. 1, 6–8, 10), 30/31 (vv. 15–16), 37/38 (v. 23), 66/67 (v. 7), 33/34 (v. 9)
Duration: *c*.35′
Commission: Cardinal Karol Wojtyła, 1977
Dates of composition: 2 April – 19 May 1979, Katowice
Dedication: 'To the Holy Father, John Paul II'
Publishers: PWM, B&H
Première: 9 June 1979, Kraków: Jerzy Mechliński, Kraków PO and Chorus, Henryk Mikołaj Górecki (conductor)
Recordings: PN Muza SX 2072 = PN CD 233, Jerzy Artysz, Kraków PO and Chorus, Jerzy Katlewicz (conductor); Argo 436 835-2, Nikita Storojev, Prague Philharmonic Choir, Czech PO, John Nelson (conductor); Stradivarius STR 33324, Tamás Altorjay, Bartók Chorus, Fricsay PO, Tamás Pál (conductor)

*Szeroka woda* (Broad Waters), Op. 39, for unaccompanied mixed choir (1979)
1. 'A ta nasza Narew' (O our river Narew)
2. 'Oj, kiedy na Powiślu' (Oh, when in Powiśle)
3. 'Oj, Janie, Janie' (Oh, Johnny, Johnny)
4. 'Polne róże rwała' (She was picking wild roses)
5. 'Szeroka woda' (Broad waters)
Texts and melodies: trad., Nos. 1, 2, and 5 taken from Jadwiga Gorzechowska, *Szeroka woda* (Warsaw, 1967), Nos. 3 and 4 from Jadwiga Gorzechowska and Maria Kaczurbina, *Jak to dawniej na kurpiach bywało* (As it was Long Ago in Kurpie) (Warsaw, 1969)
Duration: *c*.16′
Dates of composition: 2–11 December 1979, Katowice
Dedication: 'To Kraków friends'
Publisher: B&H
Première: 28 April 1987, 27th Poznań Musical Spring Festival, Schola Cantorum Gedanensis, Jan Łukaszewski (conductor)
Recording: Elektra Nonesuch 79348-21, Lira Chamber Chorus, Lucy Ding (conductor)

*Koncert na klawesyn—lub fortepian—i orkiestrę smyczkową* (Concerto for Harpsichord—or Piano—and String Orchestra), Op. 40 (1980)
Instrumentation: hpd - str (6.6.4.4.2); pf - str (min. 8.8.6.6.4)

1. Allegro molto; 2. Vivace, marcatissimo
Duration: *c*.9′
Commission: Polish Radio and Television
Dates of composition: 7–29 January 1980, Katowice
Dedication: 'To Elżbieta Chojnacka'
Publishers: PWM, B&H
Premières: (harpsichord version) 2 March 1980, Katowice: Elżbieta
    Chojnacka, Polish Radio SO, Katowice, Stanisław Wisłocki (conductor);
    (piano version) 22 April 1990, 30th Poznań Musical Spring Festival,
    Jarosław Siwiński, Poznań Music Academy SO, Marcin Sompoliński
    (conductor)
Recordings: (harpsichord version) PN Muza SX 2387, Elżbieta Chojnacka,
    Polish CO, Jerzy Maksymiuk (conductor); Adda 581233, Elżbieta
    Chojnacka, Concerto Avenna, Andrzej Mysiński (conductor); Elektra
    Nonesuch 7559-79362-2, Elżbieta Chojnacka, London Sinfonietta,
    Markus Stenz (conductor); (piano version) AMF ST-104 =Conifer
    CDCF 246, Anna Górecka, Amadeus CO, Agnieszka Duczmal (conduc-
    tor); MQCD 4003, Julian Gallant, Oxford Orchestra da Camera, Stefan
    Asbury (conductor); Erato WE 810, Alexei Lubimov, German CO
    (Bremen), Heinrich Schiff (conductor)

*Mazurki* (Mazurkas), Op. 41, for piano (1980)
Dates of composition: 28–31 May 1980, Katowice
Incomplete and unpublished

*Dwie pieśni* (Two Songs), Op. 42, for medium voice and piano (1980)
Texts: Federico García Lorca, trans. Mikołaj Bieszczadowski
1. Nokturn (Nocturne)
Date of composition: January 1956, Rydułtowy; revised 14 June 1980,
    Katowice
2. Malagueña
Date of composition: 23 June 1980, Katowice
Unpublished

*Błogosławione pieśni malinowe* (Blessed Raspberry Songs), Op. 43, for
    voice and piano (1980)
1. 'Błogosławione pieśni malinowe' (Blessed raspberry songs), from 'Pięć
    Zarysów' (Five Outlines)
2. 'Co ranek, skoro ustępują cienie' (Each morning, when the shadows
    recede)
3. 'Litość' (Compassion), from *Vade-mecum*, poem 14
4. 'O! Boże . . . jeden, który JESTEŚ,' (Oh, God . . . the one, who IS), from
    'Pierwszy list, co mnie doszedł z Europy (First letter, which reached me
    from Europe), NY, USA, 10 April 1853'
Texts: Cyprian Kamil Norwid (1821–83)
Duration: *c*.20′

Dates of composition: 29 October – 22 December 1980, Chochołów and Katowice
Unpublished

*Miserere*, **Op. 44, for unaccompanied mixed choir (1981)**
Text: 'Domine Deus noster, MISERERE NOBIS'
Duration: *c*.35′–37′
Dates of composition: 23 February – 27 June 1981, Katowice and Chochołów, and 3 January – 6 April 1987, Katowice
Dedication: 'I dedicate this to Bydgoszcz'
Publishers: PWM, B&H
Première: 10 September 1987, 15th Bydgoszcz Music Festival, Włocławek: Kraków Philharmonic Chorus, members of Bydgoszcz Arion choir, Stanisław Krawczyński (conductor)
Recordings: Elektra Nonesuch 79348-21, Chicago Symphony Chorus and Lyric Opera Chorus, John Nelson (conductor); Caprice CAP 21515, Swedish Radio Choir and Eric Ericson Chamber Choir, Tõnu Kaljuste (conductor)

*Wieczór ciemny się uniża* **(Dark Evening is Falling), Op. 45, five folksongs for unaccompanied mixed choir (1981)**
1. 'Pytają się ludzie' (People are asking)
2. 'Uwiją, wianuszki' (They will make little garlands)
3. 'Ścięli dąbek' (They felled the little oak tree)
4. 'Depce konik' (The little horse paws the ground)
5. 'Wieczór ciemny się uniża' (Dark evening is falling)
Texts and melodies: trad., taken from Jadwiga Gorzechowska and Maria Kaczurbina, *Jak to dawniej na kurpiach bywało* (As it was Long Ago in Kurpie) (Warsaw, 1969)
Date of composition: October 1981, Katowice
Unpublished

*Wisło moja, Wisło szara* **(My Vistula, Grey Vistula), Op. 46, folksong for unaccompanied mixed choir (1981)**
Text and melody: trad., taken from Jadwiga Gorzechowska, *Szeroka woda* (Broad Waters) (Warsaw, 1967)
Duration: *c*.4′–4′30″
Date of composition: 29 October 1981, Katowice
Dedication: 'To Ms Maria Wacholc'
Publisher: B&H
Première: 28 April 1987, 27th Poznań Musical Spring Festival, Schola Cantorum Gedanensis, Jan Łukaszewski (conductor)
Recording: Elektra Nonesuch 79348-21, Lira Chamber Chorus, Lucy Ding (conductor)

*Kołysanki i tańce* **(Lullabies and Dances), Op. 47, for violin and piano (1982)**

Duration: *c*.15'
Date of composition: 18–28 January 1982, Katowice
Dedication: 'For Mikołaj, on his 11th birthday'
Unpublished

*Śpiewy do słów J. Słowackiego* (Songs to Words by J. Słowacki), Op. 48, for voice and piano (1983)
1. 'We łzach, Panie, ręce podnosimy do Ciebie' (In tears, Lord, we raise our hands to You), from *Odpowiedź na 'Psalmy przyszłości'* (Response to 'Psalms of the Future'), pt. 19
2. 'Panie! o którym na niebosach słyszę' (Lord! of whom in the heavens I hear)
Texts: Juliusz Słowacki
Duration: *c*.19'
Dedication: 'To Andrzej Bachleda'
Unpublished
Première: 14 September 1985, Zakopane: Andrzej Bachleda (baritone), Henryk Mikołaj Górecki (piano)

*Trzy kołysanki* (Three Lullabies), Op. 49, for unaccompanied mixed choir (1984)
1. 'Uśnijże mi, uśnij' (Sleep for me, sleep)
2. 'Kołysz-że się kołysz' (Rock, rock)
3. 'Nie piej, kurku, nie piej' (Don't crow, cock, don't crow)
Texts: trad., Nos. 1 and 3 taken from Hanna Kostyrko, *Chodzi, chodzi Baj po ścianie* (There goes the Imp across the walls) (Warsaw, 1958), No. 2 from Oskar Kolberg, *Dzieło wszystkie* (Complete Works), xxvi: 'Mazowsze', No. 549
Duration: *c*.10'30"
Dates of composition: 18–19 March 1984, Katowice; revised 1991
Publisher: B&H
Première: 2 August 1991, Lerchenborg Music Days: Ars Nova, Bo Holten (conductor)

*Ach, mój wianku lewandowy* (O, my Garland of Lavender), Op. 50, seven folksongs for unaccompanied mixed choir (1984)
Texts and melodies: trad., taken from Oskar Kolberg, *Dzieło wszystkie* (Complete Works), xxxix: 'Pomorze':
1. 'Ach, mój wianku lewandowy' (O, my garland of lavender), No. 22
2. 'Wędrowali trzy panienki' (Three lasses were wandering), No. 45
3. 'Taiłam się' (I have kept silent), No. 145
4. 'Bzi, bzi, bzibziana', No. 147
5. 'Chcecie wiedzieć' (Do you want to know), No. 219
6. 'Po cożeś mę, matuleńku, za mąż wydała' (Why did you marry me off, mummy), No. 27
7. 'Dajże, Boże, plonowało' (Give us, God, good harvest), No. 6

Dates of composition: 6–11 March 1984, Katowice
Unpublished

*Idzie chmura, pada deszcz* (Cloud Comes, Rain Falls), Op. 51, five folksongs for unaccompanied mixed choir (1984)
Texts and melodies: trad., taken from Oskar Kolberg, *Dzieło wszystkie* (Complete Works), xxxix: 'Pomorze':
1. 'Idzie chmura, pada deszcz' (Cloud comes, rain falls), No. 14
2. 'Gdzie to jedziesz, Jaszu?' (Where are you going, Johnny?), No. 81
3. 'Kiedy będzie słońce i pogoda' (When it will be sunny and warm), No. 48
4. 'Szła sierotka po wsi' (An orphan girl walked through a village), No. 213
5. 'Czas nam do domu, dziewczyno' (Time for us to go home, girl), No. 26
Dates of composition: 12–16 March 1984, Katowice
Unpublished

**Sundry Pieces, Op. 52, for piano**
*Recitativo i mazurek* (Recitative and Mazurka) (1956)
*Dwa utwory* (Two pieces) (1957)
*Trzy miniatury dodekafoniczne* (Three Dodecaphonic Miniatures) (1957)
*Quasi walc* (Quasi-Waltz) (1961)
(for details on these pieces, see individual entries above)

*Recitativa i ariosa 'Lerchenmusik'* (Recitatives and Ariosos 'Music of Larks'), Op. 53 for clarinet, cello, and piano (1984–6)
Duration: *c*.40′
Commission: Countess Louise Lerche-Lerchenborg
Dates of composition: July 1984, Katowice and Chochołów; revised December 1984 – January 1985, Katowice; further revised October 1985 – 22 January 1986, Katowice and Chochołów
Dedication: 'Der lieben Louise Lerche-Lerchenborg gewidmet'
Publishers: B&H, PWM
Premières: (as work in progress: part of 2nd movement and complete 3rd movement) 28 July 1984, Lerchenborg Music Days: Danish Trio—Jens Schou (clarinet), Svend Winsløv (cello), and Rosalind Bevan (cello); (first revised version, complete) 25 September 1985, 28th Warsaw Autumn Festival: Danish Trio; (second revised version) 12 April 1986, 26th Poznań Musical Spring Festival: Piotr Szymyślik (clarinet), Piotr Janosik (cello), and Eugeniusz Knapik (piano)
Recordings: PN Muza SX 2431, Danish Trio; Olympia OCD 343, Camerata Vistula; Elektra Nonesuch 7559-79257-2, Michael Collins (clarinet), Christopher van Kampen (cello), and John Constable (piano); Kontrapunkt 32175, LINensemble: Jens Schou (clarinet), John Ehde (cello), and Erik Kaltoft (piano); Philips 442 533-2, Pierre Wondenberg (clarinet), Larissa Groeneweld (cello), Reinbert de Leeuw (piano)

*Pieśni Maryjne* (Marian Songs), Op. 54, five Marian songs for unaccompanied mixed choir (1985)
Texts and melodies (except 'Zdrowaś bądź Maria!'): trad., taken from Jan Siedlecki, *Śpiewnik kościelny* (Church Songbook)
1. 'Matko niebieskiego Pana' (Mother of the heavenly Lord)
2. 'Matko Najświętsza!' (Most Holy Mother!)
3. 'Zdrowaś bądź Maria!' (Hail Mary!)
4. 'Ach, jak smutna jest rozstanie' (Oh, how sad is the parting)
5. 'Ciebie na wieki wychalać będziemy' (We shall praise You for ever)
Date of composition: February 1985, Katowice
Unpublished
Première: (No. 3) 3 June 1985, Warsaw: Catholic Theological Academy Choir, Warsaw, Kazimierz Szymonik (conductor)
Recording: (No. 3) PN ECD 036, Catholic Theological Academy Choir, Warsaw, Kazimierz Szymonik (conductor)

*O Domina nostra*, Op. 55, 'Medytacje o Jasnogórskiej Pani Naszej' (Meditations on Our Lady of Jasna Góra) for soprano and organ (1985)
Text: Henryk Mikołaj Górecki
Duration: *c*.33′–34′
Dates of composition: October 1982 and 23 February 1985, Katowice
Dedication: 'To Stefania Woytowicz-Rudnicki'
Publishers: PWM, Chester
Première: 31 March 1985, 25th Poznań Musical Spring Festival, Stefania Woytowicz, Michał Dąbrowski
Recordings: ECM 1459 437956-2, Sarah Leonard, Christopher Bowers-Broadbent; Kontrapunkt 32223, Anne-Lise Berntsen, Jens E. Christensen

*Pod Twoją obronę* (Under Your Protection), Op. 56, for eight-part unaccompanied mixed choir (1985)
Text: trad., taken from Jan Siedlecki, *Śpiewnik kościelny* (Church Songbook)
Duration: *c*.12′
Date of composition: April 1985
Unpublished

*Na Anioł Pański biją dzwony* (The Bells Ring out for the Angelus Domini), Op. 57, for unaccompanied mixed choir (1986)
Text: Kazimierz Przerwa Tetmajer (1865–1940), from *Nie wierzę w nic* . . . (I Believe in Nothing . . . , 1898)
Duration: *c*.11′
Dates of composition: April–May 1986
Unpublished

*Pieśni kościelne* (Church Songs), twenty-one songs for unaccompanied mixed choir (1986)

Texts and melodies: trad., taken from Jan Siedlecki, *Śpiewnik kościelny*
(Church Songbook), listed (as of November 1991) in order of composition:
1. 'Zdrowaś bądz Maryja' (Hail Mary)
2. 'Idźmy, tulmy się, jak dziatki' (Let us go, hugging, like children)
3. 'Szczęśliwy, kto sobie Patrona Józefa ma za opiekuna' (Fortunate is he,
   who has St Joseph as his protector)
4. 'Ludu, mój ludu' (People, my people)
5. 'Witaj Pani, Matko Matki Jezusa Pana' (Welcome Lady, Mother of the
   Mother of Lord Jesus)
6. 'Zawitaj Pani świata' (Hail, Lady of the world)
7. 'Bądź pozdrowiony' (Praise be to Thee)
8. 'Jezu Chryste, Panie miły' (Jesus Christ, good Lord)
9. 'Dobranoc, Głowo święta' (Good night, holy Head)
10. 'O Matko miłościwa' (O merciful Mother)
11. 'Pozdrawiajmy wychwalajmy' (Let us praise, let us hail)
12. 'Święty, Święty, Święty' (Holy, holy, holy)
13. 'Tysiąc kroć bądź pozdrowiona' (Be praised a thousand times) [not in
    Siedlecki]
14. 'Krzyknijmy wszyscy' (Let us shout together)
15. 'Witaj, Jutrzenko' (Hail, morning star) [incomplete]
16. 'Wstał Pan Chrystus z martwych ninie' (Lord Jesus is now risen from the
    dead)
17. 'Sliczny Jezu, miły Panie' (Beautiful Jesus, good Lord)
18. 'Twoja cześć, chwała' (Your glory and praise)
19. 'Ojcze Boże wszechmogący' (God the Father Almighty)
20. 'Krzyżu Chrystusa' (O cross of Christ)
21. 'Ciebie wzywamy, Ciebie błagamy' (We call on You, we beseech You)
    [unfinished]
Dates of composition: May–June 1986, Katowice
Unpublished
Premières: (Nos. 12 and 18) April 1987, Eucharistic Congress, Warsaw:
    Warsaw Music Academy Choir, Romuald Miazga (conductor)
Recordings: (No. 12) Veriton SXV 922, Warsaw Music Academy Choir,
    Romuald Miazga (conductor); PN ECD 036, Catholic Theological
    Academy Choir, Warsaw, Kazimierz Szymonik (conductor); (No. 18)
    Veriton SXV 922, Warsaw Music Academy Choir, Romuald Miazga
    (conductor)

**Dla ciebie, Anne-Lill (For you, Anne-Lill), Op. 58, for flute and piano
(1986)**
Duration: c.12′
Commission: Louise Lerche-Lerchenborg
Dates of composition: September–October 1986, Chochołów; revised May
    1990
Publisher: B&H

Première: 4 August 1990, Lerchenborg Music Days: Anne-Lill Ree and Ellen Refstrup
Recording: Amiata ARNR 0496, Andrea Ceccomori (flute), Fabrizio Ottaviucci (piano)

*Aria*, Op. 59, 'scena operowa' (operatic scene) for tuba, piano, tam-tam, and bass drum (1987)
Duration: *c*.15′
Date of composition: Easter Saturday, 18 April 1987, Katowice
Publisher: B&H
Première: 28 May 1987, 11th ASPEKTE Salzburg Festival, Zdzisław Piernik (tuba), Andor Losonczy (piano), Rudolf Schingerlin (percussion)

*Totus Tuus*, Op. 60, for unaccompanied mixed chorus (1987)
Text: Maria Bogusławska
Duration: *c*.11′
Date of composition: 3 May 1987, Katowice
Dedication; 'To His Holiness Pope John Paul II on his third pilgrimage to his homeland'
Publisher: B&H
Première: 19 July 1987, Warsaw: Catholic Theological Academy Choir, Warsaw, Kazimierz Szymonik (conductor)
Recordings: Argo 436 835-2, Prague Philharmonic Choir, John Nelson (conductor); Proudsound PROU CD 129, Schola Cantorum of Oxford, Jeremy Summerly (conductor); United 88021 CD, BBC Singers, Bo Holten (conductor); Proudsound PROU CD 136, Oxford Pro Musica Singers, Michael Smedley (conductor); EMI 5 55096 2, King's College Choir, Stephen Cleobury (conductor); Telarc 80406, Robert Shaw Festival Singers, Robert Shaw (conductor); ASV WHL 2096, London Oriana Choir, Leon Lovett (conductor); RCA 09026 68255 2, The King's Singers; EMI CD EMX 2251, Vasari Singers, Jeremy Backhouse (conductor); Erato 0630-14634-2, New College Choir, Edward Higginbottom (conductor); PN ECD 057, Warsaw Cathedral Choir, Andrzej Filaber (conductor)

*Przybądź Duchu Święty* (Come Holy Spirit), Op. 61 for unaccompanied mixed choir (1988)
Text: 'Veni Sancte Spiritus' sequence
Duration: *c*.11′
Date of composition: 29 March 1988, Katowice
Unpublished
Première: 11 October 1993, Warsaw: Catholic Theological Academy Choir, Warsaw, Kazimierz Szymonik (conductor)
Recording: PN ECD 036, Catholic Theological Academy Choir, Warsaw, Kazimierz Szymonik (conductor)

*'Już się zmierzcha', muzyka na kwartet smyczkowy* ('Already it is Dusk', Music for String Quartet), Op. 62, String Quartet No. 1 (1988)
Duration: *c*.16′
Commission: Doris and Myron Beigler and the Lincoln Center for the Performing Arts, for the Kronos Quartet
Dates of composition: 20 October – 30 November 1988, Chochołów and Katowice
Dedication: 'To the KRONOS Quartet as a token of appreciation'
Publisher: B&H
Première: 21 January 1989, Minneapolis: Kronos Quartet (David Harrington, John Sherba, Hank Dutt, Joan Jeanrenaud)
Recordings: Elektra Nonesuch 7559-79257-2 = Elektra Nonesuch 7559-79819-2, Kronos Quartet; Olympia OCD 375, Silesian Quartet

*Good Night*, Op. 63, for soprano, alto flute, 3 tam-tams, and piano (1990)
1. Lento (Adagio)–Tranquillo; 2. Lento tranquillissimo; 3. Lento–largo, dolcissimo–cantabilissimo
Text (3rd movement): 'Good night . . . flights of angels sing thee to thy rest': William Shakespeare (1564–1616), *Hamlet* (1601), Act V, Scene ii
Duration: *c*.30′
Dates of composition: 11 March – 1 June 1988 and 10–19 February 1990, Katowice
Dedication: 'In memoriam Michael Vyner'
Publisher: B&H
Premières: (3rd movement only) 6 May 1990, London: Margaret Field and members of the London Sinfonietta; (complete) 4 November 1990, London: Nicole Tibbels and members of the London Sinfonietta
Recordings: Elektra Nonesuch 7559-79362-2, Dawn Upshaw and members of the London Sinfonietta; Telarc CD 80417, Elżbieta Szmytka and members of I Fiamminghi

*Intermezzo* for piano (1990)
Duration: *c*.2′30″
Commission: Louise Lerche-Lerchenborg
Date of composition: 23 April 1990, Katowice
Dedication: 'Andenken an Poul Rovsing Olsen'
Unpublished
Première: 3 August 1990, Lerchenborg Music Days: Rosalind Bevan

*Quasi una fantasia*, Op. 64, String Quartet No. 2 (1991)
1. Largo, Sostenuto-mesto; 2. Deciso–energico, Marcatissimo sempre; 3. Arioso: Adagio cantabile, ma molto espressivo e molto appassionato; 4. Allegro, sempre con grande passione e molto marcato
Duration: *c*.38′30″–39′

Commission: Beigler Trust, Lincoln Center for the Performing Arts, New York, and the Kościuszko Foundation for the Kronos Quartet
Dates of composition: 6 December 1990 (St Nicholas's Day) – 19 March 1991 (St Joseph's Day), Katowice
Dedication: 'To the KRONOS Quartet—David Harrington, John Sherba, Hank Dutt, Joan Jeanrenaud'
Publisher: B&H
Première: 27 October 1991, Cleveland: Kronos Quartet
Recordings: Elektra Nonesuch 7559-79819-2, Kronos Quartet; Olympia OCD 375, Silesian Quartet

**Concerto-Cantata, Op. 65, for flute/alto flute solo and orchestra (1992)**
Instrumentation: 2 picc.4 (III+IV picc.).4.4.4 - 6.4.3.1 - perc (3) - hp - str (16-18.14-16.12-14.10-12.8-10)
1. Recitativo; 2. Arioso; 3. Concertino; 4. Arioso e Corale
Duration: c.22'
Commission: Frederick S. Upton Foundation for Carol Wincenc
Dates of composition: 30 November 1991 – 12 January 1992 and 28 July – 10 September 1992, Katowice
Dedication: 'Carol Wincenc dedicato'
Publisher: B&H
Première: 28 November 1992, Amsterdam: Carol Wincenc, Dutch Radio PO, Eri Klas (conductor)

**Kleines Requiem für eine Polka (Little Requiem for a Polka), Op. 66, for piano and thirteen instruments (1993)**
Instrumentation: 1.1.1.1 - 1.1.1.0 - perc (1) - pf - 1.1.1.1.1
1. Tranquillo; 2. Allegro impetuoso–marcatissimo; 3. Allegro–deciso assai; 4. (Largo)
Duration: c.24'
Commission: Holland Festival and the Schönberg Ensemble
Date of composition: May 1993, Katowice
Dedication: 'Schönberg Ensemble dedicato'
Publisher: B&H
Première: 12 June 1993, Holland Festival, Amsterdam: Schönberg Ensemble, Reinbert de Leeuw (conductor)
Recordings: Elektra Nonesuch 7559-79362-2, London Sinfonietta, David Zinman (conductor); Philips 442 533-2, Schönberg Ensemble, Reinbert de Leeuw (conductor); Telarc CD 80417, I Fiamminghi, Rudolph Werthen (conductor)

'U okienka, u mojego' (By my Little Window) for voice and piano (1995)
Text: Maria Konopnicka
Date of composition: April 1995 (Easter), Katowice
Unpublished

Première: 28 May 1995, New York: Andrzej Bachleda (baritone), Henryk Mikołaj Górecki (piano), alongside two early songs to texts by Konopnicka (1954–5; see Juvenilia)

*Valentine Piece* for flute and little bell (1996)
Duration: c.4′30″
Commission: Carol Wincenc
Date of composition: 1 February 1996, Katowice
Unpublished
Première: 14 February 1996, New York, Carol Wincenc

*Trzy fragmenty do słów Stanisława Wyspiańskiego* (Three Fragments to Words by Stanisław Wyspiański) for voice and piano (1996)
I. Jakżeż ja się uspokoję (How on earth can I be at peace)
II. Może z mętów się dobędzie człowieka (Perhaps from these dregs a man will emerge), from *Wesele* (The Wedding, 1901), Act II, Scene viii
III. Poezjo! -tyś to jest spokojną siestą (Poetry!—you are a calm siesta), from *Wesele*, Act II, Scene viii
Duration: c.24′
Commission: Wanda Warska
Unpublished
Première: 23 February 1996, Zakopane: Wanda Warska (singer), Henryk Mikołaj Górecki (piano)

# SELECT BIBLIOGRAPHY

BACULEWSKI, KRZYSZTOF, *Polska twórczość kompozytorska 1945–1984* (Polish Composers and their Works 1945–1984) (Kraków, 1987).

BYLANDER, CYNTHIA E, 'The Warsaw Autumn International Festival of Contemporary Music, 1956–1961: Its Goals, Structures, Programs and People', Ph.D. thesis (Columbus, Ohio, 1989).

CHOMIŃSKI, JÓZEF MICHAŁ, *Muzyka Polski Ludowej* (Music in People's Poland) (Warsaw, 1968); ch. 7, trans. as 'The Contribution of Polish Composers to the Shaping of a Modern Language of Music', *Polish Musicological Studies*, 1 (1977), 167–215.

—— 'Muzyka polska po 1956 roku' (Polish Music since 1956), in Elżbieta Dziębowska (ed.), *Polska współczesna kultura muzyczna 1944–64* (Polish Contemporary Musical Culture 1944–64) (Kraków, 1968), 61–119.

—— 'Przemiany techniki kompozytorskiej w trzydziestoleciu PRL' (Changes in Compositional Techniques in the First Thirty Years of the Polish People's Republic), *Muzyka*, 3 (1975), 16–27.

CHYBIŃSKI, ADOLF, 'Wacław z Szamotuł', *Kwartalnik muzyczny* (1948), nos. 21–2, 11–34; no. 23, 7–22; no. 24, 100–31.

DREW, DAVID, 'Górecki's Millions', *London Review of Books*, 16/19 (6 Oct. 1994), 9–10.

DROBA, KRZYSZTOF, 'Henryka Mikołaja Góreckiego technika komponowania na wielkie zespoły instrumentalne na przykładzie *Refrenu* i *Canticum graduum*' (Henryk Mikołaj Górecki's Compositional Technique in Large Instrumental Ensembles as Seen in *Refrain* and *Canticum graduum*), MA thesis (Kraków, 1971).

—— 'Dwie pieśni sakralne' (Two Sacred Songs), *Zeszyty naukowe zespołu analizy i interpretacji muzyki* (Academic Notebook of the Group for the Analysis and Interpretation of Music (at the Higher School of Music)), 2 (Kraków, 1977), 185–97.

—— 'Droga do sensu tragicznego' (The Path to a Sense of Tragedy [on Symphony No. 3]), *Ruch muzyczny* (1978), no. 15, 3–4.

—— 'Wielkość-Dziwność' (Greatness–Strangeness [on Symphony No. 3 and Harpsichord Concerto]), *Ruch muzyczny* (1980), no. 10, 7–8.

—— 'Słowo w muzyce Góreckiego' (The Word in Górecki's Music), *Ruch muzyczny* (1981), no. 22, 3–4.

—— 'The Music of Henryk Mikołaj Górecki', *Music in Poland*, 1 (1984), 27–36.

—— 'Od *Refrenu* do *Beatus vir* czyli o redukcjoniźmie konstruktywistycznym i ekspresjoniźmie muzyki Henryka Mikołaja Góreckiego'

(From *Refrain* to *Beatus vir*, or Concerning Constructivist Reductionism and Expressionism in the Music of Henryk Mikołaj Górecki), in Leszek Polony (ed.), *Przemiany techniki dźwiękowej, stylu i estetyki w Polskiej muzyce lat 70* (Changes in Sound Technique, Style, and Aesthetics in Polish Music in the 1970s) (Kraków, 1986), 85–97.

——'Górecki', *Encyklopedia muzyczna PWM*, vol. efg (Kraków, 1987), 420–30.

ERHARD, LUDWIK, *Music in Poland* (Warsaw, 1975).

FILAR, ALFONS, and LEYKO, MICHAŁ, *'Palace': Katownia Podhala* ('Palace': Place of Torture in Podhale) (Warsaw, 1970).

GALESKI-WILD, CHRISTIANE, 'Henryk M. Górecki et ses œuvres symphoniques', MA thesis (University of Strasburg, 1986).

GĄSIOROWSKA, MAŁGORZATA, 'Symfonia pieśni żałosnych' (Symphony of Sorrowful Songs), *Ruch muzyczny* (1978), no. 3, 3–5.

——'Czas zatrzymany Henryka Góreckiego' (Henryk Górecki's Stopped Time), *Ruch muzyczny* (1983), no. 25, 3–4.

GÓRCZYCKA, MONIKA, 'Diagramy H. Góreckiego' (H. Górecki's *Diagrams*), *Ruch muzyczny* (1961), no. 21, 8.

GÓRECKI, HENRYK MIKOŁAJ, 'Powiem państwu szczerze . . .' (I shall Tell you Frankly . . .), *ViVO*, 1 (Kraków, 1994), 43–8.

HŁAWICZKA, KAROL, 'Ze studiów nad muzyką polskiego Odrodzenia' (From Studies into the Music of the Polish Renaissance), *Muzyka*, 1–2 (1958), 53–71: part III, 'Cantus firmus pieśni "Już się zmierzcha" Wacława z Szamotuł' (The Cantus Firmus in Wacław of Szamotuły's Song 'Already Dusk is Falling'), 65–8; part IV, 'Dwie Pieśni o życiu króla Zygmunta Augusta' (Two Songs on the Life of King Sigismund Augustus), 69–71.

HOMMA, MARTINA, 'Das Minimale und das Absolute: Die Musik Henryk Mikołaj Góreckis von der Mitte der sechziger Jahre bis 1985', *MusikTexte—Zeitschrift für neue Musik*, 44 (1992), 40–59.

HRABOVSKY, LEONID, 'Mikołaj from Katowice: Henryk Mikołaj Górecki and his Work, 1955–1972' (unpublished essay, 1973).

JACOBSON, BERNARD, *A Polish Renaissance* (London, 1996).

JURSKI, MAREK, 'Technika dźwiękowa w wybranych utworach symfonicznych Henryka Mikołaja Góreckiego' (Sound Technique in Selected Symphonic Works by Henryk Mikołaj Górecki), MA thesis (Gdańsk, 1975).

——'Kantata op. 26 Henryka Mikołaja Góreckiego na organy—technika dźwiękowa i ekspresja' (Henryk Mikołaj Górecki's Cantata Op. 26 for organ—Sound Technique and Expression), in Pawel Podejko (ed.), *Organy i muzyka organowa* (Gdańsk, 1977), 227–38.

KACZYŃSKI, TADEUSZ, and POCIEJ, BOHDAN, 'Dwugłos o *Refrenie*' (Dialogue on *Refrain*), *Ruch muzyczny* (1966), no. 23, 6–7.

KOLBERG, OSKAR, *Dzieło wszystkie* (Complete Works), xxxix: 'Pomorze' (Kraków, 1965).

Kopacz, Anna, 'Symfonie Henryka Mikołaja Góreckiego' (Henryk Mikołaj Górecki's Symphonies), MA thesis (Kraków, 1981).

Lee, Jan Patrick, 'Musical Life and Sociopolitical Change in Warsaw, Poland: 1944–1960', Ph.D. thesis (Chapel Hill, NC, 1979).

Malecka, Teresa, 'O Koncercie klawesynowym Góreckiego' (On Górecki's Harpsichord Concerto), in Teresa Malecka (ed.), *Mieczysławowi Tomaszewskiemu w 60-lecie urodzin* (For Mieczysław Tomaszewski on his 60th Birthday) (Kraków, 1984), 108–13.

Marek, Tadeusz, 'Composer's Workshop: Henryk Mikołaj Górecki', *Polish Music* (1968), no. 2, 25–8. Reprinted, with corrections, in Marek and Drew, 'Górecki in Interview'.

——'The Copernican Year in Polish Music', *Polish Music* (1973), no. 1, 3–9.

——and Drew, David, 'Górecki in Interview (1968)—and 20 Years After', *Tempo*, 168 (Mar. 1989), 25–9 (includes a corrected reprint of Marek, 'Composer's Workshop').

Markiewicz, Leon, 'O Zderzeniach, radości i . . . katastrofiźmie' (On *Collisions*, joy and . . . catastrophism), *Ruch muzyczny* (1960), no. 21, 10–11.

——'Rozmowa z Henrykiem Góreckim' (Conversation with Henryk Górecki), *Ruch muzyczny* (1962), no. 17, 6–8.

——'Choros I Henryka Góreckiego' (Henryk Górecki's *Choros I*), *Ruch muzyczny* (1964), no 21, 8–9.

——'Elementy H. Góreckiego' (H. Górecki's *Elementi*), *Ruch muzyczny* (1965), no. 17, 9.

——'Główne tendencje twórcze w katowickim środowisku kompozytorskim' (The Principle Creative Trends among Katowice Composers), *Muzyka*, 2 (1974), 22–30.

Mellers, Wilfrid, 'Round and About Górecki's Symphony No. 3', *Tempo*, 168 (Mar. 1989), 22–4.

Moody, Ivan, 'Górecki: The Path to the *Miserere*', *Musical Times*, 133 (1992), 283–4.

Morton, Brian, 'Symphony No. 3', *The Blackwell Guide to Recorded Contemporary Music* (Oxford, 1996), 238–44.

Nagórska, Aleksandra, 'Trzy Symfonie Henryka Mikołaja Góreckiego: Przemiana Elementów Muzycznych' (Henryk Mikołaj Górecki's Three Symphonies: The Transformation of Musical Elements), MA thesis (Katowice, 1981).

Ochlewski, Tadeusz (ed.), *An Outline History of Polish Music* (Warsaw, 1979).

Pociej, Bohdan, 'Epitafium Henryka Góreckiego' (Henryk Górecki's *Epitafium*), *Ruch muzyczny* (1959), no. 6, 10–13.

——'Świt awangardy: Na marginesie III Warszawskiej Jesieni' (The Dawn of the Avant-Garde: Notes in the Margin from the 3rd Warsaw Autumn), *Ruch muzyczny* (1960), no. 1, 9–10, 24.

——'*Zderzenia* Henryka Góreckiego' (Henryk Górecki's *Scontri*), *Ruch muzyczny* (1960), no. 18, 7.

——'Opis—analiza—interpretacja' (Description—Analysis—Interpretation [on *Elementi* and *Canti strumentali*]), *Res facta*, 4 (Kraków, 1970), 151–65.

——'*Ad matrem* Henryka Mikołaja Góreckiego' (Henryk Mikołaj Górecki's *Ad matrem*), *Ruch muzyczny* (1973), no. 3, 3–5.

——'Kosmos, Tradycja, Brzmienie' (Cosmos, Tradition, Sound [on Symphony No. 2]), *Ruch muzyczny* (1973), no. 15, 3–5.

——'Wielkość i prostota' (Greatness and Simplicity [on *Ad matrem*]), *Polska w kaleidoskopie* (Kaleidoscopic Poland) (Warsaw, 1977), 33–5.

——'Górecki', *The New Grove Dictionary of Music and Musicians*, ed. Stanley Sadie (London, 1980), vii. 539–40.

——'*Recitatywy i ariosa* Henryka Mikołaja' (Henryk Mikołaj's *Recitatives and ariosos*), *Ruch muzyczny* (1986), no. 3, 6–7.

——'Elément religieux dans la nouvelle musique polonaise' (Religious Element in the New Polish Music), *Polish Art Studies*, 11 (Wrocław, 1990), 143–53.

RAPPOPORT-GELFAND, LIDIA, *Musical Life in Poland: The Postwar Years 1945–1977* (New York, 1991).

SCHÄFFER, BOGUSŁAW, 'Od dodekafonii do muzyki elektronowej' (From Dodecaphony to Electronic Music), *Ruch muzyczny* (1958), no. 1, 9–19.

SCHILLER, HENRYK, 'Najmłodsza generacja kompozytorów polskich na III Międzynarodowym Festiwalu Muzyki Współczesnej "Warszawska Jesień"' (The Youngest Generation of Polish Composers at the 3rd International Warsaw Autumn Festival of Contemporary Music), *Horyzonty muzyki* (Kraków, 1970), no. 2.

SIEDLECKI, JAN, *Śpiewnik kościelny* (Church Songbook) (jubilee edn., Lwów, Kraków, and Paris, 1928; 39th edn. Kraków, 1990).

SKWARNICKI, MAREK, 'Introit, Gradual, Offertorium, Communio', *Tygodnik powszechny*, 1168 (13 June 1971), 1.

SUTKOWSKI, ADAM, 'Nieznane zabytki muzyki wielogłosowej z polskich rękopisów chorałowych XIII i XV wieku' (Unknown Monuments of Polyphonic Music from Thirteenth- and Fifteenth-Century Polish Chorale Manuscripts), *Muzyka*, 3 (1958), 28–36.

——'Organum "Surrexit Cristus hodie" i inne zabytki średniowiecznej muzyki wielogłosowej' (The Organum 'Surrexit Cristus hodie' and Other Monuments of Medieval Polyphonic Music), *Ruch muzyczny* (1958), no. 19, 2–6.

——'"Benedicamus Domino"—nieznany zabytek wczesno-średniowiecznej polifonii' ('Benedicamus Domino'—an Unknown Monument of Early Medieval Polyphony), *Ruch muzyczny* (1960), no. 18, 16–17.

——'Początki polifonii średniowiecznej w Polsce w świetle nowych żródeł' (The Beginnings of Medieval Polyphony in Poland in the Light of New Sources), *Muzyka*, 1 (1961), 3–22.

THOMAS, ADRIAN, 'The Music of Henryk Mikołaj Górecki: The First Decade', *Contact*, 27 (1983), 10–20.

—— 'A Pole Apart: The Music of Górecki since 1965', *Contact*, 28 (1984), 20–31.

—— 'Górecki: A Place at the Top', *Classic CD*, 32 (1992), 20–22.

—— 'Granieten monumentaliteit en heldere lucht' (Granite Monumentalism in the Clear Air), *Holland Festival Almanak* (Amsterdam, 1993), 52–8.

WILCZYŃSKI, MAREK, 'Percussione batteria w twórczości Henryka Mikołaja Góreckiego' (Percussion in the Works of Henryk Mikołaj Górecki), MA thesis (Kraków, 1974).

WOZACZYŃSKA, ANTONINA, *Pieśni Kurpiowskie: Ich struktura i charakterystyka w świetle zbiorów W. Skierkowskiego* (Kurpian Songs: Their Structure and Characteristics in the Light of W. Skierkowski's Collections) (Wrocław, 1956).

# INDEX

*Note*: Bold figures denote major entries and references to examples or figures